Mormon and Maori

Mormon and Maori

Marjorie Newton

GREG KOFFORD BOOKS
SALT LAKE CITY, 2014

Greg Kofford Books
P.O. Box 1362
Draper, UT 84020
www. koffordbooks.com

Also available in ebook.

2018   17   16   15   14   5   4   3   2   1

Library of Congress Cataloging-in-Publication Data

Newton, Marjorie, author.
 Mormon and Maori / Marjorie Newton.
     pages cm
 Includes bibliographical references and index.
   ISBN 978-1-58958-639-0 (alk. paper)
 1. Church of Jesus Christ of Latter-day Saints--New Zealand. 2. Maori (New Zealand people) 3. Mormon Church--New Zealand. I. Title.
  BX8617.N45N48 2014
  289.3089'99442--dc23
                        2014003730

For Cecily

> . . . in strange way
> To stand inquiring right, is not to stray;
> To sleep, or runne wrong, is.
>   — John Donne, *Third Satyre*

Contents

Preface   xi

Introduction   xvii

Time Line   xxiii

Chapter 1 Mormon Beliefs and the Maori   1

Chapter 2 Mormon Schools in New Zealand   37

Chapter 3 Mormon Legends in New Zealand   79

Chapter 4 Mormon Leaders and Maori Culture   113

Chapter 5 Mormon and Maori?   149

Glossary of Maori Words   183

Glossary of LDS Terminology   187

Bibliography   191

Index   213

Preface

Since February 1996, most members of the Church of Jesus Christ of Latter-day Saints (Mormons) are to be found in countries outside North America. Just twenty-five years earlier, 85 percent of LDS Church members were American or Canadian.[1] There are now fifteen million Mormons located in more than 160 countries throughout the world, and the LDS Church today is attracting not only converts from a wide variety of religious and cultural backgrounds but also attention from scholars in a variety of disciplines.

"Foreign" missions are not new to the Latter-day Saints, but never before have their leaders and missionaries faced the problems associated with socialising converts from such a wide spectrum of cultures. Resurgent nationalism and indigenisation philosophy in many nations also pose problems for Mormon leaders, and recent attempts to strip the LDS Church of its American cultural overtones have been only partially successful. Thus, the history of Mormonism's impact on its Maori converts and their culture is surprisingly relevant to the wider Church today.

The New Zealand Mission[2] of the Church of Jesus Christ of Latter-day Saints was unusual among nineteenth-century and early twentieth-century Mormon missions in that it was really two missions: one conducted among Pakeha (European) New Zealanders, and another among the indigenous people of the islands of Aotearoa/New Zealand. American missionaries assigned to "European" work moved among the European

---

1. Lowell C. "Ben" Bennion and Lawrence A. Young, "The Uncertain Dynamics of LDS Expansion, 1950–2020," 8.

2. Until 1 January 1898, the New Zealand Mission was actually part of the Australasian Mission, which included both Australia and New Zealand, but for convenience I refer to it as the New Zealand Mission for the entire period.

immigrants and their descendants. Those assigned to Maori work learned to love a noble, proud, but disgruntled race, a people smarting from the confiscation of their land and their consequent loss of mana (authority, prestige, influence), disenchanted with orthodox Christian churches, and whose numbers were shrinking to the point where extinction or amalgamation seemed in the eyes of many Europeans, at the time of the Mormon approach, their only future prospect.

While the first Mormon missionaries arrived in New Zealand in 1854, it was not until the 1880s that Mormonism began to flourish among the Maori. As Maori conversions began to escalate, most of the scanty resources of the Mormon mission in New Zealand were perforce channelled into Maori work, and efforts among the Pakeha diminished, though never ceased. During the next six decades, about 90 percent of Mormons in New Zealand were Maori (though only about 10 percent of all Maori were Mormons). Post-World War II Mormon Church leaders in New Zealand made vigorous efforts to overcome the public perception that Mormonism was a "Maori Church," with some success. By the end of the twentieth century, the ratio was approximately 70 percent Maori and 30 percent Pakeha, and the LDS Church ranked sixth in number of adherents of all churches in New Zealand.

The LDS Church's success in New Zealand was not achieved without cost to the culture and traditional way of life (Maoritanga) of its Maori converts. In *Tiki and Temple: The Mormon Mission in New Zealand, 1854–1958,* I have traced the story of the introduction, growth, and development of the LDS Church in Aotearoa/New Zealand. That book, addressed primarily to a Latter-day Saint audience, was honoured by the Mormon History Association with its Best International Book Award for 2012. However, it did not deal with deeper or more scholarly issues. *Mormon and Maori* was originally written as a Ph.D. thesis (dissertation) for the School of Studies in Religion at the University of Sydney and is accordingly a more objective and more academic examination of the interaction of Mormonism and Maoritanga.

As the first two chapters of my dissertation were expanded to become *Tiki and Temple*, these chapters do not appear in this volume, though a few topics briefly mentioned there are discussed in more depth here. The third chapter of my dissertation discussed the not inconsiderable early Mormon success among the Pakeha and argued that the Mormon missionaries did not turn to the Maori because of lack of success among them. This chapter has likewise been published elsewhere[3] so is not included in this book.

---

3. Marjorie Newton, "Nineteenth-century Pakeha Mormons in New Zealand,"

Instead, as previously stated, this book explores the interaction of Maori culture and Mormonism, the topic that formed the main thrust of my dissertation. As my doctorate was awarded in 1998, these chapters have been revised and updated for this volume. Because this book was originally written as a religious studies dissertation, I did not attempt to relate many of the matters I discussed to the wider issues of New Zealand history, either secular or religious. I feel confident that a growing generation of scholars who are both Mormon and Maori will find much more to say on many topics raised here and on many which could have been raised here had space permitted.

As a lifelong and committed Mormon, I accept the LDS doctrine that "the glory of God is intelligence, or, in other words, light and truth,"[4] and consequently I believe that faith and sound scholarship are not mutually exclusive. But as a Mormon who is neither Maori, Pakeha, nor American, I felt very diffident about attempting this work when I began my research in the early 1990s at the suggestion of Dale Robertson, then Editor of Publications at the Institute for Polynesian Studies at Brigham Young University-Hawaii Campus.[5] However, I have come to hope that my nonalignment with any of the protagonists in this story might have strengthened rather than weakened the resulting analysis.

My completed dissertation, titled "Mormonism in New Zealand: A Historical Analysis," was to be published by the Joseph Fielding Smith Institute for Church History at Brigham Young University, Provo. When it was suggested that I should write a chronological history of the New Zealand Mission first, publication of my dissertation was delayed until the manuscript of *Tiki and Temple* was completed. Both books were still in the early stages of copy-editing when the institute was closed in 2005. I am grateful to Dale Robertson for his initial suggestion, to Richard L. Jensen for his preliminary editing at the JFS, and to Greg Kofford, who immediately offered to publish both books when the institute closed.

Throughout this book, the Church of Jesus Christ of Latter-day Saints is variously referred to by its full name, as the "LDS Church," or as the "Mormon Church." Whenever the exclusivist phrase "the Church" is used, it refers to the Mormon Church. No disparagement of other churches is intended: it is simply less cumbersome to refer in this way to the particular denomination that is the subject of this book. Members of the Church of

in *Proclamation to the People: Nineteenth-century Mormonism and the Pacific Basin Frontier,* 228–54.

4. Doctrine and Covenants 93:36.

5. The Institute for Polynesian Studies is now the Pacific Institute.

Jesus Christ of Latter-day Saints are referred to as "Latter-day Saints," "Mormons," or simply as "Saints."

Spelling throughout this book is inconsistent, as I have used English spelling except in quotations, where the original spelling of both primary and secondary sources has been retained. Spelling accordingly switches between American and English (including Australian and New Zealand English). In order to avoid further confusion, I have refrained from using the macron unless it appeared in the original source of a quotation.[6] Given that I do not speak the Maori language, this is doubly necessary, as I am unqualified in the correct use of macrons and double vowels and do not want to cause offence by any misuse of the language. As Maori is now an official language of New Zealand, I do not italicise Maori words, except in quotations or references where they were italicised in the original.

All dates have been standardised in the international day, month, and year format. Distances are given in miles, as imperial measurements prevailed for most of the period discussed, but one kilometre equals five-eighths of a mile. Monetary sums are expressed in either American dollars, or in New Zealand pounds (£) until 1967, and in New Zealand dollars thereafter, according to the context.

I wish to acknowledge with gratitude the staffs of the LDS Church History Library in Salt Lake City, Utah; the Harold B. Lee Library at Brigham Young University, Provo, Utah; the New Zealand Government Archives, and the former Church College of New Zealand, for their friendly, willing help. The Institute for Polynesian Studies at BYU–Hawaii and the Joseph Fielding Smith Institute for Church History at BYU–Provo provided small grants that made research trips possible. The Mormon History Association awarded me a travel scholarship in 1995 which allowed me to do further research in the LDS Church Archives in Salt Lake City as well as present part of this book as a paper at its 1995 meeting in Kingston, Ontario.[7] I am grateful for this help.

I also acknowledge my gratitude to Dr Ian G. Barber for advising me on points of Maori anthropology (with the disclaimer that any errors are mine, not his). Numerous friends helped me in various ways, from giving

---

6. Under the Māori Language Act of 1987, Māori was declared an official language of New Zealand and the Māori Language Commission (Te Taura Whiri i te Reo Māori) was set up. Since that date, the Māori Language Commission has strongly advocated use of the macron. However, it was seldom used for most of the period covered by this book.

7. This paper was published as "From Tolerance to 'House-Cleaning': LDS Leadership Response to Maori Marriage Customs, 1890–1990," *Journal of Mormon History* 22, no. 2 (Fall 1996): 72–91.

scholarly advice to solving computer problems and providing accommodation for extended research visits to Utah; I wish I could name them all, but special thanks go to Lavina Fielding Anderson, Patricia Lyn Scott, and Loyd Ericson. My husband, Don, and my daughters Cecily and Jenny, gave practical help and never doubted my capacity to cope despite the overwhelming health problems our family faced while I was researching and writing both my original dissertation and *Tiki and Temple*. Finally, I would like to acknowledge and thank Dr. Jan Shipps, Dr. Lawrence Foster, and Dr. Peter Lineham—each an eminent non-LDS scholar of Mormonism—who were appointed in 1997 by the University of Sydney as my examiners.

I am deeply grateful to them all, but the last to be named is my supervisor, the late Professor Eric J. Sharpe of the School of Studies in Religion at the University of Sydney. Without his interest and encouragement, not only would my thesis not have been completed, it would never have been begun.

Introduction

The islands of Aotearoa lay undisturbed by Western visitors for more than a century after their "second discovery" by seventeenth-century Dutch navigator Abel Tasman.[1] Then, during the last thirty years of the eighteenth century, Tasman was followed by the British expeditions of James Cook (1769, 1773, and 1777) and the French explorers Jean Francois Marie de Surville (1769) and Marion du Fresne (1772). Perhaps inhibited by the violence that accompanied these early encounters with the Maori inhabitants, no serious attempt was made by either Dutch, British, or French to annex and settle the islands of Aotearoa. The Maori tribes of coastal regions, however, soon became familiar with the British and Americans who began to visit these islands (which the Dutch had named "New Zealand") in increasing numbers as whaling, sealing, and timber-felling became important industries of the new colonies in nearby Australia.

European settlement in New Zealand was at first haphazard rather than planned. Ships and gear needed repairs. Crews needed rest, fresh water, and produce. Timber and flax beckoned the traders. Shore bases were set up in the Bay of Islands in the North Island and even, as they were frequently called as late as the 1890s, on the "Middle Island" and "South Island"—today's South and Stewart Islands. There was no sense of invasion or of permanent occupation. The Maori were happy to trade and began to cultivate potatoes to supply a growing market. Some Maori joined ships' crews, sailing to other Pacific ports and even further afield. Maori chiefs visited Australia and were vice-regally entertained in Sydney by Governor Philip Gidley King. Only gradually did the Maori tribes realise that the makeshift camps set up by the Pakeha (Europeans) in Aotearoa were

---

1. I owe this phrase to Harry Morton and Carol Morton Johnston, whose book, *The Farthest Corner*, is sub-titled *New Zealand—A Twice Discovered Land.*

being replaced by huts, and the huts by strange but permanent-looking houses; that embryo townships were growing up; and that these strange white tribesmen with their superior weapons and tools and their different language and different God had come to stay. As so often occurred in Europe's colonial ventures, the introduction of weapons and manufactured goods also signalled the introduction of Bibles and prayer books.

The first Christian missionaries to visit New Zealand came from Sydney in 1814. The Reverend Samuel Marsden was the spearhead of the Anglican invasion of Aotearoa. Appointed chaplain to the British colony in New South Wales in 1794 and appointed a magistrate soon after his arrival, Marsden was a cold, harsh administrator but one ardently committed to spreading the Christian gospel among the heathen races of the South Seas. He encountered Maori crewmen and visiting chiefs in Sydney. He was impressed; and with this personal contact added to travellers' tales of the "noble savage" genre, he soon developed a feeling of responsibility to convert the race:

> The natives of New Zealand are far advanced in Civilization, and apparently prepared for receiving the Knowledge of Christianity more than any Savage nations I have seen. . . .
> The more I see of these People, the more I am pleased with, and astonished at their moral Ideas, and Characters. They appear like a superior Race of men. Was Christianity once received amongst them, New Zealand would be one of the finest parts of the Globe.[2]

While visiting London in 1807–8, Marsden had obtained Church Missionary Society (CMS) backing for a venture to New Zealand. The strategy he recommended was that of introducing the arts of civilisation to the Maori first, as a basis for lasting conversion.[3] After recruiting missionary "settlers"—a carpenter/cum shipwright and a shoemaker/cum flax spinner, with the later addition of Thomas Kendall, a schoolteacher—Marsden returned to Sydney. Here news of the massacre of the crew of the trading vessel *Boyd* changed the climate of opinion towards the Maori, and the missionary venture was postponed for some years.

Marsden finally accompanied his missionary team to New Zealand in 1814 and preached the first Christian sermon on New Zealand soil on Christmas Day of that year before returning to Sydney. Despite the considerable early troubles of the group he left in New Zealand, other missionaries were not discouraged; by the 1830s there were three CMS mission stations

---

2. Samuel Marsden, Letter to Revd. J. Pratt, dated Parramatta, 20 November 1811, 36–38.

3. Samuel Marsden, Letter to Revd. J. Pratt, dated 8 Ivy Lane, 7 April 1808, 15.

and a Methodist settlement, all in the Bay of Islands area of the North Island. The first Roman Catholic missionary efforts began in 1838.

Rewards in the form of conversions were meagre for some time. It was not until Henry Williams (first of a Church of England missionary family of enormous influence in nineteenth-century New Zealand) took charge of the CMS missions in 1823 that the work of converting the Maori to Christianity slowly began to prosper. Many factors (such as cultural dislocation, materialistic motives, and increasing literacy coupled with translation of the Bible into Maori) are seen as contributing to Maori conversion to Christianity. During the 1830s, the missions extended south; and during this and the two following decades, an estimated two-thirds of New Zealand Maori were converted to one or other of the competing Christian denominations.[4]

The 1830s also saw the first interest in planned settlement of the islands by Europeans. Among the first were the French settlements of Charles Philip Hippolytus de Thierry (1837) in the North Island and another at Akaroa in the South Island (1840). The first planned British settlement was organised by Edward Gibbon Wakefield, whose New Zealand Company sold land the company did not yet own to prospective settlers, whom they then dispatched to the South Pacific on the *Tory* in 1839. Other ventures were planned from Sydney.

While Cook had claimed the South Island for Great Britain in 1770, there was considerable uncertainty about British rights to "ownership" of all New Zealand. It was not until 1839 that the boundaries of New South Wales were officially extended to include New Zealand. Captain William Hobson, appointed lieutenant-governor, negotiated the Treaty of Waitangi with the chiefs of as many Maori tribes as could be consulted. Dated 6 February 1840, this treaty, poorly interpreted to Maori, became the legal basis for European claims to the land for more than a century.[5] By signing it, the Maori chiefs yielded sovereignty to Queen Victoria of England and agreed to give the British government first option on land purchase; in return, they were guaranteed "full and undisturbed possession" of their lands and the rights and privileges of British subjects. No one bothered to point out that these clauses were mutually exclusive. A few months after the treaty was signed, Britain claimed sovereignty over the whole of New

---

4. K. R. Howe, *Where the Waves Fall: A New South Sea Islands History from First Settlement to Colonial Rule*, 222, 224; Claudia Orange, "The Maori People and the British Crown (1769–1840," 32; Bronwyn Elsmore, *Like Them That Dream: The Maori and the Old Testament*, 12–13.

5. The most widely recognised authority on the Treaty of Waitangi is Claudia Orange, *The Treaty of Waitangi*.

Zealand, and in 1841 New Zealand was formally separated from New South Wales.

A treaty that in essence defrauded the Maori, a mixture of authorised and unauthorised land purchases by ever-increasing numbers of white settlers, and the rapid acquisition of firearms by the Maori led to the New Zealand Land Wars of the 1860s. By the time the dust settled, much Maori land in the North Island was alienated from its tribal owners. Ironically, the tribes that remained neutral or supported the British lost most; unsubdued tribes occupying marginal lands were left in possession of what the Pakeha did not yet want.

With peace restored and a British garrison guaranteeing security, British and Scandinavian immigrants began to pour into the islands. Existing towns grew into cities, and new towns sprang up. Responsible government, banks, schools, and universities were founded. By 1890, all the institutions of Western civilisation were established to regulate Pakeha life in this far-distant outpost of the British Empire.

During the 1890s, New Zealand was at the forefront of world movements for female franchise and social welfare legislation. Most of the land was well watered and fertile; wheat, sheep, and dairy farms prospered. Towards the end of the century refrigeration made possible a new and lucrative export industry, and New Zealand butter, cheese, mutton, and beef were shipped in large quantities to England. The government borrowed heavily to finance capital works and its pioneering social programs, with the result that the struggling colony soon found itself deeply in debt.

European diseases introduced into New Zealand had a devastating effect on the Maori population. Intertribal wars in the 1820s and the Land Wars of the 1860s also contributed to shrinking Maori numbers so that, by the beginning of the twentieth century, Pakeha settlers outnumbered the indigenous Maori inhabitants, whose numbers had shrunk from Cook's estimate of 100,000 to about 40,000. Following Darwin, most Europeans mistakenly assumed that the Maori were a dying race whose demise was to be regretted and whose passing was to be eased by the care and ministrations of the now predominant Pakeha. Land courts were established to deal with Maori claims, and four Maori seats were designated in the colonial parliament. New Zealanders began to pride themselves on their exemplary race relations, a pride that persisted for half a century till post-World War II urbanisation of the Maori brought the two races into really close contact for the first time since the Land Wars.

Nevertheless, compared with the treatment of Aborigines in Australia, New Zealand's record was good, if far from blameless. As in the Australian colonies, a national identity began to emerge and strengthen in New Zealand during World War I as Maori and Pakeha fought in the Dardanelles and France. New Zealanders (both Maori and Pakeha) and Australians fell together at Gallipoli, and the acronym "Anzac"[6] was untainted by racial discrimination.

A generation later, the exploits and courage of the Maori Battalion in the Second World War won the respect not only of New Zealanders but of ally and enemy alike. Maori and Pakeha servicemen and women returned to New Zealand after the war to take up the opportunities offered by a grateful country. In unprecedented numbers, Maori qualified for trades and professions. As the European Common Market eroded New Zealand's agricultural prosperity, Maori movement to the cities for education and employment accelerated, and the Treaty of Waitangi became a focal point for increasing racial tension. Contemporary New Zealanders are still struggling to reconcile resurgent Maori identity with now firmly entrenched Pakeha values.

Mormon missionaries sent from America to serve in the Australasian Mission (Australia and New Zealand) first visited New Zealand from Sydney in 1854, and the first New Zealand branch of the LDS Church was organised at Karori, near Wellington, the following year. Another branch was organised by immigrant European converts in Kaiapoi, near Christchurch, in 1867. Despite the lack of a consistent American missionary presence in New Zealand until the late 1870s, Mormon converts in both small branches proved remarkably faithful. Although many of their number joined the body of the LDS Church in Utah, these small branches provided a foundation in the 1880s when the headquarters of the Australasian Mission changed from Australia to New Zealand and the mission's main thrust changed from proselytising among the European population to intensive work among the indigenous Maori.

This volume examines various aspects of the interaction of an American church and its Maori flock from 1881 until today, when it claims more than 100,000 adherents in New Zealand, about 70 percent of them Maori and Pacific Islanders. While the story of the Mormon mission in New Zealand is told in *Tiki and Temple: The Mormon Mission in New Zealand, 1854–1958*, the principal milestones of this history are listed in the following timeline for the convenience of readers of this volume.

---

6. Australian and New Zealand Army Corps.

Time Line

1851   Official opening of the Australasian Mission, headquarters Sydney

1854   First Mormon missionaries visit New Zealand (from Sydney)

1855   Karori Branch organised near Wellington, North Island

1867   Kaiapoi Branch organised near Christchurch, South Island

1878   Beginning of continuous Mormon missionary presence in New Zealand

1879   First Relief Society organised in New Zealand in Christchurch

1881   Mission headquarters changed from Sydney to Auckland

       First systematic preaching by Mormon elders to Maori

       First LDS tract translated into Maori

1883   First Maori LDS branches organised

1885   First Hui Tau (annual mission conference) held

1886   First Mormon schools opened in New Zealand

1889   First Maori edition of Book of Mormon published

1897   Australasian Mission divided into Australian and New Zealand Missions, effective 1 January 1898

1901   79 branches with 4,457 members including 1,287 children under eight

       First Maori Relief Societies organised

1903   First LDS marriage celebrant gazetted by New Zealand government

1907   First issue of the *Elders' Messenger* (later *Te Karere)*

1909   Auckland meetinghouse and Mission Home dedicated

1913   Maori Agricultural College opened

1914 World War I begins

1917 American missionaries refused visas to enter New Zealand

1918 World War I ends

Second Maori edition of Book of Mormon published

1919 Maori edition of Doctrine and Covenants and Pearl of Great Price published

1921 Visit of Apostle David O. McKay

1925 Ratana Church organised

1928 First Maori district presidents appointed

1930 Fifteen districts totalling 7,256 Latter-day Saints in New Zealand

1931 Maori Agricultural College closed

1932 Missionary numbers depleted to eleven by Great Depression

1938 Visit of Apostle George Albert Smith

1939 World War II begins

1940 American missionaries evacuated

1941 United States enters World War II after bombing of Pearl Harbor

1945 World War II ends

1946 Missionaries from Canada/U.S. return to New Zealand

1947 Matthew Cowley's first visit as an apostle

1948 Replacement for Maori Agricultural College announced

1953 New Auckland meetinghouse dedicated

1955 Church President David O. McKay visits New Zealand

New Zealand Temple announced

First elders' quorums organised

Total membership 13,000, of whom 11,000 were Maori

1958 Church President David O. McKay dedicates the Hamilton New Zealand Temple and the Church College of New Zealand

Auckland New Zealand Stake organised

New Zealand Mission divided

1960 Annual mission conferences (Hui Tau) discontinued

Publication of *Te Karere* discontinued

Hamilton and Hawkes Bay stakes organised

1967   Church administrative offices open in Auckland

1970   Seminary and Institute of Religion programs introduced

1975   Area Supervisor for South Pacific appointed, based in New Zealand

1976   Church President Spencer W. Kimball visits New Zealand

1984   Pacific Area Presidency announced, headquarters in Sydney

1989   Maori edition of Book of Mormon reprinted

1991   Census results list LDS Church as sixth largest Christian denomination in New Zealand

1998   Australia/New Zealand Area announced

2005   New Zealand/Pacific Area and Australia Area announced

2008   New Zealand, Australia, and South Pacific islands reunited as Pacific Area, headquarters in Auckland

2009   Church College of New Zealand closed

2012   LDS membership 102,574 in twenty-five stakes and three mission districts

Chapter 1

Mormon Beliefs and the Maori

Although Mormon missionary work began among the Pakeha (Europeans) in New Zealand as early as 1854, only sporadic attempts were made to preach to Maori before 1883. From that time, Mormon missionaries systematically tried to learn the Maori language and convert Maori, with considerable success. By January 1887, there were 2,292 Latter-day Saints in the Australasian Mission, 2,055 (89.7 percent) of them Maori, and approximately fourteen pairs of American Mormon missionaries were giving pastoral care to the converts who were organised into districts and branches.[1]

Why the early Mormon missionaries found success among the Maori is a question that has long intrigued both LDS and non-LDS writers. Answers have ranged from the extremes of a nineteenth-century Anglican historian who considered the Maori to be superstitious and credulous enough to accept something as bizarre as he perceived Mormonism to be,[2] to the Mormon "faithful history" interpretation that "the Maoris appear to have been prepared in special ways for the coming of the Mormon missionaries."[3]

Like many other generalisations, there is an element of truth in both assertions. Depending on one's definition of the word, Maori *were* superstitious. But "one man's superstition is another man's religion, . . ." cautions James Axtell. "*Superstition* has no objective reality; it is merely an aspersion used by one group to denigrate the religion of another."[4] In traditional

---

1. John Ephraim Magleby, New Zealand Mission Journal, introduction to Volume 4 (27 March–12 April 1888), 4–6.

2. Eugene Stock, *The History of the Church Missionary Society, Its Environment, Its Men and Its Work*, 3:556.

3. R. Lanier Britsch, "Maori Traditions and the Mormon Church," 38.

4. James Axtell, *The Invasion Within: The Contest of Cultures in Colonial North America*, 13; emphasis his.

terms, *religio* described a rational, moral, and public system of belief; *superstitio* was regarded as irrational, private, and probably immoral.

Many Maori were willing to believe what Pakeha (European, non-Maori) churchmen found unbelievable, to find credible what they found incredible. The traditional taha Maori (Maori worldview) was compatible with Mormon belief in revelation, prophecy, and other gifts of the Spirit.[5] In the 1880s and 1890s, the leap of faith necessary for a Pakeha Anglican or Methodist to accept this American church that claimed continuing revelation and living prophets was much greater than for a Maori. Ian Barker contrasted the Mormon claim to continuing revelation with the teachings of Protestant churches which believed that revelation had ceased. "In the eyes of Polynesians, the Mormon Church possessed God's favour for He continued to reveal His will to it," he wrote.[6]

Maori Prophecies and Mormonism

At the other end of the spectrum, the belief that the Maori race was specially prepared to receive the Mormon gospel also has an element of truth. This Mormon claim was originally made in the context of comparing a slower response to Mormonism in some other Polynesian missions than in New Zealand, where, Mormons believe, indigenous prophets had foretold the coming of a new religion. Several such prophecies are celebrated by Mormons.[7]

But interpretation of prophecy is a subjective art. Some Maori religions, such as Ringatu and Ratana, have likewise been seen as the fulfilment of these prophecies.[8] Particularly is this true of the prophecy most frequently quoted by Mormons, that of Paora Potangaroa, made at Te Oreore, near Masterton in the Wairarapa Valley, in 1881, one version of which reads: "There is a religious denomination coming for us; perhaps it will come from the sea, perhaps it will emerge here."[9] Mormon accounts usually give a slightly different translation, omitting "perhaps it will emerge here"; it is this latter phrase that undoubtedly legitimised the establishment of the

5. James Irwin, *An Introduction to Maori Religion: Its Character before European Contact and Its Survival in Contemporary Maori and New Zealand Culture*, 6–7; Bronwyn Elsmore, *Like Them That Dream: The Maori and the Old Testament*, 86.

6. Ian R. Barker, "The Connexion: The Mormon Church and the Maori People," 32.

7. See, for example, *He Poropititanga Enei: Na nga Poropiti Maori o nga wa o mua*, and Britsch, "Maori Traditions and the Mormon Church."

8. Peter Lineham, "The Mormon Message in the Context of Maori Culture," 87–88.

9. Bronwyn Elsmore, *Mana from Heaven: A Century of Maori Prophets in New Zealand*, 284.

Ratana Church in the eyes of its adherents. But to Mormons, Te Potanga-roa's prophecy and covenant explicitly identified Mormonism.[10]

As well, Maori prophecies variously foretold that those bringing the true church to the Maori would come from the east, across the ocean, and travel in twos. They could be recognised because they would pray with their arms raised to the square; they would record genealogy, teach salvation for the dead, and live among the Maori.[11] Many Mormons have not confront-ed the fact that not all these characteristics were unique to Mormonism. Perhaps what is most significant about these prophecies is not their spe-cific subject matter but that Maori were accustomed to living prophets;[12] it was not too difficult for them to accept another, just as two generations earlier they had not found it difficult to add another god to their pantheon.

"Top-Down" Conversion Pattern

To a significant degree, Mormon success depended on the conversions of influential rangatira.[13] Elders Alma Greenwood and Ira N. Hinckley welcomed the prospect of baptising Manihera Te Whenuanui Rangitakai-waho, a Wairarapa rangatira; and not just for the sake of his personal salva-tion. "If he would embrace the truth it would be of great utility in opening our way to the natives," wrote Elder Greenwood.[14] The Mormon elders were also pleased when they baptised Hohepa Otene Meihana, a rangatira of the Ngati Kahungunu, and still more pleased when his father, an even more important rangatira, was also baptised.[15] In July 1881, King Tawhaio

---

10. Matthew Cowley, "Maori Chief Predicts Coming of L.D.S. Missionaries," 696–98, 754–56; Stuart Meha, "A Prophetic Utterance of Paora Potangaroa," 298.

11. Britsch, "Maori Traditions and the Mormon Church," 41; Brian W. Hunt, *Zion in New Zealand: A History of the Church of Jesus Christ of Latter-day Saints in New Zealand, 1854–1977*, 9–11.

12. Elsmore, *Mana from Heaven*, 160–89.

13. Lineham, "The Mormon Message in the Context of Maori Culture," 73–74. It is important to note that "it is misleading to translate rangatira as chief . . . for only a few rangatira had as much influence as this word implies. Early observers often referred to them as either freemen or gentlemen, using this word to refer to well-to-do men of good birth and high social standing." Margaret Orbell, "The Traditional Maori Family," 115 note 3. This is confirmed by H. W. Williams, *Dic-tionary of the Maori Language*, which gives, as well as "chief," "a person of good breeding" and "well-born, noble," in other words, a gentleman. See also Pieter Hendrik de Bres, *Religion in Atene: Religious Associations and the Urban Maori*, 41.

14. "Our New Zealand Letter," Alma Greenwood to Editor, dated 1 December 1883, *Territorial Enquirer*, 11 January 1884, in Journal History, 11 January 1884, 11.

15. Correspondence: Interesting Letter from New Zealand to the YMMIA [Young Men's Mutual Improvement Association] of Elsinore [Utah] from Charles

invited Elder John S. Ferris to visit him the following December. Ferris was elated at the invitation; he noted in his journal that whichever church the king and the prophet Te Kooti joined, all their people would join also.[16]

Elders Amasa Aldridge and Edwin L. Davies deliberately sought out the prophet Te Whiti in 1885. Te Whiti was an important chief as well as being regarded as a prophet by the people. "It is a curious fact, yet nevertheless true, that where a people place so much confidence in one man as in this case, a person might talk for a week, bringing any amount of truth to substantiate his argument, yet in nine cases out of ten, they would never heed it if their 'Rangatira' did not take the lead," the elders wrote. "We found it but little use to preach to them as they were firm believers in their prophet and said they would believe none of the Pakehas. . . . We were told by them to go to the 'Home of the Lord' that if he would believe us, they would."[17] Elder John E. Magleby talked to an old chief who favoured the LDS Church but would not join it unless the Maori king did. "Where the King went was where he were [sic] going even if it were to hell," wrote Magleby. "His faith was pinned to man and not to God."[18] These experiences provide near-classic, if microcosmic, examples of "top-down" conversion patterns found throughout Christian mission history from medieval times.[19]

It became Mormon custom to ordain baptised chiefs to the priesthood and appoint them to preside over Maori branches; but this did not happen automatically. "There was a bad spirit manifested on account of one of the chiefs not getting ordained to the office of an elder," wrote William Gardner after an 1885 conference at Napier, "but it was talked over and the most of them left feeling well."[20] Another exception was Hare Teimana, the first chief converted to Mormonism and baptised in the Waikato on Christmas Day, 1882. Two months later when the Waotu Branch was organised, Teimana declined the office of branch president, feeling unworthy. His brother-in-law, Harry Carter, was appointed instead.[21]

The influence of the rangatira could also, of course, have negative effects. In 1887, Elder Magleby complained that the people in the Waiapu district were "too chief-ridden" for Mormon success.[22] A decade later, missionaries

Anderson," *Deseret News*, 28 April 1885, in Journal History, 28 April 1885, 4.

16. John Solomon Ferris, Journals, 1880–82, 4 June 1881.

17. "Correspondence: A Maori 'Prophet': Amasa Aldridge to Editor, dated 29 March 1885," *Deseret Evening News*, 25 April 1885, 3.

18. Magleby, Journal, 27 January 1901.

19. Carol M. Cusack, "Towards a General Theory of Conversion," 5–19.

20. William Gardner, Diary, 19 January 1885.

21. New Zealand Mission, Manuscript History, 25 February 1883.

22. John E. Magleby, "Among the Maoris, Funeral of a Chief—Queer Native

were cautioned to consult the mission president before excommunicating or otherwise imposing church discipline on any chief.[23] Half a century later again, a rangatira was so offended when the mission president released him from his calling as branch president that he threatened to leave the Church and take his whole hapu (kinship group, sub-tribe) with him.[24]

To cite the importance of the conversion of important rangatira and the networking of chiefly influence as reasons for Mormon success is not, however, to answer the question, but merely to make it necessary to delve one layer deeper: What features of Mormonism appealed to the rangatira? While some factors are undoubtedly more important than others, and some perhaps of doubtful authenticity in the light of modern scholarship, there were many features that set Mormonism apart from the mainstream Christian churches in New Zealand, and its appeal to Maori may be traced to a combination of these factors.

Perceived Mormon/Maori Parallels

The Maori propensity for "top-down" conversions, discussed above, illustrates the importance of group or collective experience in Polynesian socio-religious organisations.[25] Nineteenth-century Mormonism was a "collective" religion, and as such had a greater appeal for many Maori than those mainstream churches that stressed individual salvation and a personal relationship with Christ.[26] Communitarianism was still a Mormon ideal in the late nineteenth century when large numbers of Maori joined the LDS Church. Today, the Mormon Church teaches a more individualistic doctrine and of building a personal relationship with Christ, and the Mormon communities formerly established under the "United Order" are now seen only as symbols of a hoped-for millennial state.[27]

However, the nineteenth-century Mormon Church was first and foremost a millennialist religion that offered hope of redemption—individual and national, temporal and spiritual—to the Maori. Anthropologist Erik G. Schwimmer demonstrates the continuing appeal of millennialism to Maori by quoting twentieth-century adherence figures: in 1961, 4 percent of the general population of New Zealand identified with millenarian

Customs," Letter to the Editor, *Deseret Evening News*, 30 November 1887, [2].

23. Ezra Foss Richards, Journal, 1 April 1897.

24. Gordon Claridge Young, Journal, 26 April 1951.

25. Tony Swain and Garry Trompf, *The Religions of Oceania*, 7–8. The "top-down" pattern of conversion was most frequent when Maori embraced Christianity fifty years before the appearance of Mormonism among them.

26. Cusack, "Towards a General Theory of Conversion," 8.

27. L. Dwight Israelson, "United Orders," 4:1493–95.

churches, but among Maori the relevant statistic was 26 percent.[28] "During the nineteenth century the people had lost their tribal way of life, their lands, their traditional religion and their mana or prestige," wrote J. M. Henderson. "At the beginning of the twentieth century it was unlikely that a faith would appeal to the remnants and survivors unless it expressed their deepest feelings and offered the hope of recovering that which had been lost."[29] Latter-day Saint interpretations of Book of Mormon prophecies confirmed Maori identity as chosen people, heirs to the choicest of all promised lands. Mormonism appealed to dispossessed Maori in much the same ways as it did to depressed labourers suffering the effects of enclosure and industrialisation in England half a century earlier.

Mormon missionaries soon noted other parallels between traditional Maori cosmology and religion and Mormonism. Among these was the Maori concept of multiple, anthropomorphic gods, with a supreme God, Io, and other "high gods," plus lesser or departmental gods.[30] The scholarly debate over whether Io is a pre- or post-European-contact element of Maori religion is irrelevant to the present discussion; even if the concept was post-European-contact, Io was firmly established by the time Mormonism penetrated Maoridom.[31] As modern scholars have noted, Mormonism's vertical and anthropomorphic theology was attractive to Polynesians.[32] Mormon missionaries in New Zealand quickly equated Io with Elohim; and Mormon teachings that Elohim (God the Father), his Son Jesus Christ, and the Holy Ghost are separate divine beings fitted well with the Maori concept of "high gods." Mormons believe that each of several resurrected biblical and Book of Mormon prophets restored different parts of the true gospel to Joseph Smith and that Mormon men and women who participate in temple ceremonies and remain faithful to the covenants they make there will eventually achieve godhood and have the opportunity of creating their own worlds. To the unsophisticated Maori of the late nineteenth century, this teaching offered a simple equation, perhaps, with "departmental gods."

Mormons often compared LDS emphasis on researching genealogy with Maori veneration of long-departed ancestors and recitation of whakapapa (ceremonial oral recitation of ancestry). Another concept common to

---

28. Erik G. Schwimmer, "Mormonism in a Maori Village: A Study in Social Change," 40.

29. J. McLeod Henderson, *Ratana: The Man, the Church, the Political Movement*, 10.

30. Swain and Trompf, *The Religions of Oceania*, 126–27.

31. For a discussion of Io as an innovation, see Margaret Orbell, *The Illustrated Encyclopedia of Maori Myth and Legend*, 72–74. There is ongoing debate on this question.

32. Swain and Trompf, *The Religions of Oceania*, 219.

both Mormon and Maori was the idea of opposition in all things: to the Mormon, good and evil; to the Maori, noa and tapu.[33] Neither Maori nor Mormons distinguished between sacred and secular;[34] to both, religion was not simply an aspect of culture (or vice versa), their religion *was* their culture. While there was philosophical similarity, the difference of praxis led to inevitable conflict after Maori conversion, as some American Mormon leaders failed to understand that "human cultures ... provid[e] foundations for people's lives, and ... a person's culture is an essential part of them."[35] "At the grass roots," wrote Swain and Trompf, "evangelisation or formal education do not result in a strong acculturation into Western (or global) styles of thinking."[36] Mormon acculturation of their Maori converts will be discussed more fully in succeeding chapters.

Cultural Immersion of Mormon Missionaries

In the nineteenth century, Mormon elders could share their message with most Maori only if they spoke "te reo Maori" (the Maori language). Accordingly, they lived in whare raupo (rush huts) in Maori villages, sleeping on rush mats spread on the floor and eating from communal pots with their fingers. The Anglican Church Missionary Society (CMS) missionaries in earlier decades had kept aloof, maintaining the niceties of civilisation; their European-style houses and customs were thought to be models for their "barbarian" congregations. "The Pakeha settlers and the occasional missionary who lived in the villages with the Maori people, were criticized by the missionaries for their lapse in social and moral standards," wrote Bronwyn Elsmore.[37]

Most Mormon elders adjusted well to Maori culture, eating, sleeping, and living with the people. It has been suggested that this cultural immersion was forced on them by lack of means to do otherwise.[38] To some extent this is true. They did not have the funds to build European-style homes, but this ultimately worked to their advantage. Cultural immersion not only helped them learn the language quickly and so facilitate their evangelistic success, it also won the hearts of the Maori, who were accustomed to Anglican and other Protestant ministers building European-style houses and

33. Book of Mormon, 2 Nephi 2:11–15; Irwin, *An Introduction to Maori Religion*, 23–31.
34. Irwin, *An Introduction to Maori Religion*, 5–6; Doctrine and Covenants 29:34–35.
35. Cusack, "Towards a General Theory of Conversion," 8.
36. Swain and Trompf, *The Religions of Oceania*, 205.
37. Elsmore, *Like Them That Dream*, 17.
38. Lineham, "The Mormon Message in the Context of Maori Culture," 71.

living apart from their flocks.[39] It is true that not all enjoyed the experience; but some degree of culture shock was inevitable and should not be taken as evidence of what is today perceived as racism.

To build homes, schools, and churches, the early Christian missionaries required land and labour from their flocks; the Mormon elders, at least at first, asked for neither. When small LDS meetinghouses and "elders' homes" were built in Maori pa from the 1880s, they were invariably built by Maori initiative on Maori land and remained the property of local Maori. When construction of the Maori Agricultural College began in 1912, LDS Church officials purposely bought the land from Pakeha owners so that it could not become the subject of Maori grievance. Nor were collections taken at Mormon services.

However, the perception that Mormon missionaries were young single men and for this reason did not need Maori donations to house and support their families is anachronistic.[40] Until 1900, Mormon missionaries were overwhelmingly older, married men.[41] The difference was not marital status but the relatively brief time (usually three years for a foreign-language mission) that Mormon men spent in the mission field. Ordained Protestant ministers became "career missionaries," dedicating much of their lives to missionary service, and taking it for granted that their wives and children would accompany or follow them. Mormon families were cared for by their home ward or stake in America during the temporary absence of missionary husbands and fathers, or they were supported by the independent efforts of the wives; only four Mormon women accompanied their missionary husbands to New Zealand before 1900.

Maori Alienation from Mainstream Christian Churches

Mormon missionaries also profited by the alienation of many Maori tribes from the mainstream Christian churches. CMS missionary promotion of the Treaty of Waitangi (1840) was a long-standing grievance, as was some CMS missionary involvement in large-scale land purchases. When CMS missionaries aided British regiments during the Land Wars of the 1860s, many Maori withdrew from the missions and developed hybrid versions of Christianity; indigenous Maori churches and prophet-movements proliferated.

---

39. Hunt, *Zion in New Zealand*, 18; Elsmore, *Like Them That Dream*, 17, 19.

40. Barker, "The Connexion," 42; Lineham, "The Mormon Message in the Context of Maori Culture," 69.

41. Before 1895, 82 percent of Mormon missionaries were married; between 1895 and 1900, the percentage dropped to 51 percent. William G. Hartley, "From Men to Boys: LDS Aaronic Priesthood Offices, 1829–1996," 113.

Coincident with declining Maori participation in mainline Christian mission institutions came a paucity of CMS funding for New Zealand. The CMS eventually withdrew in 1902, expecting local Church of England dioceses to carry on.[42] Instead, Anglican missionary work was largely left to the corps of frequently unordained Maori ministers, leaving the field open for the Mormon missionaries. Newspaper editors were not slow to highlight the irony of New Zealand Pakeha congregations supporting missions to indigenous people overseas while allowing American Mormons to minister to the local Maori tribes.[43]

As others have pointed out, the Mormons arrived after the hard work was done.[44] By the time the Mormons began to proselytise among the Maori, the mainstream churches had changed the Maori way of life forever. When the Maori became Christian, they forsook such customs as cannibalism, suicide of the widows of chiefs, female infanticide, slavery, and, to some extent, polygamy. The Mormons basically recruited converts from existing Maori congregations of the different Christian denominations and from the indigenous Maori/Christian hybrid churches.

Mormon missionaries frequently referred to Maori disillusionment with the Protestant churches, especially the Church of England, over land ownership. "It was not that the land issue turned Maori towards the Latter-day Saints but rather that it dented the credibility of the Mihinare church [Missionary church, i.e., the Church of England-sponsored Church Missionary Society]," wrote Peter Lineham, citing specific disputes over Church of England failure to build promised schools on donated Maori land at Porirua and in the Wairarapa. After the Porirua Maori community lost an historic court battle over the failure of the Church of England to build a promised school on land the local Maori tribes had donated for this

---

42. W. P. Morrell, *The Anglican Church in New Zealand: A History*, 121.

43. See, for example, "Mormons and Maori," letter to editor signed by "Alpha," *Wairarapa Standard*, 20 August 1883, clipping pasted in Alma Greenwood, Scrapbook, [11]; *Wairarapa Standard*, quoted in "Mormonism among the Maoris," *Deseret Evening News*, 10 February 1891, 4; *Marlborough Express*, 28 November 1893, quoted by Benjamin Goddard to Mrs. Benjamin Goddard, "Mormons in Maoriland," *Deseret News*, 25 January 1894, in Journal History, 25 January 1894, 5; "The Mormons and the Maori," Christchurch *Evening News*, n.d., reprinted in *Te Karere (The Messenger)* 7, no. 10 (7 May 1913): 111; unidentified newspaper article reported by Esther Linford, "Gospel Grows in New Zealand," *Deseret Evening News*, 21 March 1908, in Journal History, 7 February 1908, 3.

44. Schwimmer, "Mormonism in a Maori Village," 79; Barker, "The Connexion," 41.

purpose, there was what Lineham calls a "wholesale secession" of the local Maori iwi (tribe) to the Mormon Church.[45]

The land question, inextricably connected in Maori minds with CMS missionary promotion of the Treaty of Waitangi, was and remains the most complicated issue of Maori/Pakeha relations. It has been suggested that most Mormon elders were unaware of the deeper issues at stake and consequently did not realise that these had any bearing on their mass conversions at Porirua and in the Wairarapa.[46] It would be more accurate, perhaps, to say that many Mormon *historians* have been unaware of the land issue as a factor in Mormon success in these areas.

Elders Alma Greenwood and Ira N. Hinckley, who baptised many Maori in the Wairarapa in the mid-1880s, certainly understood the connection between the land question and Maori conversion to Mormonism there; Greenwood carefully clipped and saved local newspaper commentary on the subject, including his own lengthy published correspondence with an opponent identified only by the pseudonym "Alpha." A few years later, another Mormon missionary, Charles Anderson, was convinced that Maori prophet-movements were a reaction to the "ministers who have through strategy stolen their lands from them. Especially are they down on the Church of England."[47]

In fact, most early Mormon missionaries were well aware that Maori disenchantment with the CMS missionaries, specifically over land, worked to their advantage. Their journals contain many accounts of preaching to large gatherings assembled for land court hearings and frequent repetitions of Maori accusations against the mainstream Christian missionaries. Few Mormon missionaries did not hear the classic "look up to heaven and pray" story. The version recorded in 1895 by Assistant LDS Church Historian Andrew Jenson in a village near Gisborne is typical. "Tamati Waka related some of his experience in the land courts, and denounced the actions of the Church of England missionaries," wrote Jenson, "who, he said, had taught the Maori to pray to God; but while the confiding Maori was engaged in his devotion, the missionaries and other pakehas (Europeans) stole his land from under him."[48]

---

45. Lineham, "The Mormon Message in the Context of Maori Culture," 78.

46. Ibid.

47. Charles Anderson, "The New Zealand Mission, 3 December 1884, Waotu," *Deseret Evening News*, 9 February 1885, [4].

48. New Zealand Mission, Manuscript History, 7 November 1895, reversion to 1895 inserted after 1900; Andrew Jenson, "Jenson's Travels: Letter No. XXXVIII," *Deseret News Weekly*, 28 March 1896, 465. Versions of this story also featured in earlier accounts of Native American/missionary relations. It seems to have been

Although Benjamin Goddard seems to have been the only nineteenth-century Mormon missionary to publish an account of the land question, many others referred to it in their journals and their letters home. Nelson S. Bishop typifies missionary awareness of the problems. "There is considerable feelings existing among [the Maori] over their land troubles," he recorded in his journal one day in 1888. Bishop worried that the result would be some kind of Antipodean *Bleak House*. "I sometimes think that they will spend the whole value of the land in fighting in the court," he wrote.[49] Francis W. Kirkham summarised the Maori position in a long journal entry in 1898. "The Maori side of the war will never be told," he concluded, "how with poor arms and little ammunition, with scanty food, they fought and held at bay for so many years the troops of England."[50] Later mission presidents such as John E. Magleby, Matthew Cowley, and Gordon C. Young urged Maori to beware of land consolidation schemes, to keep or acquire and, where possible, work their land.

Several commentators have suggested that an American church provided an attractive alternative for Maori tribes disillusioned with things British.[51] Well-known Presbyterian leader John G. Laughton (1891–1965), speaking of Mormon success in Nuhaka after the disintegration of the CMS mission there, stated that the early American missionaries deliberately capitalised on anti-British feeling.[52] But most scholars also agree that the iwi most responsive to Mormonism were, on the whole, loyalist or neutral tribes such as Ngati Kahungunu, tribes that had actively fought alongside the British or remained neutral during the Land Wars.

While there was initial Mormon success in the Waikato, the American missionaries found the King Country Maori among the most unreceptive to their message. As late as 1914, missionaries were quoting Maori land

---

imported from America into New Zealand and adopted by Maori. According to Vine Deloria Jr., "It has been said of missionaries that when they arrived they had only the Book and we had the land; now we have the Book and they have the land." *Custer Died for Your Sins: An Indian Manifesto*, 101.

49. Nelson Spicer Bishop, New Zealand Mission Diaries, 20 November 1888, 400.
50. Francis W. Kirkham, Diaries, 28 February 1898, 8:22.
51. Pieter H. de Bres, "The Religious Affiliation and the Religious Behaviour of the New Zealand Maori—A Sociological Study of the Religious Life of the Maori in a Suburban Area," 46; Ian G. Barber, "Between Biculturalism and Assimilation: The Changing Place of Maori Culture in the Twentieth Century New Zealand Mormon Church," 142; Lineham, "The Mormon Message in the Context of Maori Culture," 79.
52. J. G. Laughton, *From Forest Trail to City Street: The Story of the Presbyterian Church among the Maori People*, 13.

grievances, "real or imaginary," as the cause of earlier Maori hostility to *all* Pakeha, including American Mormons, in Taranaki.[53] In the light of this perception, it is at least possible that to see Maori tribes embracing an American church in the nineteenth century as a reaction to things British is to credit them with a degree of discrimination and sophistication many did not then possess.

On the other hand, both Peter Lineham and Ian Barber point out that the Kotahitanga mo Te Tiriti o Waitangi, or Maori parliament, was centred in the Wairarapa and two of its leaders were prominent Mormon converts, Hamiora Mangai Kahia and Te Whatahoro (John A. Jury).[54] Post-war confiscation of land from loyal or neutral tribes eroded their allegiance to the British government and the Church of England. But it should also be kept in mind that American Mormonism was only one alternative available to disenchanted Protestant Maori. Maori prophets Te Kooti (on the East Coast) and Te Whiti (on the West Coast) both had larger followings than did the Mormons; a generation later, the Ratana Church (which soon became politicised in order to pursue the land question) provided another religious focus for Maori discontent over land issues.[55]

The Book of Mormon and Maori Origins

Undoubtedly the Mormon doctrine that had the greatest impact on Maori conversion and that underlay most other reasons for the appeal of the Mormon message for Maori, was the belief that Polynesians are descendants of the expatriate Israelites of the Book of Mormon and are therefore eligible for the redemptive blessings promised to scattered Israel. This belief defined Mormon perceptions of Maori origins and destiny and led the early Mormon missionaries to disregard contemporary wisdom that forecast the continuing decline and eventual disappearance (or at least absorption) of the Maori race. Book of Mormon prophecies, they believed, would be fulfilled, and the Lamanites on the isles of the sea, like those in the Americas, would be regenerated.

The origins of the Polynesian people have been debated since the first European ships ventured into the Pacific, as the large volume of literature on the subject attests.[56] Although many Mormons (including many

53. New Zealand Mission, Manuscript History, 5 July 1914.

54. Lineham, "The Mormon Message in the Context of Maori Culture," 78; Barber, "Between Biculturalism and Assimilation," 145.

55. Barber, "Between Biculturalism and Assimilation,"150–55; Michael Hill and Wiebe Zwaga, "Religion," 284.

56. One of the best summaries of the literature to the mid-1960s is Alan Howard, "Polynesian Origins and Migrations: A Review of Two Centuries of Specula-

Maori Mormons) think that the LDS Church is unique in its belief that Polynesians are related to Native Americans and that both are remnants of the house of Israel,[57] such beliefs were neither new nor unique when the Book of Mormon was published in 1830. Only the specific but uncanonised Mormon belief that the various Polynesian peoples are descended from Hagoth, a Nephite shipbuilder who lived about 54 B.C. on the west coast of either Central or South America, is really unique.[58] It was upon the basis of this fragmentary Book of Mormon story that Mormon missionaries found success among the Maori, but prior widespread acceptance by Maori of Christian speculation about their Israelitish origin provided a fertile field in which the Mormon message flourished.

Historian M. P. K. Sorrenson notes that pre-Darwin explanations of Polynesian origins were strongly influenced by the Judeo/Christian theology that all races must have descended from one of Noah's three sons. "The blackest and apparently most primitive of them, like the American negroes and Australian aborigines, were classed as the sons of Ham. But others of lighter hue and more advanced culture, including the American Indians and the Polynesians, were considered to be the sons of Shem."[59] Evidence was sought to confirm their prehistoric journeying from the Middle East to their present abodes.

This categorisation of newly discovered peoples in terms of Western sacred history was likewise not new. Anthropologists and historians have long noted a similar phenomenon in fifteenth-, sixteenth- and seventeenth-century European encounters with the inhabitants of the Americas. "What was profoundly unsettling and thereby unimaginable to many Europeans colonizing the Americas was the possibility that people could exist outside

tion and Theory," 45–101. A highly respected addition to the literature is Geoffrey Irwin, *The Prehistoric Exploration and Colonisation of the Pacific* (1992). Numerous articles and books published since 1992 discuss modern theories of Polynesian origins in the light of contemporary scientific findings.

57. For example, a well-educated and highly respected Maori Latter-day Saint, Stuart Meha, thought this was a purely Mormon belief. In 1948, he stated that former LDS mission president William T. Stewart addressed a Church of England Synod in the 1880s, telling an audience of 2,000 that "the Maoris were a remnant of the House of Israel." The people were surprised, noted Meha, "for although Christianity had been with them 70 years, that was the first occasion when such a claim was advanced." Meha, "A Prophetic Utterance of Paora Potangaroa," 299.

58. Hagoth, a "curious man," led two emigrations into "the west sea, by the narrow neck which led into the land northward." His ships never returned to the parent colony. See Book of Mormon, Alma 63:5–8.

59. M. P. K. Sorrenson, *Maori Origins and Migrations: The Genesis of Some Pakeha Myths and Legends*, 11, 83.

of history, especially outside of the sacred history of the Bible," writes American anthropologist Thomas W. Murphy. "The threat posed by the existence of people beyond the limits of the history and knowledge of the Old World was overcome by incorporating the American Indians into a grand narrative and then establishing the certainty of that narrative. . . . With the Old Testament as the only well-documented account of a 'primitive' way of life, the earliest European explorers and historians tended to favor the hypothesis that the original inhabitants of the Americas were descended from the lost tribes of Israel." Murphy cites Francisco Lopez de Gomara in the early sixteenth century and a long list of English and American writers including Thomas Thorowgood, Charles Beatty, John Eliot, Cotton Mather, William Penn, and Jonathan Edwards, all of whom "advocated an Israelitish origin for American Indians." This thesis was still popular in the United States in 1830 when the Book of Mormon was published.[60]

As Sorrenson demonstrates, there is a long history of the application of the same ideas to Polynesian peoples of the Pacific. Samuel Marsden, the first to introduce the Maori of Aotearoa[61] to Christianity, was a scholarly man, well-versed in the history of European travels in the Pacific. Aware of such hypotheses, he found little difficulty in carrying their theories over to the Maori, who, he suggested after observing them, may have "sprung from some dispersed Jews." Marsden listed similarities between Old Testament Jews and early nineteenth-century Maori that ranged from warfare customs to the "great natural turn for traffic" of the Maori, who, said Marsden, would "buy and sell anything they have got."[62] The theory of Semitic origins of the Maori remained popular with scholars until at least the 1870s—much longer with followers of Maori prophets Te Kooti and Te Whiti. As Sorrenson points out, it took a new lease on life when Mormon missionaries came among the Maori.[63]

By the middle of the nineteenth century, scientists were divided among three principal theories of Polynesian origin: autochthonous origin (finally discredited by failure to find geological evidence of a missing continent); Asian origins with west-to-east migration; and American origins with east-to-west migration.[64] There were, of course, many variations on each of these themes; for example, some scholars agreed with Asian origins but

---

60. Thomas W. Murphy, "Imagining Lamanites: Constructions of Self and Other in the Book of Mormon," not paginated. See also Allen H. Godbey, *The Lost Tribes a Myth: Suggestions Towards Rewriting Hebrew History*, 2–4.

61. The Maori name for New Zealand.

62. Samuel Marsden, quoted in Sorrenson, *Maori Origins and Migrations*, 14–15.

63. Sorrenson, *Maori Origins and Migrations*, 16–17.

64. Howard, "Polynesian Origins and Migrations," 49.

suggested that the Polynesians arrived in the Pacific via the Bering Straits and the West Coast of America.

Ironically, as scientists during the twentieth century came to broad agreement on Asian origins and a west-to-east migration for the peoples of Polynesia, Mormon Church leaders stated their belief in the American origins of their Polynesian members more and more explicitly, although they stopped short of actually canonising such beliefs as official Church doctrine. "In few cases is the Mormon Church at such odds with 'the learning of men' as in its answers to the intriguing questions of Polynesian origins and migrations," wrote Mormon scholar Russell T. Clement in 1980.[65]

Early Mormon Teachings about Polynesian Origins

Joseph Smith identified Native Americans as descendants of Book of Mormon peoples and sent missionaries to the "Lamanites" in the Western Reserve and in Indian territories west of Missouri in 1830, soon after the organization of the Church. Thirteen years later, he called Addison Pratt and three companions to carry the Mormon message to the inhabitants of the islands of the Pacific. It was not the Prophet, however, but a woman who seems to have made the first Mormon identification of Polynesians as descendants of Book of Mormon people. Louisa Barnes Pratt, who accompanied her husband, Addison Pratt, during his second mission to the Pacific (1850–52), taught the native women of Tubuai in October 1851 that "the Nephites were the ancient fathers of the Tahitians."[66] It is not known how she arrived at this conclusion. Pratt family reminiscences suggest that Louisa's husband, a seaman who had formerly visited Hawaii, discussed similarities between Hawaiian Islanders and Native Americans with Joseph Smith in Nauvoo and that this discussion led Smith to assign Pratt his first Pacific mission in 1843. This sounds logical, but as Australian historian Norman Douglas pointed out, no contemporary documentary evidence has been found for this attempt to trace Louisa Barnes Pratt's ideas to Joseph Smith. That the story is apocryphal may be fairly concluded; nowhere did Pratt or his missionary companions refer to such a view of the Polynesians in their journals or letters during their first (1843) mission to the Pacific.[67]

---

65. Russell T. Clement, "Polynesian Origins: More Word on the Mormon Perspective," 88.
66. Norman Douglas, "The Sons of Lehi and the Seed of Cain: Racial Myths in Mormon Scripture and Their Relevance to the Pacific Islands," 96.
67. Ibid., 94–97.

Meanwhile, in Hawaii in 1851, Elder George Q. Cannon (later a member of the Church's First Presidency) felt strongly impressed that he and his companions should be preaching to the Polynesian population and was told by revelation that they were of the house of Israel.[68] By 1852, this belief was being taught as doctrine by all the LDS Hawaiian missionaries. As has been discussed, this was not a new idea—only the identification of the Polynesian people as descendants of the Lamanites of the Book of Mormon was unique to Mormonism. While Brigham Young referred to Hawaiians as Israelites in 1858,[69] there does not seem to be any record of his positively identifying the Hawaiian people with the Book of Mormon before 1865, by which time the missionaries had long been convinced their Polynesian converts were of Lamanite descent.[70]

These ideas were accepted without question by Mormon Church members. "Reception of the belief in a racial association between the [Native Americans and Polynesians] was an act of faith, a simple extension of literal acceptance of Mormon scripture itself, requiring no scientific proof or external evidence," wrote Norman Douglas. "It was not until much later that Latter-day Saints began to quote the observations of scientists and mythologists in support of their assumptions, and then only to provide further illustrations of what were already held to be self-evident truths." Douglas pointed out that South East Asian origins and west-to-east migration were dismissed as the work of "uninspired men" (that is, those operating without the special guidance of the Spirit believed to actuate Mormon prophets) by the LDS publication *Juvenile Instructor* as early as 1868.[71]

Almost a century later, Mormon journals reported Thor Heyerdahl's *Kon-Tiki* expedition as justification for dismissing the century's steady accumulation of anthropological, archaeological, and linguistic evidence of west-to-east Pacific migration as uninspired.[72] Some Church leaders made no apology for refusing to accept scientific evidence. Apostle Mark E. Pe-

---

68. R. Lanier Britsch, *Unto the Islands of the Sea: A History of the Latter-day Saints in the Pacific*, 97–98.

69. G[eorge] D. Watt, "Discourse by Pres. Brigham Young, Tabernacle, 7 February 1858," *Deseret News*, 17 February 1858, in Journal History, 7 February 1858, 2.

70. Douglas, "The Sons of Lehi and the Seed of Cain," 98.

71. Ibid., 98–99. *The Juvenile Instructor* was a monthly journal published by George Q. Cannon from 1866. It did not become an official Church publication until 1901.

72. Otis Peterson, "Raft Voyage 'Proves' Origin of South Sea Natives," 6–7; and Archibald F. Bennett, "Traditions of Polynesians Give Support to Book of Mormon Story of Hagoth," 6–7; John A. Widtsoe, "Does the Kon-Tiki Voyage Confirm the Book of Mormon?" 318–19.

tersen, speaking at the Church's general conference in 1962, reinforced the traditional Mormon interpretation. "As Latter-day Saints we have always believed that the Polynesians are descendants of Lehi and blood relatives of the American Indians, despite the contrary theories of other men."[73]

Mormon identification of Polynesians as Lamanites was seen as both a damnation and a dedication by Norman Douglas, "as much a promise as a warning."[74] Anthropologist Erik G. Schwimmer suggested that, to white Mormons, the "Lamanites" are "both inferior and superior, inferior, because punished and superior, because part of the Chosen People."[75] Like Douglas, Schwimmer recognised the dual message in the definition of Polynesians as Lamanites but suggested that Maori Mormons have little trouble reconciling the seemingly contradictory aspects of the doctrine. Well aware of their inferior status in the larger white society (as measured by socio-economic indicators), he said, Maori found their lower status "not only explained but validated by the mythological statement of the position of the Lamanites from whom the Maori were descended. . . . It explained why the Maori were poorer and less powerful than the whites in New Zealand. Not only did it explain, but it offered a solution: obedience to the Church."[76]

Similarly, Douglas felt that early Mormon identification of Polynesians with Book of Mormon people was "a rationalization of and a compensation for their initial lack of success with the whites of various island groups and their failure to make much impression on the American Indian, at least in the nineteenth century."[77] However, it is not necessary to assume, as Douglas did, that Mormon attempts to convert the European population of the Pacific islands before they addressed the indigenous people is evidence that they had no prior intention of proselytising among the native people. Such proselytising among the Polynesians was not "second best" nor was its ensuing success some kind of consolation prize. Concentrating first on the European population of each island group was simply the easiest and most natural procedure for the English-speaking missionaries.

First Mormon Interaction with Maori

Latter-day Saint records make it clear that, as early as 1832, the Maori of New Zealand were perceived to be an important objective for future Mormon proselytising activities.[78] When the Australasian Mission was

---

73. Mark E. Petersen, "Polynesians Came from America," 112.

74. Douglas, "The Sons of Lehi and the Seed of Cain," 93.

75. Schwimmer, "Mormonism in a Maori Village," 150; emphasis his.

76. Ibid., 149–50.

77. Douglas, "The Sons of Lehi and the Seed of Cain," 100.

78. W. W. Phelps, "We accidentily [sic] came across...," *Evening and the Morn-*

organized in 1851, nearly twenty years later, each early mission president had the Maori as firmly in mind as the Pakeha.[79] The first Mormon missionaries visited New Zealand in 1854, but a chronic shortage of both missionaries and funds inevitably postponed a serious approach to the Maori for three decades. The Land Wars of the 1860s would have made Mormon proselytising among the Maori impossible even had there been missionaries available, so it was not until the 1870s that the first tentative Mormon approaches were made to the Maori, and consistent missionary work among them did not begin until the 1880s.

In 1876, William McLachlan, one of the first four missionaries sent directly to New Zealand from Utah, was intrigued when he learned of a Maori tradition that their ancestors had come to New Zealand in a fleet of canoes from Hawaiki, a large island in the Pacific, but neither McLachlan nor his informant was able to identify "the direction or position of Hawaiki." Elder McLachlan reported that "many of the colonists of New Zealand believe the natives to be of Malay origin, but have no evidence or proofs to offer in support of this belief."[80] He himself thought that the Maori "resemble our Indians very much and are undoubtedly of the same race."[81] Four years later, the First Presidency is reported to have told William M. Bromley, in setting him apart as the new president of the Australasian Mission that "the Gospel should be preached to the Lamanite branch of the House of Israel."[82] President Bromley does not seem to have speculated on Maori origins, nor did his Maori tract inform his potential Maori audience of any Mormon belief regarding their origins.

Elder John S. Ferris was the first Mormon missionary known to have specifically taught a group of Maori that they were Book of Mormon people. "Thursday, 2 June 1881. Working in the field today and intend to take

---

ing Star 1, no. 6 (November 1832): 44.

79. John Murdock, "Extracts from a Letter from John Murdock to First Presidency," *Deseret News*, 24 July 1852, 2; John Murdock, Letter to Parley P. Pratt, 17 January 1852, copy in John Murdock, Journal and Autobiography, 158; Augustus A. Farnham, "Extracts of a Letter from Elder Augustus A. Farnham to Brigham Young, dated 14 August 1853," *Deseret News*, 8 December 1853, [96]; John Jones, "To the Aboriginals of New Zealand," 200. For a fuller discussion of this point, see Marjorie Newton, *Tiki and Temple: The Mormon Mission in New Zealand, 1854–1958*, ch. 1.

80. William McLachlan, Letter to the Editor, dated Christchurch, 28 June 1876, *Juvenile Instructor* 11, no. 15 (1 August 1876): 172–73.

81. "New Zealand Missionaries—William McLachlan, Letter to George Goddard, 10 January 1876," *Deseret Evening News*, 5 March 1876, [3].

82. William M. Bromley, "Introduction of the Gospel to the Maories," 6.

the Bible tonight and the Book of Mormon to the Maories camp and tell them of the stick of Judah and the stick of Ephraim being joined in one and of the natives of America that must be related to them in the Cherokee Nation," he wrote in his journal.[83] Next day, he recorded his visit of the previous evening: "They seemed to be moved upon to wonder and seemed to understand me and to have faith in the work as the true way and some say that they want to join my church." In July, Elder Ferris reported teaching Maori at Opotiki that they were "of the blood of Ephraim."[84]

Alma Greenwood, serving in the New Zealand Mission between 1882 and 1884, referred to the Maori as "lost sheep of the House of Israel," who had "wandered in gross darkness." He spoke of their forefathers who had been prompted to leave "the land of Jerusalem" for America[85] and of their own belief that they were "a portion of the House of Israel." Elder Greenwood noted that "many of their traditions and religious customs bear them out in this belief. . . . Some of the practices, religious and otherwise which characterized the ancient Nephites and Lamanites are extant among the aborigines of the South sea [sic] islands."[86] Although Greenwood most frequently taught potential Maori proselytes from the Bible, he several times expounded the Book of Mormon origins of the Maori in answer to questions.[87]

Elder Henry McCune, redirected to New Zealand in 1885 when his mission to India was aborted, was sure the Maori were "of the House of Israel, True Descendants of Lehi."[88] In 1886, Elder Nelson S. Bishop was saddened to note the "low" condition of these descendants of the Nephites and recorded his gratitude that "God in his goodness and mercy has preserved and brought forth to the world of this generation a history of their ancestors and that had been a mystery to the world so long as to the origin of these and our American Indians and was revealed through the instrumentality of the prophet Jos[eph] Smith."[89] When some disgruntled Maori Latter-day Saints objected to paying for publication of the first Maori

83. Ferris, Journal, 2 June 1881, fd. 2, 119–20. The stick of Judah and the stick of Ephraim (Ezekiel 37:16) are believed by Mormons to be the Bible and the Book of Mormon respectively.

84. Ibid., 3 July 1881, 123.

85. Alma Greenwood, "My New Zealand Mission," *Juvenile Instructor* 20, no. 13 (1 July 1885), 207; and no. 17 (1 September 1885), 258; Alma Greenwood, Diary, 30 January, 1 February 1883, 38.

86. Greenwood, "My New Zealand Mission," 207.

87. Greenwood, Diary, 15 May, 16 August, 13 October 1883, 96–97, 171, 198–99.

88. Henry Frederick McCune, Autobiography and Diaries, 1919–24, 27 July 1885, 70.

89. Bishop, Diary, 2 November 1886, 20.

edition of the Book of Mormon in 1888, mission president William Paxman (1886–89) "took great pains to show them that this sacred and holy Book concerned them especially, as it was a history of God's dealings with their forefathers."[90] In 1893, Piripi Te Maari, an "intelligent and influential chief" from the Wairarapa, spoke "at great length" in an LDS conference session, referring to "the ancient history of the Maori people connecting them with the House of Israel."[91]

By the end of the century, the Book of Mormon was freely promoted as an historical record of the ancestors of the Maori. When mission president Ezra T. Stevenson (1898–1900) told a Christchurch reporter in 1899 that the Mormons felt a great interest in the Maori because they believed them to be some of the Book of Mormon people, the reporter was incredulous. "'You surely do not mean to say that you regard the Maori as a descendant of the Redskin?' 'Yes, sir, we do,'" replied President Stevenson.[92]

Maori converts absorbed Book of Mormon teachings, reconciled these with their own migration legends and their prior self-identification as Israelites, and passed these legends on to the missionaries; the amount and degree of cross-fertilisation is impossible to ascertain. "I gleaned the following valuable information from Manihera respecting the history of the Maori, where they came from," Elder Alma Greenwood wrote in May 1883, shortly before Manihera's baptism. "Tawhiti nui is the ancient name for Fiji, the place the Maoris were at before coming to New Zealand. Tawhiti roa the ancient Maori name for the Sandwich Islands, means far away, the country where the Maoris were before coming to Fiji. Tawhiti pamamao, the ancient Maori name for America, means still farther away, the country where the Maoris were before they went to the Sandwich Islands. Te Wairua tapu is the ancient Maori name for Palestine meaning the place where the Maoris were first before going to America. This is very significant information amply furnished in the Book of Mormon," Greenwood commented, totally ignoring the post-European-contact knowledge on which Manihera's account rested.[93]

Elder Greenwood's account appears to be the earliest appearance of this Maori tradition in Mormon sources. More than twenty years later, the legend was published in the mission paper, *The Messenger*, and reprinted

90. William Paxman, Journal, 7 April 1888, quoted in New Zealand Mission, Manuscript History, 7 April 1888.

91. New Zealand Mission, Manuscript History, 29 January 1893.

92. Unidentified article from *Christchurch Press* in Journal History, 31 October 1899, 12.

93. Greenwood, Diary, 15 May 1883, 1:96–97. The wording is repetitive because the Maori language does not cope well with superlatives.

in the same journal seven years later. This version listed only three stages, omitting Fiji and identifying "tawhiti pamamao" as Jerusalem rather than America.[94] Fifty years later again, Stuart Meha rendered it: "'I HAERE MAI TAUA I HAWAIKI; TAWHITI NUI, TAWHITI ROA, TAWHI-TI PAMAMAO; I TE HONO I WAI RUA.' No more, no less. Translation: 'You and I had come from Hawaiki; a great distance away, an extended distance away, an extremely remote distance away; I te hono I wai Rua—even from the joining of the two waters.'" Meha was sure that earlier versions erred in their translation of the final phrase, which took "wairua" as one word and rendered it "even from the joining of the spirit." Meha insisted that his translation was correct and that the "joining of the waters" clearly meant the Isthmus of Panama rather than Palestine. He thus accommodated the Book of Mormon story of Hagoth as the origin of the Maori, rather than the earlier direct link to Palestine and the Old Testament history of the Jews.[95]

Mormon missionaries in New Zealand assiduously collected what they saw as evidence to bolster the Mormon claim that Maori were Israelites. "This people . . . are evidently a branch of the House of Israel," wrote Elder Charles Anderson in 1885. "There are many things of their habits and customs which correspond with the customs of ancient Israel." Elder Anderson cited Maori body lacerations as a sign of mourning, referring his readers to Leviticus 19:28 (where the practice is forbidden) and added that there were many other similarities "too numerous to mention."[96]

Elder Benjamin Goddard thought that the Maori tangi (ceremonial weeping) was "undoubtedly an ancient Israelitish custom," an exact counterpart of Israel's "mourning women" who were to make haste and "take up a wailing for us, that our eyes may run down with tears, and our eyelids gush out with waters" (Jer. 9:17–18). Elder Goddard quoted New Zealand

94. "Are the Maoris of Israelitish Origin?" *Te Karere*, 9 September 1914, 212–16. This article was first printed in *The Messenger* (*Te Karere*), 31 October 1907, but copies of that issue do not appear to have survived. In June 1959, it was reprinted yet again. See "Are the Maoris of Israelitish Origin?" *Te Karere*, June 1959, 251–53, 256.

95. Stuart Meha, "A Request Talk for Sunday Evening the 15 April 1962," copy in my possession, courtesy of Robert P. Manookin; and Stuart [Tetuati] Meha, Letter to Elder Francis W. Kirkham, Salt Lake City, Utah, dated Waiapa, 14 March 1961. See also Grant Underwood, "Mormonism, the Maori and Cultural Authenticity," 137–41.

96. Charles Anderson, "Correspondence: Interesting Letter from New Zealand; Letter to YMMIA (Young Men's Mutual Improvement Association) of Elsinore," *Deseret Evening News*, 28 April 1885, [4].

governor Sir George Grey's theory that the Maori may have originated in Mexico, and speculated, "Is it possible that the southern G.O.M. [Grand Old Man] can have read of Hagoth building his ships . . . ?" Elder Goddard pointed out that Grey had owned a copy of the Book of Mormon.[97]

In 1886, Charles Hardy,[98] an Englishman converted to Mormonism on the Australian goldfields in the 1850s and now living in New Zealand, sent a list of twenty-nine Maori "customs" to a friend in Utah, assuring his friend that these customs were "identical with those of the ancient Israelites." The list was published in the *Deseret News* to demonstrate that the Maori were descended from ancient Israel.[99] Two years later, Brother Hardy became president of the LDS branch in Auckland, a calling he held for the next twenty-six years. He continued to study Maori ethnography until his death in 1914, acquiring a large library on the subject which, rather than fieldwork, was the source of his information. Hardy's list, expanded to fifty "Israelitish" Maori practices (the majority annotated with appropriate Old Testament references), was published in the New Zealand mission paper in 1907, together with his version of the migration chant discussed earlier. The full article was reprinted in the same journal in 1914[100] and included an assurance that the items on the list had been "collated from reliable authorities," sources dating back to, if not copied verbatim from, Samuel Marsden and other early Christian missionaries.[101] Typewritten copies, headed "Fifty Reasons Why the Maoris and American Indians Are of Israelitish Origin," circulated among the Mormon missionaries in New Zealand for several decades.[102]

Elder John W. Kauleinamoku, who had emigrated from Hawaii to Utah and from thence was called to serve a mission in New Zealand in the late 1880s, could be understood by the Maori, and his Hawaiian Book of Mormon was used in the process of translating this Mormon scripture

---

97. New Zealand Mission, Manuscript History, 19 April 1893; 8 September 1894.

98. No relation to Rufus K. Hardy.

99. "Interesting from New Zealand," *Deseret News,* 28 July 1886, 13.

100. "Are the Maoris of Israelitish Origin?" *The Messenger* 8, no. 18 (9 September 1914): 212–16.

101. In Hardy's letter to his unnamed friend, published in the *Deseret News* in 1886, he disclaimed original research and said the information he supplied was "merely compilations from old works, principally published many years ago when the Maoris and their customs were but little changed by contact with Europeans." *Deseret News,* 28 July 1886, 13. See note 106.

102. Slightly abridged, the article was reprinted in *Te Karere* in 1959. "Are the Maoris of Israelitish Origin?" *Te Karere,* June 1959, 251–53, 256.

into Maori in 1887–88.[103] At least one mission president naively assumed that, because the Eastern Polynesian languages of Hawaii, Tahiti, and New Zealand were more or less intelligible to native speakers of each, Native American languages must also be related to these. A newly arrived missionary, Elder Jacob B. Workman, was assigned to Maori rather than European work in 1901, "he being a speaker of the Ute language."[104] It is not known whether Elder Workman was of Native American descent or how this assumption of linguistic compatibility worked out.

Physical resemblances between Maori and Native Americans were frequently noted by Mormon missionaries. "We were struck with the remarkable resemblance the women have to the American Indians," wrote Elder M. M. Johnson in 1911. "This is another of the many evidences of the truth and divine authority of the only history extant of these people, viz., the Book of Mormon."[105] Thirty years earlier, William McLachlan had exhibited photographs of Maori on his return to Salt Lake City. The *Deseret News* commented on the "marked similarity" between the Maori and the "aborigines" of the American continent, and postulated that the Hagoth story was the connecting link.[106] Matthew Cowley, during his first New Zealand mission (1914–19), reversed the process, showing Maori "views of some Indians who are the ancestors of the Maoris. They were very much interested," he noted.[107]

Unfortunately for those Mormons who search for a scientific basis for their theology, scientists do not accept physical and cultural similarities between people as evidence of ethnic relatedness. Similarities of customs of people as varied as the Zulus, Bantus, Japanese, Burmese, and Malays with Old Testament ritual have been compiled by travellers and Christian missionaries over a very long period, and physical resemblances between indigenous peoples and "Jews" have likewise long been reported from many parts of the world.[108] More specifically, Maori have been compared, "on the basis of language similarities and cultural parallels," with people on every continent.[109]

---

103. Richards, Journal, 24 August 1885, 16 July 1887; Magleby, Journal, 11 October 1885, 1:82.

104. New Zealand Mission, Manuscript History, 4 January 1901.

105. M. M. Johnson, "New Zealand," *Deseret News*, 10 June 1911, in Journal History, 29 March 1911, 3.

106. "New Zealand," *Deseret News Weekly*, 8 August 1877, in Journal History, 3 August 1877, 4.

107. Matthew Cowley, Journal, 18 January 1915, 1:28.

108. Godbey, *The Lost Tribes a Myth*, 1–2.

109. Elsmore, *Like Them That Dream*, 71.

An Uncanonised Doctrine

In 1979, a question in the Church's *New Era* magazine for youth asked: "Is there any reference in scripture or other sources of information that tells where Hagoth and his ships, referred to in Alma 63, went?" The answer, written by an instructor at the LDS Institute of Religion at the University of Utah, stated that "the theories are still speculation as far as scientists are concerned and unsettled as far as the prophets are concerned," adding, "They have not seen fit to comment on the matter. Several have stated that the Polynesians are descendants of Lehi, but we have no comments from them on the fate of Hagoth."[110] As the contemporary Church president and prophet Spencer W. Kimball had specifically told congregations in Hawaii, Tonga, Samoa, and New Zealand that Hagoth was their common ancestor during his tour of the South Pacific only three years earlier (1976), the appearance of this statement in a Church publication was surprising.

However, a decade later a paper on "Hagoth and the Polynesians" was presented by retired BYU professor of religion Robert E. Parsons at the Sixth Annual Book of Mormon Symposium at Brigham Young University. Professor Parsons promoted the Hagoth theory and quoted modern Church leaders such as Mark E. Petersen, Hugh B. Brown, David O. McKay, Spencer W. Kimball, and Gordon B. Hinckley identifying Polynesians as descendants of Lehi. Parsons concluded by saying: "It seems fair to state that although the Church has no official, published declaration on the origin of the Polynesians, there have been enough semi-official statements by prophets of the Lord to leave little doubt that the Church believes that the Polynesians are direct blood relatives of Lehi's colony and that Hagoth's lost ships provide at least one connection between the Americas and Polynesia." Parsons's paper was extensively quoted in the *Church News*.[111]

While there is still no authoritative, canonised doctrine about Polynesian origins, at least five LDS Church presidents (Brigham Young, Jo-

---

110. Dale C. LeCheminant, "Questions and Answers: 'Is There Any Reference in Scripture . . . ,'" 14–15. The "Questions and Answers" column in the *New Era* was always headed by the disclaimer that "answers are for help and perspective, not as pronouncements of Church doctrine."

111. Robert E. Parsons, emeritus professor of ancient scripture at Brigham Young University, quoted in (no author identified) "Hagoth Believed to Be Link between Polynesia and Peoples of America," [LDS] *Church News*, 25 July 1992, 10; see also, (no author identified) "Latter-day Prophets Have Indicated that Pacific Islanders Are Descendants of Lehi," [LDS] *Church News*, 9 July 1988, 14. Both articles were prepared for use as enrichment material for a Church-wide adult Sunday School course on the Book of Mormon.

seph F. Smith, Heber J. Grant, David O. McKay, and Spencer W. Kimball) publicly indicated their belief that Polynesians are descendants of Lehi during their individual terms of office as "prophets, seers, and revelators." At least two apostles who later became presidents of the Church (George Albert Smith and his third cousin Joseph Fielding Smith) also made specific statements linking Polynesian origins to the Book of Mormon, as did numerous other General Authorities, including Gordon B. Hinckley, future LDS Church president, when he was a newly called Assistant to the Twelve in 1958.[112]

Most of these General Authorities confined themselves to linking the Polynesian peoples to Lehi, identifying them as either Nephites or, more commonly, Lamanites. Only two Church presidents—Joseph F. Smith (1901–18), and Spencer W. Kimball (1973–85)—seem to have definitely stated that Hagoth was the connecting link.

Joseph F. Smith was the LDS prophet and Church president when a group of six prominent and wealthy Maori Latter-day Saints visited Salt Lake City in 1913. Stuart Meha, Luxford Peeti, Wiremu and Takare Duncan, and Takerei and Ema Ihaia sailed on the *Niagara* on 10 May that year. Disembarking in Vancouver, they found a welcoming letter from former New Zealand missionary Benjamin Goddard waiting for them. Meha telegraphed a reply to Goddard, the president of Zion's Maori Association in Salt Lake City, and thanked him for his welcome.[113] "In the wire I also said 'Who knows but that some of Hagoth's people have arrived, pea [perhaps],'" said Meha, retelling the story many years later. The Maori party was given an almost royal reception in Salt Lake City, where Church president Joseph F. Smith and his counsellors were hosts at a welcome banquet on 3 June. "At the reception tendered us ... in Salt Lake City, President Joseph [F.] Smith and his counsellors ... and many of the leading citizens of the city were present," Meha continued. "President Smith in his welcome said, inter alia, 'You brethren and sisters from New Zealand, I want you to know that you are from the people of Hagoth and there is no pea about it.'" For Meha, if not for LDS leaders and scholars today, there was no further doubt. "This is the word of a prophet of God and we need go no further to look for proofs of the Origin of the Maori," he said.[114]

---

112. Elwin W. Jensen, "Polynesians Descend from Lehi, According to Statements of the Prophets," 1977; Gordon B. Hinckley, "Temple in the Pacific," 509. Many other General Authorities have also spoken of Native Americans as descendants of Lehi.

113. Zion's Maori Association was an association of Mormon missionaries who had formerly served in New Zealand.

114. Meha, "A Request Talk for Sunday Evening the 15th April, 1962." See also Meha, Letter to Kirkham, 14 March 1961.

In his speech at this banquet, President Smith recalled that, as a very young missionary in Hawaii some sixty years previously, he had found on the beach "great saw[n] timbers which had been driven from the mouth of the Columbia river or other points along the west coast of America, by sea currents and winds directly to the shores of Hawaii." It was "very probable," he continued, "that Hagoth's ships, which never returned, may have followed the currents likewise to the Pacific islands."[115] A century after President Smith's experience in Hawaii, Thor Heyerdahl documented similar sightings, reinforcing Mormon belief.[116]

As previously mentioned, six decades after the first Maori visit to Utah, President Spencer W. Kimball explicitly linked Hagoth's voyage with the peopling of Polynesia during his tour of Pacific missions in early 1976. Speaking to students and faculty at the Brigham Young University-Hawaii campus, President Kimball "[made] it clear that Hagoth came first to Hawaii, then these descendants of Lehi 'moved from here (i.e., Hawaii) to the Southland,' eventually colonizing many of the South Sea islands," wrote Russell Clement, special collections librarian at BYU-Hawaii, in 1980. Clement then commented: "This concept of Polynesian migration from Hawaii southward is as contrary to scientific thought and findings as the Church's belief of ultimate American origins for Polynesians." As President Kimball travelled on to Church area conferences in Samoa and Tonga, he repeated these statements to his largely Polynesian congregations before continuing to New Zealand and Australia. In New Zealand, President Kimball was quite specific. "The Maori people came from the north country, from Hawaii," he said. "Their origin is recorded in the Book of Mormon where Alma gives an account of their journeys. Their common ancestor was Hagoth."[117]

Rethinking Polynesian Origins

In contrast to the celebration of Polynesians as Lamanites before and during the administration of Church president Spencer W. Kimball (1973–85),[118] many Mormon scholars—and some, but not all, Church leaders—

115. "Reception for Visiting Maoris," *Deseret Evening News*, 3 June 1913, in Journal History, 3 June 1913, 2.

116. Thor Heyerdahl, *American Indians in the Pacific: The Theory behind the Kon-Tiki Expedition*, 162–64.

117. Clement, "Polynesian Origins," 92–97.

118. John-Charles Duffy, "The Use of 'Lamanite' in Official LDS Discourse," 143–44, lists fourteen General Authorities who, among others, referred to American Indians, Latin Americans, or Pacific Islanders as Lamanites in addresses delivered between 1948 and 1982. Duffy's list included two Church presidents, nine

gradually became more cautious. In 1976, shortly after President Kimball specifically identified Polynesians as descendants of Hagoth, LDS scholar Jerry K. Loveland suggested that, although scientific evidence pointed to Southeast Asian origins of the Polynesians, scientists also admitted American contact. "In most scholarly circles now the argument is not whether there was American influence in the Pacific, but upon how it got there and how significant it was," he wrote. Loveland acknowledged that "no archaeological evidence has yet been found which specifically substantiates the Hagoth story," and postulated that genealogies and oral traditions were (at that date) the only other possible source of confirmation of the story; however, he acknowledged, Polynesian traditions are unreliable as scientific evidence.[119]

DNA sequencing was still in its infancy in 1976 when President Kimball visited Church members in the Pacific. By the mid-1980s, Mormon apologists and opponents alike were becoming aware of its implications for Mormon identification of Native Americans as descendants of Book of Mormon peoples and, as an inevitable corollary, their widely held beliefs about Polynesians. Coupled with increasing scientific evidence of multiple migrations to America, and continuing lack of archaeological and linguistic evidence for the existence of Book of Mormon peoples in the Americas, many Mormon apologists began to re-examine traditional assumptions about the Book of Mormon. "The weight of evidence has forced Mormon scholars to rethink the scale, location, and nature of the historical account in the Book of Mormon," wrote molecular biologist and ex-Mormon Simon Southerton in 2004. "Currently, there is scant molecular evidence for migrations from the Americas to Polynesia."[120]

John L. Sorenson, professor of anthropology at Brigham Young University, published a two-part article, "Digging into the Book of Mormon:

---

apostles, and three Assistants to the Twelve.

119. Jerry K. Loveland, "Hagoth and the Polynesian Tradition," 59–73. Loveland later became Director of the Institute for Polynesian Studies, Church College of Hawaii. The Institute for Polynesians Studies is now known as the Pacific Institute, and the Church College of Hawaii has been renamed BYU–Hawaii.

120. Simon G. Southerton, *Losing a Lost Tribe: Native Americans, DNA, and the Mormon Church*, xv, 88, 115. For Mormon scientists' and scholars' discussions on DNA and associated fields as they relate to the Book of Mormon, see also D. Jeffrey Meldrum and Trent D. Stephens, *Who Are the Children of Lehi? DNA and the Book of Mormon*, as well as publications of the Foundation for Ancient Research and Mormon Studies (FARMS), now part of the Neal A. Maxwell Institute for Religious Scholarship at Brigham Young University. See also FAIR (the Foundation for Apologetic Information and Research) and associated websites.

Our Changing Understanding of Ancient America and Its Scripture," in the Church's official magazine, the *Ensign*, in September and October 1984.[121] Sorenson referred to "one problem some Latter-day Saint writers and lecturers have had is confusing the actual text of the Book of Mormon with the traditional interpretation of it. For example," he wrote, "a commonly heard statement is that the Book of Mormon is 'the history of the American Indians.' This statement contains a number of unexamined assumptions—that the scripture is a history in the common sense—a systematic, chronological account of the main events in the past of a nation or territory; that 'the' American Indians are a unitary population; and that the approximately one hundred pages of text containing historical and cultural material in the scripture could conceivably tell all the entire history of a hemisphere."[122]

Professor Sorenson proceeded to outline his thesis that Book of Mormon events occurred in a limited territory in the New World (Mesoamerica), instead of in all of North and South America. He acknowledged that scientific evidence made it incontrovertible that many groups other than the three Book of Mormon colonies were present in ancient America. Although Sorenson prefaced his article with a disclaimer that his limited-region thesis was not Church doctrine, the appearance of such ideas in the official Church organ was remarkable. Joseph Smith and several Mormon prophets who had succeeded him clearly believed in a whole-America setting for the Book of Mormon; that Sorenson's article appeared in the *Ensign* indicates an official tolerance of Mormon scholars' attempts to accommodate the findings of archaeologists, anthropologists, scientists, and historians about pre-European Americans. Professor Sorenson's subsequent book, *An Ancient American Setting for the Book of Mormon*, is devoted to Book of Mormon geography and was published by the Church-owned Deseret Book Company.[123] However, both Sorenson's *Ensign* article and his book went virtually unnoticed by most rank-and-file Mormons, especially those outside the United States—including, apparently, most Polynesian Mormons.

Only cautious and minimal official rethinking of the Mormon theory of Maori origins was evident until recently. For some years, the closest explicit approximation to accommodation by a Church General Authority came from Elder Robert L. Simpson, long-time Church representative

121. John L. Sorenson, "Digging into the Book of Mormon: Our Changing Understanding of Ancient America and Its Scripture," Part 1, September 1984, 27–37 and Part 2, October 1984, 12–24.

122. Sorenson, "Digging into the Book of Mormon," Part 1, September 1984, 27.

123. Today Sorenson's Mesoamerican setting for the Book of Mormon is widely accepted by Mormon intellectuals and many Church authorities.

in New Zealand (as missionary, mission president, Area Supervisor, and Area President). Speaking in 1978, Elder Simpson admitted to changes in his own thinking on the subject. "I remember in my early missionary days [1937-40] ... in a nineteen-year-old mind something is either black or white ... [and] we'd say, 'You know, the Polynesians came from the Americas.' Science was saying, 'Well, no, we have Polynesian influences from Asia and even some from the Oriental countries.' I was always willing to argue, 'No, sir, it was from the Americas and no other way.' But now I can see that there were influences from both directions. But certainly the influence from the Americas was a very important one, and this is why we have the strong Israel influence throughout Polynesia that gives rise to their total and immediate acceptance of the gospel on such ready terms."[124]

Elder Simpson's recollections were recorded in 1978; three years later, the LDS Church published a new edition of the Book of Mormon—the first since 1920. It included an introduction that stated that the Book of Mormon "is a record of God's dealings with the ancient inhabitants of the Americas," who were eventually all destroyed "except the Lamanites, and they are the principal ancestors of the American Indians." That the Lamanites were described as the "principal" ancestors of the American Indians seemed to indicate cautious acceptance of the idea that early inhabitants of the Americas included peoples other than those featured in the Book of Mormon.

A decade later, the *Encyclopedia of Mormonism* was published. It includes an entry on "Polynesians" written by Eric Shumway, former president of BYU-Hawaii, an Area Seventy, and a temple president. Shumway's article suggests continuing accommodation of scientific findings: "A basic view held in the Church ... [is] that Polynesians have *ancestral connections* with the Book of Mormon people who were descendants of Abraham." Shumway quotes Brigham Young on the subject, then continues, "Other Church leaders have since affirmed the belief, some indicating that *among* Polynesian ancestors were the people of Hagoth. ... Church leaders, who have attested to Polynesian roots in the Nephite peoples, have not elaborated on the likelihood of other migrating groups in the Pacific or of social mixing and intermarriage."[125]

Another article in the *Encyclopedia of Mormonism* acknowledges that none of the proposed geographical locations of Book of Mormon sites has been positively confirmed by archaeology, and that attempts to identify

---

124. Robert Leatham Simpson, Oral History, 28.
125. Eric B. Shumway, "Polynesians," 3:1110–12; emphasis mine.

such sites must therefore be regarded as merely "intellectual conjectures."[126] While not an LDS Church publication, the *Encyclopedia of Mormonism* was edited by a team of scholars led by BYU professor of religion, Daniel H. Ludlow. Ludlow worked closely with two LDS apostles before the encyclopedia was published by Macmillan in 1992.[127]

More recent changes have been noted. For example, the 1978 lesson manual *Gospel Principles*, originally written to instruct those investigating Mormonism or recently baptised as Mormons, was reprinted in 2009 to serve as a lesson manual for Melchizedek Priesthood and Relief Society classes (in essence, all adult members of the Church) for 2010 and 2011. It no longer states: "Great numbers of Lamanites in North and South America and the South Pacific are now receiving the blessings of the gospel," as did the 1978 edition.[128]

Perhaps the most significant changes made by LDS leaders to date are the small but important alterations to the wording of the introduction to the previous (1981) edition of the Book of Mormon when the 2013 edition was released. As the existing plates were wearing and needed to be replaced, Church leaders took advantage of the opportunity to incorporate numerous minor changes—and a few of more significance—resulting from recent scholarship, including, but not limited to, the findings of scholars working in the Church History Department on the Joseph Smith Papers.

The introduction to the 2013 edition states that the Book of Mormon "is a record of God's dealings with ancient inhabitants of the Americas," who were all destroyed "except the Lamanites, and they are among the ancestors of the American Indians."[129] The omission of the definitive "the" before "ancient inhabitants" and the substitution of "among" for "principal" are more than minor changes to the 1981 edition, but it is likely that most LDS Church members, for whom purchase of the new print edition is optional, will remain unaware of these amendments or of their significance.

There has been considerable discussion over the last decade of the implications of DNA research findings for commonly taught beliefs of the LDS Church about Native American and Polynesian origins. Molecular biologist Simon Southerton summarised current scientific conclusions

126. John E. Clark, "Book of Mormon Geography," 1:176–79.

127. "News of the Church: *Encyclopedia of Mormonism* Released," *Ensign*, March 1992, 79.

128. *Gospel Principles*, 1978, 268.

129. Introduction, Book of Mormon: Another Witness of Jesus Christ, http://www/lds.org/scriptures/bofm/introduction?lang=eng (accessed 12 April 2013). The 1981 introduction was earlier altered as quoted above in the *Book of Mormon: Another Witness of Jesus Christ*, in the edition published by Doubleday, 2006. See Meldrum and Stephens, *Who Are the Children of Lehi?* 5–6, 20.

when he wrote, "In agreement with anthropological and archaeological research, the molecular pedigrees of Native Americans cluster on the Asian branch of the human family tree."[130]

D. Jeffrey Meldrum, professor of anatomy and anthropology at Idaho State University, and Trent D. Stephens, professor of anatomy and embryology at the same university, suggest that "the apparent contradiction [between] the written record of the children of Lehi with the genetic legacy of native American populations studied to date ... stems from imposing simplistic generalizations onto the primary account, placing undue significance on speculations by early Church officials, or failing to recognise the limitations on the interpretation of the genetic legacies of populations." While accepting that "genetic findings among Native Americans have failed to link Native American populations to ancient Israelites," Meldrum and Stephens point out that the lack of "modern genetic connections between Native American and Middle Eastern populations does not justify a statement that no such connections ever existed or that the Book of Mormon is a work of nineteenth-century fiction." They then present cogent arguments to support their position, but conclude: "Ultimately, ... the fundamental question of the veracity of Book of Mormon claims lie beyond the ken of modern DNA research ... in the realm of personal faith and individual testimony."[131]

Early Mormon Attitudes to Maori "Lamanites"

LDS records show that, while some Mormon missionaries working in New Zealand from the early 1880s called the Maori people Nephites, most referred to them as Lamanites. There seems to have been little, if any, resentment manifested by Maori converts towards the latter title, although "Nephites" were commonly understood to be the righteous, and "Lamanites" the wicked, protagonists of the Book of Mormon. At a conference in 1894, for example, Ngawawaea Poipoi, a "native Demosthenes" from the Mahia District, "fluently reviewed the history of Lehi and his sons, showing how the Maoris inherited the dark skin through the disobedience of their ancestors."[132] Some early Mormon leaders occasionally made comments about New Zealand Maori which, while reflecting the views of their times, today seem offensive. For example, Apostle Franklin D. Richards congratulated his son Ezra Foss Richards on his "great condescension

---

130. Southerton, *Losing a Lost Tribe*, 88.

131. Meldrum and Stephens, *Who Are the Children of Lehi?*, 2–3, 128. While my *Mormon and Maori* was in final proofs, the Church posted "Book of Mormon and DNA Studies," which discussed DNA studies but affirmed that secular evidence neither proves nor disproves Book of Mormon historicity. https://www.lds.org/topics/book-of-mormon-and-dna-studies (accessed 2 February 2014).

132. New Zealand Mission, Manuscript History, 6 April 1894.

[in] stooping to the low condition of poor degraded humanity" and saw his son's 1880s mission among the Maori as a type of the Saviour's atonement.[133]

Most Mormons believed (and many still believe) that the distinction between Nephites and Lamanites in the Book of Mormon was that the latter were cursed with a dark skin because of their wickedness. It is curious that many Mormons designate the dark-skinned Polynesians "Lamanites" while still regarding them as descendants of Hagoth—for Hagoth was a Nephite.[134] But while Hagoth himself is usually referred to as the ancestor of the Polynesian peoples, the Book of Mormon makes it clear that Hagoth did not sail away alone but led a fleet of ships filled with Nephite men, women, and children. If "Nephite" in this context was a political or religious rather than a genealogical classification, as will be discussed later, there may well have been some dark-skinned adventurers on board Hagoth's ships.

Nephites or Lamanites?

While Church leaders visiting the Pacific missions and stakes in the middle decades of the twentieth century almost invariably referred to Polynesian Saints as Lamanites, some Polynesians had a different self-perception. Samoan James Southon joked wryly about Apostle Spencer W. Kimball's visit to organise the Hawkes Bay stake in 1960. "He called it the first Lamanite stake in all the Church," said Southon. "He called it a Lamanite stake, although everybody had thought they were all Nephites."[135] Occasionally Maori (and Pakeha) Mormons use the term "Lamanites" with pejorative overtones when referring to less active or less reliable Maori Mormons. "In [the Church in] New Zealand the term Lamanite referred to a type of people, or one who is not as good as another," said Edwin Nepia, a Maori student at Brigham Young University-Provo in 1986. "I hated being called a Lamanite [but] it does not bother me now. I understand the term Lamanite and accept it as a term of distinction rather than a curse. I define a Lamanite as anyone known as a descendant of Lehi."[136]

President Spencer W. Kimball could not understand anyone objecting to the term "Lamanite." "I have met some who are a little bit ashamed that they are Lamanites," he wrote in 1975. "How can it be? Some would rather

---

133. Franklin D. Richards, Letter to Ezra F. Richards, dated Salt Lake City, 26 June 1885, copied into Ezra Foss Richards, Journal, between 13 and 14 August 1885.

134. Alma 63:5–8.

135. James Southon, Oral History, 1971. Southon served as a counselor in the new stake's presidency, then as its second president. The Hawkes Bay Stake was renamed the Hastings Stake in 1974.

136. "'Lamanite' Viewed as 'Term of Distinction,'" *Daily Universe*, 24 November 1986, 6.

define themselves as Nephites ... or something else. Surely there must be a misunderstanding. Would they separate themselves from the great blessings the Lord has promised to his covenant people?" President Kimball reassured the 350,000 "Lamanite" members of the LDS Church (some 10 percent of total Church membership in 1975) that their ancestors "were no more rebellious than any of the other branches of the house of Israel. All the seed of Israel fell into apostasy and suffered the long night of spiritual darkness."[137]

In another controversial area where the Church's official position is that it *has* no official position, it is possible to be a Latter-day Saint in good standing and not believe in a literal interpretation of the creation story in the Bible.[138] Today, this is generally interpreted as freedom to believe in a vastly extended time-frame for the creation of the earth, and even in pre-Adamites, as long as belief in Adam as the "primal parent" of the human race is maintained.[139] However, orthodox Mormons are still expected to subscribe to the literal historicity of the Book of Mormon. "On this issue we draw a line in the sand," stated Mormon Apostle Jeffrey R. Holland in 1994.[140]

Tied to acceptance of the historicity of the Book of Mormon is the uncanonised Mormon belief about Polynesian origins. The recent scholarly debate over conclusions reached by scientists researching the DNA of Native Americans and Polynesians—that they are unrelated—has added another layer to the unquestioning faith required of those Maori Mormons aware of the arguments and counter-arguments presented.

White and Delightsome

Mission president William Paxman had no qualms about promising the Maori at a district conference in 1889 that the time was "nigh at hand" when they would become "a white and delightsome people in the sight of the Lord."[141] Even Maori leaders repeated such statements. Wi Duncan Sr. spoke on this promise at Hui Tau in 1927, promising that, if the Maori

---

137. Spencer W. Kimball, "Our Paths Have Met Again," *Ensign*, December 1975, 2–8. President Kimball stated that there were "nearly 130 million Lamanites worldwide" and rejoiced that he personally had been privileged to "carry the gospel to the Lamanites from the Pacific Ocean to the Atlantic, from the reaches of Canada to southern Chile, and in the islands from Hawaii to New Zealand."

138. President David O. McKay, Letter to Professor William Lee Stokes, 15 February 1957; photocopy in my possession.

139. William E. Evenson, "Evolution," 2:478.

140. Jeffrey R. Holland, "True or False," *New Era*, June 1995, 66. This line was omitted when an edited version of this address was published by Elder Holland in *Christ and the New Covenant: The Messianic Message of the Book of Mormon* (1997).

141. New Zealand Mission, Manuscript History, 7 July 1889.

Saints obeyed the gospel, "they would become a white and delightsome people, as they are descendants of Jacob who was white."[142]

The Book of Mormon prophecy that the dark-skinned Lamanites would return to Christ and become "white and delightsome"[143] caused problems for the Mormon mission in New Zealand in the 1950s, when the international magazine *Time* reported the opening of the Church College of New Zealand near Hamilton.[144] The article quoted a local Presbyterian spokesman who objected to Mormon proselytising and who accused the Mormons of promoting racist doctrine, citing the "white and delightsome" Book of Mormon verse.[145] *Time* commented on the clergyman's accusations of "sheep stealing" by saying: "The Mormons reply that the sheep are simply returning to their proper fold after centuries astray." The reporter summarised the Book of Mormon story and concluded, "Though the Church gives no official interpretation of the Hagoth legend, it has served Mormon missionaries from Hawaii to New Zealand to give thousands of natives hope that they may once again become 'white and delightsome.' According to New Zealand Mission President Ariel S. Ballif, the way is simple: 'As they take up the righteous way of living, they become more attractive and acceptable to white people and lose their dark skin [by intermarriage].'"[146]

Fifteen years later, President Ballif vehemently insisted that the last phrase was inserted by the reporter, with whom, he said, he had had only a short interview. "My point of view was that the LDS Maori was becoming a better person, that he was more acceptable to people because of the way of life that the Church taught him."[147] The explanation scarcely helped his cause, if by "acceptable to people" one understands him to mean "acceptable to white people." The reporter's explication seems the only logical interpretation of Ballif's meaning, even as clarified in 1973; perhaps Ballif was subconsciously looking for a way to retreat from the traditional understanding of this Book of Mormon passage.

When the 1981 edition of the Book of Mormon was published, the term "white and delightsome" was changed back to "pure and delightsome." Eugene England, among other scholars, noted that "pure," not "white," was the term used by Joseph Smith in the first edition of the Book of Mormon. Any racism, England insisted, was human weakness on the part of editors

142. Minutes of Annual Mission Conference, Friday, 15 April 1927, New Zealand Mission, Manuscript History.

143. 2 Nephi 30:6, editions prior to 1981.

144. "Hagoth's Children," *Time [Magazine]*, 26 May 1958, 65 and 67.

145. Ibid., 67.

146. Ibid., brackets in original.

147. Ariel S. Ballif, Oral History, interviewed by R. Lanier Britsch, 1973, 65.

of intermediate editions, who simply reflected the views of contemporary American society.[148]

In the last half-century, Mormon exegetes have pointed out that the traditional definition of "Lamanites" as lineal descendants of Lehi's eldest son and his followers, who were distinguished from the Nephites by the curse of a dark skin, is only one meaning of the term used in the Book of Mormon. Initially applied to the literal family of Laman, wrote Lane Johnson (an assistant editor of the *Ensign*) in 1975, the name *Lamanite* "very soon took on a broader application" and eventually referred to "a religious/political faction whose distinguishing feature was its opposition to the church" rather than skin colour.[149] This interpretation was taught at least a decade earlier, notably by Mormon scholar Hugh Nibley, but Johnson's article on the subject was one of the first to be published in the official Church magazine, the *Ensign*.

The most recent scholar to confirm this reading of the text is Brant Gardner, whose detailed verse-by-verse exegesis of the Book of Mormon makes it clear that the terms "Nephites" and "Lamanites" to designate the major political and tribal categories were in use very early in Nephite history. Gardner states that "Lamanite" quickly became a generic term, describing anyone who was not a follower of Nephi and was therefore an enemy. "Being a Nephite meant living in a distinct place, being ruled by a single individual, and sharing the same religion," Gardner notes. "Because of the necessary social distinctions developed within the Nephite community, all outsiders were seen negatively and labeled with this collective name of 'Lamanites.'"[150] While Nibley, Johnson, and Gardner all give textual Book of Mormon references, this definition was actually confirmed *before* publication of the Book of Mormon, when a revelation to Joseph Smith referred to the Lamanites as not only the descendants of Laman, but "also all that had become Lamanites because of their dissensions."[151]

A third interpretation was taught by some Mormon leaders after several generations of faithful Maori Latter-day Saints failed to become white: that Lamanite "whiteness" would be restored during the Millennium.[152] But there is little doubt that Maori Latter-day Saints customarily

148. Eugene England, Response to Eduardo Pagan, "An Innocent Racism," 8–9.

149. Lane Johnson, "Who and Where Are the Lamanites?" 15; Hugh W. Nibley, *Since Cumorah*, 246–51.

150. Brant A. Gardner, *Second Witness: Analytical and Contextual Commentary on the Book of Mormon*, 2:477–78; see also 1:353–56.

151. Doctrine and Covenants 10:48.

152. For more information on this point, see Schwimmer, "Mormonism in a Maori Village," 149; Lineham, "The Mormon Message in the Context of Maori

interpreted the prophecy more literally and, at least at first, looked for more immediate fulfilment. Ariel S. Ballif's attitudes towards Maori were not, after all, too far removed from those of an earlier mission president, William T. Stewart, who in 1892 wrote back to Church headquarters of his satisfaction as he noted "the improvement in progress among Maori members of the Church. They are gradually adopting the manner of dress and other customs of white people."[153] Ten years later, Auckland Branch president Charles Hardy reported in an Auckland newspaper: "The [Mormon] elders realize that if they can elevate the women into a higher plane of civilized life, the children will profit in more than an equal degree."[154]

Because the Maori were perceived to be descendants of Lehi and heirs of the promised regeneration of his descendants, the equation of "progress" with the adoption of white culture underpinned the entire philosophy of the Mormon mission to the Maori. As has been shown, in this approach the Mormons did not differ greatly from the attitudes of the mainstream Christian missionaries who saw the Maori as Israelites.[155] The history of the Maori Agricultural College makes it clear that pre-World War II Mormon missionaries did not just promote a new religion among the Maori but encouraged their converts to adopt Western culture, specifically white American Mormon culture.

Culture," 82; Barker, "The Connexion," 41.

    153. New Zealand Mission, Manuscript History, 20 August 1892.
    154. "The Mormon Mission in New Zealand," *Auckland Weekly News*, 24 April 1902.
    155. Lineham, "The Mormon Message in the Context of Maori Culture," 82.

Chapter 2

Mormon Schools in New Zealand

For more than a century, the Mormon Church attempted to provide secular as well as spiritual education for the children of its Maori converts. Its efforts between 1886 and 1931 were sincere and well-meant, but most students obtained little academic benefit from attendance at either the small number of Mormon primary schools or the Maori Agricultural College. Whether these schools brought other benefits to their Maori students is a question that can be answered more positively. After a quarter-century hiatus following the closing of the Maori Agricultural College in 1931, the Latter-day Saint mission in New Zealand again ventured into secular education, this time fully backed by the resources of a now wealthy church. The Church College of New Zealand achieved a reputation for academic success and considerable sporting renown. By the 1990s, however, free secondary education of a very high standard was available for almost all Maori students, and the lavishly appointed school had become an unnecessary financial drain on the Church, but one from which it could not easily extricate itself. The school finally closed in November 2009.

Mormon attempts to provide schooling for the children of its Maori converts absorbed an inequitable amount of the time, manpower, and financial resources of the Mormon mission from 1886 to 1931, and building the Church College of New Zealand in the 1950s cost millions of dollars. The story of the Maori Agricultural College and its successor is told in the companion volume to this work, *Tiki and Temple: The Mormon Mission in New Zealand, 1854–1958*. This present chapter examines the motives for and assesses the success (or otherwise) of Mormon educational efforts.

Maori Schools in New Zealand

Christian Missionary Society (Church of England) schools in New Zealand predated Mormon efforts by nearly three-quarters of a century.[1] Maori enthusiasm for literacy at first excited much interest in the schools established by CMS missionaries,[2] who devised a written language from an oral one. By 1845, it was estimated that 50 percent of adult Maori could read and write a little in their own language, though few had thoroughly mastered either skill.[3] Even fewer were fluent in English.

Recognising that Maori needed literacy in order to cope with the settler society rapidly encroaching upon their traditional culture, Governor George Grey instituted an Education Ordinance (1847) that provided subsidies for the struggling mission schools if they taught in English and included industrial training in their curricula. Several new co-educational boarding schools were begun under this scheme, and offered courses such as carpentry and agriculture as well as more traditional subjects. Although about 700 Maori students were enrolled in these schools by 1852,[4] they represented only a small fraction of potential Maori students. However, at this time, schooling opportunities for Pakeha children were not universal either and varied widely among the diverse New Zealand provinces.[5]

Governor Grey's education policy was continued by the Stafford ministry, whose 1858 Native Schools Act introduced a proficiency criterion and what amounted to a capitation subsidy for church boarding schools.[6] A decade later, the Native Schools Act (1867) sanctioned the establishment of government primary schools for Maori children, to be administered by the Department of Native Affairs. This effectively began a dual school system, although there was never any prohibition against Maori children attending Pakeha schools or vice versa, and some cross-enrolment occurred, especially in isolated areas. Under the new act, schools were provided on condition of considerable input from the communities that

---

1. The first Christian mission school was established in 1816. J. C. Dakin, *Education in New Zealand*, 18.

2. Bronwyn Elsmore, *Like Them That Dream: The Maori and the Old Testament*, 23–24; J. M. Barrington, "Maori Scholastic Achievement. A Symposium: A Historical Review of Policies and Provisions," 1.

3. M. P. K. Sorrenson, "Māori and Pākehā," 143–45.

4. Keith Sinclair, *A History of New Zealand*, 84.

5. George Thomas Kurian, *Facts on File—National Profiles: Australia and New Zealand*, 187–88.

6. W. P. Morrell, *The Anglican Church in New Zealand: A History*, 45; Roger Openshaw, Greg Lee, and Howard Lee, *Challenging the Myths: Rethinking New Zealand's Educational History*, 38–39.

wanted them: Maori villages had to provide land, half the cost of erecting a suitable building and maintaining it, all books and one quarter of the teacher's salary. Only thirteen Maori primary schools opened under this act before government participation was increased in 1871; by the end of the 1870s, there were still only fifty-seven government native schools, all staffed by European teachers with a few Maori assistants.[7]

A wider state school system was formally established when abolition of the provincial governments in 1876 forced the central government to take over responsibility for education. By the 1877 Education Act, New Zealand enshrined the ideals of "free, compulsory and secular education" becoming popular around the world, although Maori children were specifically exempted from the "compulsory" provisions. School attendance for Maori children did not become compulsory until 1905, and progress in providing schools in Maori villages was slow. Where the 1891 census showed that four out of five of the colony's Pakeha children were now attending school, it seems likely that an inverse ratio applied to Maori children. While many Maori tribes petitioned for schools as stepping-stones to equality with Pakeha, some regions—especially the Waikato, the King Country, and Taranaki—saw active resistance to the establishment of schools. This resistance, largely overcome by the turn of the century, reflected post-Land Wars hostility to the British and the subsequent conscious decisions by some Maori tribes to have as little as possible to do with Pakeha.[8]

It was in this climate that the Mormon mission began to establish primary (elementary) schools from 1886. Ironically, by this date, the mainstream Christian missions (with the exception of the Catholic Church) had largely retreated from the primary education field. This was partly because of greatly decreased attendance (a carry-over from Maori disillusionment with the Christian missionaries following the 1860s Land Wars and the consequent virtual collapse of the missions in several areas); partly because financial support from CMS headquarters in England was being withdrawn from the Church of England in New Zealand; and partly because, from 1877, church schools were excluded from state subsidies for primary education.[9] Except for Roman Catholic schools, denominational efforts became concentrated on the provision and maintenance of a small number of secondary boarding schools for Maori youth. There were few

7. Sorrenson, "Māori and Pākehā," 163.

8. J. M. Barrington, "Maori Attitudes to Pakeha Institutions after the Wars: A Note on the Establishment of Schools," 25–28; Openshaw, Lee, and Lee, *Challenging the Myths*, 43–44.

9. Jeanine Graham, "Settler Society," 132; Morrell, *The Anglican Church in New Zealand*, 102.

state secondary schools for either Maori or Pakeha students in New Zealand at this time; as late as 1900, only 10 percent of European youth had the opportunity of progressing to secondary school.[10] Accordingly, some subsidies were still available for church secondary schools for Maori children, provided these schools met basic educational standards.

In an idealistic effort to fill a pronounced void in a few predominantly Mormon villages, the Mormon Church in 1886 opened primary schools at Nuhaka on the Mahia peninsula and at Taumata-o-Tapuhi in the Waiapu district; another was opened at Puketapu near Huntly in the Waikato the following year. Two or three others soon followed. These schools survived for a decade or so and then closed because of lack of interest or because a state school opened nearby. Another ten Mormon primary schools were established in the first two decades of the twentieth century, making a total of fifteen or sixteen Mormon primary schools that functioned for short periods in New Zealand between 1886 and the early 1920s.[11]

In 1886, the LDS Church owned no land or church buildings in New Zealand and had no permanent headquarters there. The mission had no capital and no income. Few of its full-time missionaries were sufficiently well-educated to be capable of effective pedagogy. Mormon missionary success among the Maori was beginning to expand faster than mission leaders could staff the burgeoning number of LDS Church branches. To assign American missionaries to teach school in remote Maori villages must have been a sacrifice of valuable manpower unless overriding motives compelled the new venture.

Mormon Motives for Establishing Schools

The most pressing and immediate motive of the Mormon elders was probably that of meeting Maori expectations. For forty years, Christian missions had provided schools. Maori who converted to Mormonism undoubtedly thought that their new church should provide schools as the "Mihinare Church" had done; there is at least one record of a Maori village petitioning a mission president for a school on these grounds.[12] No doubt some element of "keeping up with the Joneses" entered into the mission presidents' ready agreement. It can also be assumed that they were following the example of the first Mormon missionaries to Polynesia, who had established schools among the children in Tubuai and Hawaii in the early 1850s.[13]

---

10. Kurian, *Facts on File*, 188.
11. New Zealand Mission, Manuscript History, passim.
12. New Zealand Mission, Minutes, 16 April 1910.
13. R. Lanier Britsch, "Latter-day Saint Education in the Pacific Islands," 198.

The Mormon missionaries fervently believed in the benefits of education. Early Mormon leaders stressed the place of education in a church that made no distinction between spiritual and temporal matters. Founding Church president and prophet Joseph Smith proclaimed that "the glory of God is intelligence" (once painted on the wall behind many Mormon pulpits) and that men could not be "saved in ignorance." Mormons, Joseph Smith announced in another revelation at the end of 1832, should study astronomy, geology, history, political science, and current affairs as well as the principles and doctrines of the Church.[14]

Almost from its inception in 1830, the LDS Church sponsored adult education as well as common schools for children wherever the Saints settled long enough for these to function. Joseph Smith's successor, Brigham Young, vigorously promoted both intellectual and practical education in the Rocky Mountains settlements where the Saints were located from 1847. By default, the first primary schools in Utah were Church-sponsored rather than government-sponsored, though some were supported by local taxes. Most were at least nominally fee-paying. A state school system supported by taxation was not fully established in Utah until 1890, at first providing only elementary schools. As the government took over elementary schooling in Utah, the LDS Church Board of Education set about establishing academies (secondary schools), junior colleges and universities. Mainstream churches becoming established in Utah also founded their own denominational schools there in the latter decades of the nineteenth century.[15]

Mormon commitment to education reflected a theology that stressed human perfectibility.[16] As discussed in Chapter 1, Mormon elders were convinced that their mission was to raise the Maori from a degenerate state of ignorance and savagery to their former status as a "white and delightsome" branch of the house of Israel, and they believed that the Maori were not only capable of, but desired, such regeneration. The Mormons, of course, were not unique in their beliefs about Maori origins, nor were they alone in their desire to "reclaim" the Maori. Early ethnological discussions of Maori stressed their intelligence and aptitude for such civilizing efforts, and many contemporary commentators acknowledged that Maori "degeneration" was simply a result of the European invasion.[17]

---

14. Doctrine and Covenants 93:36, 131:6, 88:78–79.

15. William E. Berrett, "Church Educational Systems (CES)," 1:274–76; A. Garr Cranney, "Schools," 3:1267–69.

16. David P. Gardner, "Education," 2:441–46.

17. See, for example, S. J. Brittan, G. F. Grace, C. W. Grace, and A. V. Grace, eds., *A Pioneer Missionary among the Maoris, 1850–1879: Being Letters and Journals of Thomas Samuel Grace*, 18, 61–62; Report of 1891 Royal Commission, quoted in Sinclair, *A*

The Mormons, like the early Protestant missionaries, subscribed to idealistic but inevitably ethnocentric visions of their mission to raise Maori to Western concepts of civilisation. Mormon mission president Charles B. Bartlett (1902–5) deplored the introduction of European vices and their effect on Maori: "The problem of how to regenerate the race is one of a serious nature, and, so far as our Maori Saints are concerned, demands a solution at our hands," he wrote in 1904.[18] Regeneration apart, the Mormon elders, like New Zealand government leaders, mainstream church ministers and many Maori themselves, recognised that Maori needed European education in order to cope with European society.[19] "We will be compelled to take direction of their temporal as well as of their spiritual affairs. We will have to give them technical instruction in every department of life," wrote President Bartlett.[20]

There were additional motives for the establishment of the Maori Agricultural College in 1913. By the turn of the century, Mormon youth attending denominational secondary schools were, in the view of the Mormon elders, "becoming indoctrinated with sectarianism" instead of Mormonism.[21] As a lay church, the Mormon Church depended heavily for its progress on the availability of a local lay priesthood, that is, a corps of literate men capable of reading and passing on instructions, keeping financial and membership records, compiling reports, and teaching Church doctrine and procedure to others. The Maori Agricultural College reflected Church leaders' anticipation of a continuing need for educated male Maori Latter-day Saints, preferably literate in both English and Maori.

Early Mormon Schools

The early Mormon day schools were very primitive, often conducted in existing village meetinghouses.[22] Furniture was virtually nonexistent, but the lack of desks and benches scarcely registered with Maori pupils unaccustomed to such European artefacts. Basic equipment consisted of a few slates and slate pencils, a blackboard, and some chalk. Discipline imposed by the American teachers—discipline virtually unknown in Maori child-

History of New Zealand, 143.

18. Charles B. Bartlett, "The New Zealand Mission," *Millennial Star* 66, no. 32 (11 August 1904): 501.

19. Openshaw, Lee, and Lee, *Challenging the Myths*, 43, cite several Maori petitions that stressed that schools would enable Maori to achieve social and economic parity with Pakeha.

20. Bartlett, "The New Zealand Mission," 501.

21. New Zealand Mission, Manuscript History, 3 April 1904.

22. New Zealand Missionary Society, "Book Prepared for David O. McKay and Hugh J. Cannon."

care[23]—led both to some degree of absenteeism and to confrontations with indignant relatives as culturally unaware American teachers occasionally violated Maori tapu by, for example, administering corporal punishment on a pupil's head.[24] When the schools were a novelty, they attracted eager students; as the schools became "old" with both children and parents, absenteeism increased enormously. Competing attractions tempted pupils from the schoolhouse. "There were not enough children to carry on school," Elder Ezra F. Richards recorded one day in 1887, "they having run away to the horse races."[25] The same problems had plagued the CMS and government schools from an early date.[26] With these conditions prevailing, little was accomplished by the Mormon missionary-teachers, all of whom were unqualified and some of whom freely admitted that their efforts were somewhat less than successful.[27]

Poorly equipped and badly staffed as the Mormon schools were, they did not differ significantly from the CMS schools in New Zealand a quarter of a century earlier. Several CMS schools were reported in 1863 to have "buildings shockingly inadequate, teachers poorly paid and often quite unqualified."[28] Nor were Church schools the only ones taught by unqualified teachers; even in the 1920s, despite official policy, 50 percent of teachers in government primary schools in rural New Zealand were uncertified.[29] The Mormon primary schools in New Zealand were taught by frequently rotating, untrained Americans who, nevertheless, attempted to follow the primary school syllabus prescribed in the Native School Code (1880).[30] The Mormon Church largely withdrew from primary school edu-

---

23. Margaret Orbell, "The Traditional Maori Family," 113.

24. Ezra Foss Richards, Journal, 14 March 1887; Nelson Spicer Bishop, New Zealand Mission Diaries, 3, 4, 10 December 1886.

25. Richards, Journal, 1 February 1887.

26. Openshaw, Lee, and Lee, *Challenging the Myths*, 39, 48–50.

27. Sondra Sanders Jr., Letter to President William Paxman, 25 May 1886, in Sondra Sanders Jr., Journal, 577; Bishop, Diary, 28 October 1886, 18; James Noble, Letter to Louis G. Hoagland, dated Korongata, 26 November 1905.

28. Morrell, *The Anglican Church in New Zealand*, 102.

29. Dakin, *Education in New Zealand*, 68. Nineteenth-century Mormon schools in Utah were also frequently staffed by unqualified teachers, who were often reported to be "only slightly more knowledgeable than their students." Cranney, "Schools," 1267–69. So academically impoverished were many Utah schools of this period that LDS students often attended denominational schools, which offered a higher standard of education than that available in Mormon schools in the Territory. James B. Allen and Glen M. Leonard, *The Story of the Latter-day Saints*, 341.

30. Openshaw, Lee, and Lee, Challenging the Myths, 47; Barrington, "Maori Scholastic Achievement," 4. The public school primary syllabus was adapted for

cation in New Zealand when registration (and consequently, inspection) of private primary schools became mandatory in 1922 and as state primary schools were established within the reach of most Maori communities.

Without access to inspection reports,[31] it is difficult to make an accurate assessment of the value of the Mormon primary schools. No record has been found of any pupil at any Mormon day school passing the Standard Six Proficiency Certificate examination, and a search of mission records and the mission paper, *Te Karere*, found mention of only two pupils receiving government scholarships (tenable at denominational boarding schools) that were available to Maori students who passed Standard Four.[32] It is arguable that any degree of literacy achieved by any child who had no other opportunity for schooling was worthwhile; and a degree of Western socialisation, although perhaps eroding traditional tribal values, may have served the children well in contemporary New Zealand society.

The Maori Agricultural College

As early as 1889, Elder Heber C. Cutler visualised the Mormon primary school at Taumata-o-Tapuhi in the Waiapu valley developing into a boarding school along the lines of the early denominational industrial schools.[33] Mission president Charles B. Bartlett, who is usually given credit for the idea that led to the establishment of the Maori Agricultural College, arrived in New Zealand to begin his first mission in July 1892, just nine months after Elder Cutler left the country at the completion of his three-year mission. Cutler's idea was probably still being discussed during President Bartlett's first mission; during the next decade, discussion continued intermittently, and the idea was embellished when he returned as mission president.[34]

At the mission conference (Hui Tau) in 1904, President Bartlett proposed that an LDS secondary-level boarding school should be built. At that time, Maori students who desired a secondary education applied for

---

Maori schools by the Native Schools Code (1880) mainly by the deletion of history, formal grammar, and elementary science.

31. No records pertaining to Mormon primary schools other than the MAC could be found by staff of the New Zealand government archives in March 1997, and it was suggested that this was because these primary schools were not registered.

32. "Porirua School Report," *Te Karere (The Messenger)* 4, no. 6 (13 April 1910): 70–71, and "Porirua Native School," *Te Karere* 4, no. 26 (18 January 1911): 311.

33. Heber S. Cutler, "In Maori Land," dated 27 November 1889.

34. See Louis G. Hoagland et al., to President Joseph F. Smith, dated Auckland, 24 September 1906.

places at one of the denominational boarding schools, the most important of which were the Anglican Te Aute (near Napier in Hawkes Bay) and St. Stephen's (Auckland) for boys, and Hukarere (Napier) and Queen Victoria (Auckland) schools for Maori girls. The proposed LDS school was to have sufficient land to allow the teaching of agriculture as well as other practical subjects. The missionaries expected the Maori Saints to contribute towards its construction and, further, that the farm would enable the school to become self-supporting thereafter.

Though Maori Saints attending this mission conference gave unanimous approval to the project, only $US700, most of it contributed by the missionaries, had been raised by September 1906 when President Bartlett's successor, Louis G. Hoagland, and a committee of mission leaders petitioned Church president Joseph F. Smith for a grant of $US10,000 to make the long-promised "academy" a reality. President Hoagland asserted that "the majority" of Mormon boys were ambitious for academic schooling. After "graduation" from government primary schools, he told President Smith, these youth fell "into the trap set for them by other denominations," and "their parents are placed under obligations to the denominations which educates [sic] their children." Driving home the nail with forceful blows of his rhetorical hammer, Hoagland reminded President Smith that "we are very zealous in teaching them that the 'Glory of God is intelligence,' but provide no way for them to obtain knowledge." He pointed out that (despite the failure of the Maori Saints to donate more freely), the non-appearance of the promised school was becoming an embarrassment to the mission.[35]

The First Presidency approved the proposal, and the school, officially named the Latter-day Saints Maori Agricultural College, was finally built at Korongata, a Maori pa near Hastings, and opened in April 1913. Its first catalogue (prospectus), issued shortly before the school opened, listed both spiritual and practical goals for the new school.[36] These ideals were praiseworthy, but several factors combined to undermine the efforts of missionaries, staff, and students of the Maori Agricultural College (MAC) over the eighteen years it functioned. Problems began with the choice of site and culminated with a disastrous earthquake in February 1931; but the earthquake merely precipitated an outcome that by then had become unavoidable.[37]

---

35. Ibid.

36. *Catalogue and Announcement of the Latter-day Saints Agricultural College: First Year, 1913–1914*, 13.

37. For the story of the MAC over these eighteen years, see Marjorie Newton, *Tiki and Temple: The Mormon Mission in New Zealand, 1854–1958.*

Choice of Land

It was decided to purchase land for the new school from European rather than Maori landowners in order to avoid lengthy Land Court procedures and to forestall insinuations that the Mormon Church was as land-hungry as the mainstream Christian churches were perceived to have been.[38] President Hoagland's original intention was to purchase only enough land for the actual college buildings, then lease additional land for a college farm from nearby Maori owners.[39] It is a pity that this plan was not followed. Before land was purchased, Hoagland was released to return home. He was replaced by another former missionary, Rufus K. Hardy. President Hardy was accompanied to New Zealand by yet another former New Zealand missionary, Benjamin Goddard, commissioned by the First Presidency to help President Hardy choose land for the new college.[40] That Hardy, an insurance agent, and Goddard, a journalist-cum-visitors' bureau director, were entrusted with the selection of farming acreage of such critical importance was an unfortunate error of judgment.

Debate over the suitability of the chosen land began almost at once and continued for many years after the college closed. In 1918, just five years after its opening, mission president James N. Lambert was called upon by Church officials in Salt Lake City to account for the continuing bad financial condition of the college and farm. President Lambert had the soil at the college farm tested and forwarded soil samples to Salt Lake City, together with a report which showed that 80 percent of the MAC land was unsuitable for farming. "It would not have taken much of a farmer to discover [this]," former mission president Louis G. Hoagland commented acidly many years later. "The College boys used to say [that] all the mission presidents who were city men said the soil was fine but the presidents who were farmers said the soil was very poor and only fairly productive when we had a good damp season."[41]

In November 1920, Apostle David O. McKay and Liberty Stake president Hugh J. Cannon were preparing for a world tour of LDS missions. Louis G. Hoagland wrote to Cannon, detailing the history of the MAC

---

38. New Zealand Mission, Manuscript History, 6 April 1906; New Zealand Missionary Society, "Book Prepared for David O. McKay and Hugh J. Cannon."

39. New Zealand Mission, Manuscript History, Minutes of General Priesthood Meeting, 7 April 1906.

40. *Catalogue and Announcement, First Year, 1913–1914*, 11.

41. Louis G. Hoagland, Letter to President M. C. Woods, dated Salt Lake City, 11 May 1937. In 1917, normal practice on the MAC farm was to plough only four inches deep because deeper ploughing turned up the dead pumice subsoil. John Shaw Welch, New Zealand Missionary Journals, 19 March 1917, 49.

site purchase. Rufus K. Hardy and Benjamin Goddard had, of course, vigorously defended their choice, blaming the poor crops on drought and lack of fertilisers. Hoagland was sceptical and told Cannon that the LDS Church was the laughing-stock of the Hastings district for its purchase. It was somewhat of a fiasco, Hoagland felt, for the Mormons to set out to teach Maori boys how to make their own land pay, when professors of agriculture could not make the college farm pay. He urged Cannon to test the depth of the soil at the MAC farm while he and Elder McKay were in New Zealand, and decide on its quality for himself.[42]

David O. McKay had a farming background; he and Cannon, well aware of the controversy and the coolness which existed between some past New Zealand mission presidents as a result, paid particular attention to the soil as they walked around the 266-acre property on Saturday, 30 July 1921. McKay unequivocally agreed with Lambert and Hoagland. "The farm is very poor, shallow soil and not fertile at best," he reported. "The depth of productive soil will not average more than six inches! Why such a place was selected for an agricultural college is more than I can comprehend." Elder McKay was stunned to find that, with nearly 300 acres, the school could not keep itself in vegetables, not even potatoes, and that staff took students to neighbouring properties to see good crops and stock in fine condition. McKay recommended that the present school should be converted to a boarding school for Mormon girls, and that a more fertile site should be sought for the MAC. He also wondered whether failure of the farm stemmed not only from poor soil but also from poor management.[43]

Nothing came of Elder McKay's recommendations for relocation. Years after the college closed in 1931, Rufus K. Hardy, since 1934 a member of the First Council of the Seventy, was still vitally concerned to justify his purchase. In 1938, he escorted Apostle George Albert Smith over the site of the now-defunct MAC during their South Pacific tour. Elder Smith's opinion, as Hardy pointedly wrote in his published account of their trip, was that Korongata was "the most ideal setting he had ever seen for an agricultural college."[44] Hardy did not add that Elder Smith had worked at a leading Salt Lake City store, Zion's Cooperative Mercantile Institution (ZCMI), as a clerk and bookkeeper prior to his call to the Quorum of the Twelve.

---

42. Louis G. Hoagland to President Hugh J. Cannon, Liberty Stake, dated Mesa, Arizona, 16 November 1920.

43. David O. McKay, "Journal of World Mission Tour, 1921," 30 July 1921.

44. Rufus K. Hardy, "With Church Leaders in New Zealand," 7.

Benjamin Goddard's position was particularly invidious. The farm could scarcely be classed as anything but a failure. It became increasingly obvious that either the land was infertile, or that the school principals, all "professors" of agriculture and many of them personally recommended by Goddard, were incompetent. From the late 1890s until his death in December 1930, Benjamin Goddard was clearly the "king-maker" of the New Zealand Mission. By virtue of holding office in Zion's Maori Association (later the New Zealand Missionary Society, a Utah association of returned missionaries), he was involved in the selection of several New Zealand mission presidents, MAC principals, and missionaries, and had a benevolent finger in most New Zealand mission pies. At least one college principal was related to him.[45] His position as director of the Bureau of Information on Temple Square placed him in close proximity to the First Presidency's offices, and there is every indication that Goddard took advantage of the easy access to the presidency then available. His "help" was not always appreciated in New Zealand; one mission president was frankly annoyed to be told of his own impending release by Goddard instead of through official Church channels.[46] In the matter of college principals and staff, Goddard's recommendations were not always felicitous.

An American High School in New Zealand

Disagreements that sometimes arose between mission presidents and college principals were complicated by the lack of clear guidelines from Salt Lake City about the demarcation line between their responsibilities, and also by the failure of those responsible to clarify whether the school was indeed a New Zealand college (that is, a private secondary-level high school with a staff of teachers headed by a principal) or an American college (a tertiary-level institution with a faculty headed by a president). The initial rejection of proffered New Zealand Education Department assistance allowed American influence too much sway in curriculum, lesson content, and choice of American textbooks. Even the desks came from the United States, and a picture of the United States president hung in the dining hall alongside that of the British king. It was freely—even proud-

---

45. See, for example, Journal History, 17 December 1897, 2; James Needham Lambert, Journal, 1916–19, 23 January, 11 July 1918; James N. Lambert, Letter to Matthew Cowley, dated Salt Lake City, 16 May 1924; John Johnson, Journal, 19 June, 26 September 1912; George Shepard Taylor, Private Journal, 1920-24, Book 1, 21 March 1921.

46. John Ephraim Magleby to Elder George Reynolds, copied into Magleby, Journal, 29 May 1902.

ly—stated that the school was "distinctly American" in many respects.[47] This was illustrated by such American conventions as references to the "1913-14 school year," whereas, in the southern hemisphere, each academic year was (and is) wholly contained within one calendar year. Also bewildering was the American custom of holding "commencement" at the *end* of the school year, and continual references to the "graduating class." Graduation ceremonies for high school students were foreign to New Zealand, especially when some MAC pupils were reported to have "graduated" simply by staying at the school for four years.[48]

Although the students revelled in the novelty of the American atmosphere, it did not increase the school's credibility with parents, school inspectors, members of parliament, or prospective employers of its "graduates." There were many well-deserved compliments for the school buildings, for the school's "character building" efforts and its general goals (what today would be called its "mission statement"); but the school was not praised for academic achievement.[49] For half a century, the MAC was fondly remembered by its former students for the fun and the football, the music and the men who taught there.[50] Several former students, interviewed in the 1970s, stated that their MAC graduation certificates had been virtually worthless in terms of enhancing their employability.[51]

On the other hand, nearly all former students felt they had benefited from the gospel teachings, character building, and leadership skills learned at the MAC. Even the government inspectors praised this aspect of life at the MAC. "The regular farm work under supervision, the regular life and association with earnest young white men of about their own age, the formation of habits of punctuality and tidiness and the band and choir practice, cannot but exercise a good influence upon their lives and in this respect the institution is doing good work," wrote the school's regular in-

47. "College Work Advancing," *Te Karere* 7, no. 12 (4 June 1913): 140-43; Ariel S. Ballif, Oral History, interviewed by R. Lanier Britsch, 1973, 11.

48. James Southon, interviewed by Roger Tansley, in Kenneth Wayne Baldridge, Interviews, 1971.

49. G. M. Henderson, Inspector, Native Schools, Memorandum to Director of Education, 4 October 1926.

50. For example, see Ariel Smith Ballif, Oral History, 10, interviewed by Kenneth W. Baldridge, 1972; Eruha Kawana, George Nepia, Tipi Kopua, and Nephi Wharemahihi, in Kenneth Wayne Baldridge, Interviews, 1971; James Southon, James Munday, and Daniel Williams, interviewed by Roger Tansley, in Kenneth Wayne Baldridge, Interviews, 1971.

51. See, for example, George Nepia, Heteraka Anaru, and Rupert Wihongi, in Kenneth Wayne Baldridge, Interviews, 1971.

spector, Mr. G. M. Henderson, in 1927, before adding the damning rider, "but as a scholastic institution for imparting a literary education the college is not worthy of serious consideration."[52]

In later life, very few former pupils thought that the farming and agriculture courses had been of any benefit. The American farming methods taught at the MAC were unsuitable for New Zealand conditions, the college land was not conducive to fruitful lessons in agriculture, and, even more importantly, it was very different from the farming land in the home communities of most of its pupils. As few Mormon Maori held individual land titles, even students who wanted to apply their newly learned farming knowledge in later life did not control the land and so were unable to do so,[53] a situation that should have been anticipated by the college's founders. "The care and feeding of animals cannot be taught adequately from a text-book, especially one compiled in another country," wrote Henderson.[54] Agriculture and animal husbandry lessons had little relevance for the numerous Islanders enrolled in the school (averaging about one third of the school population between 1920 and 1928).[55] Such industries were unknown and impracticable in Tonga and Samoa.[56]

Staff and Students

Not only was the land chosen for the MAC unsuitable for farming purposes, the qualifications and management skills of the American "professors" were, on the whole, inadequate. Copies of thirteen of the eighteen catalogues published by the MAC survive, as do copies of the annual reports of the school to the New Zealand Education Department for the years 1924–29.[57] Both sources list the names and qualifications (if any) of the teaching staff for the relevant years.

Altogether, nine principals were appointed during the MAC's eighteen years, compared with only two at nearby Te Aute College during the same

52. G. M. Henderson, Inspector, Native Schools, Memorandum to Director of Education, 11 October 1927.

53. John Shortland, in Kenneth Wayne Baldridge, Interviews, 1971.

54. G. M. Henderson, Memorandum to Director of Education, 4 October 1926.

55. The surviving annual Catalogues of the MAC listed the names of the previous year's students, together with their home town (if Maori) or country of origin (if Islander). Five of the eighteen catalogues have not survived.

56. Henderson, Memorandum to Director of Education, 11 October 1927.

57. Catalogues of the Maori Agricultural College, 1913–14, 1914, 1918–1926, 1929–31; New Zealand Education Department, Registered Private Primary Schools Statistics—Maori Agricultural College (copies of reports submitted by MAC Principals to the New Zealand Department of Education), 1924–29.

period. Seven of the nine MAC principals had degrees, usually in science or agriculture, but only one of the seven (Leo B. Sharp) is known to have held a higher degree. The last principal, Robert P. Hodge, was a certificated New Zealand teacher (with no farming qualifications) who was appointed principal for the second half of 1930 and for 1931, but Hodge served only six months as the school was discontinued during the first week of the 1931 academic year when the Napier earthquake struck. Although most of the eight American principals had teaching experience, none had teaching qualifications that would have satisfied the New Zealand government and none had any previous experience of farming in New Zealand.

Sixty-six teachers are listed in the thirteen surviving catalogues and six surviving annual reports;[58] of these, only fifteen (22.7 percent), held any qualification. The remaining 77.3 percent were unqualified missionaries seconded from the regular unpaid missionary force. Although designated a "college" or secondary school, in practice the MAC was forced to also offer primary education, as too few of the enrolling students had had sufficient elementary education to enable them to take high school courses. As the least qualified teachers were, by and large, assigned to teach primary grades, it is not surprising that the annual reports show poor results in the Proficiency Certificate examinations. "There is no lack of earnestness and good intention among the assistants," wrote Inspector Henderson in 1924, "but these are not an adequate substitute for training and experience."[59] Teaching methods were freely criticised. "Their invariable practice seems to be to work steadily through a text-book in each subject explaining the meaning to the pupils where necessary," wrote Henderson to the Director of Education in January 1928. "In many cases, I suspect, the subject-matter of the text-book is as new to the teacher as it is to the scholar."[60] As the missionaries were ultimately responsible to the mission president in Auck-

---

58. This total includes a few faculty wives who taught classes and were listed as teachers. Bernice Mainwaring and Artemisia Ballif were the only faculty wives known to be trained teachers, yet neither was listed in the catalogues. Ironically, Mrs. Ballif's dramatic productions were praised by Inspector Henderson as a significant aid to English language teaching at the college, and he also commented favourably on the music program with which Mrs. Mainwaring assisted. See G. M. Henderson, Inspector, Native Schools, Memorandum to Director of Education, 25 September 1928.

59. G. M. Henderson, Report of Inspection of Maori Agricultural College, Hastings, 5 September 1924.

60. G. M. Henderson, Memorandum to Director of Education, dated Ohau, 10 January 1928.

land, who had a free hand in their assignment and subsequent transfers, frequent staff changes also dismayed Education Department inspectors.[61]

Although the MAC was intended as a high school, the preparatory department consistently had the larger enrolment for several years. At first it offered only Standards Five and Six, but in 1919, it began offering Standards Three and Four also, to accommodate the low educational level of many enrolling students. Later, the lower primary grades were phased out, and over-age or unqualified pupils who enrolled were placed in Standard Six or in secondary forms, with or without a Proficiency Certificate.

The six-hour Proficiency Certificate examination, for which Standard Six primary school pupils sat, was instituted in 1899 and modified several times before it was abolished in 1936. By the time the MAC opened in 1913, the Proficiency Certificate represented a school-leaving certificate, normally earned at the age of thirteen or fourteen; it also acted as a filter for the secondary schools. By 1914, pass requirements were 60 percent for English and arithmetic plus aggregate marks for all subjects of 60 percent. A "poor relation" Certificate of Competency was issued to children who completed Standard Six but did not pass the Proficiency Examination. A Proficiency Certificate was a widely respected achievement, a passport to a free place for two years at secondary school, or a considerable help in obtaining employment. As the Junior Civil Service examination was discontinued one year before the MAC opened, and the School Certificate not introduced until four years after it closed, the Proficiency Certificate was the only recognised award for which the MAC prepared pupils; matriculation to a New Zealand university from the MAC was scarcely an option.

It was not until 1929 that the native primary school syllabus was required to be identical with that of the public primary schools. During the first three decades of the twentieth century, most native schools offered only Standards One to Four; a pass at Standard Four was regarded as satisfactory completion of primary education for Maori pupils,[62] and scholarships to denominational boarding schools were awarded to Maori pupils at this level. But, however unrealistically, ambitious Maori parents wanted their sons to obtain the Standard Six Proficiency Certificate and proceed to secondary education. The provision of secondary education for Mormon Maori youth was, after all, the whole reason for the existence of the MAC. Denominational boarding schools such as the Anglican Te Aute College

---

61. G. M. Henderson, Memorandum to Director of Education, 11 October 1927; see also Henderson's reports dated 13 October 1925, 4 October 1926; and D. G. Ball, Inspection Report, Maori Agricultural College, 14 August 1930.

62. Openshaw, Lee, and Lee, *Challenging the Myths*, 47–49.

had a proud record of academic excellence; Mormon Maori parents had been led to expect no less of the MAC.

Registration of private primary schools in New Zealand became compulsory during 1922. The MAC received registration for its primary department (though not its secondary department) during 1923, and first presented candidates for the Proficiency Certificate examination in 1924. The low pass rate (about 25%) between 1924 and 1930 indicates that parents had good reason for concern. Education Department officers, with access to statistics from comparable schools throughout the Dominion, were also concerned. "The results of the Proficiency Examination are very unsatisfactory," wrote the Director of Education to the incumbent MAC principal Albert Sells in 1926. "If the teaching has not improved by the time the Inspector makes his next visit, the Department will reluctantly be compelled to take into consideration the question of cancelling the registration."[63] Faced with continuing poor results from the MAC, Thomas Strong, Director of Education, could only comment philosophically, "The aims of the Principal appear to be quite worthy ones and no doubt the school is of a somewhat special type and its efficiency cannot readily be measured by the number of pupils passing, say, the Proficiency Examination."[64]

Eleven of the surviving school catalogues list the names and forms of the previous year's pupils. The average number enrolled each year between 1920 and 1930 was forty-four. From 1920 to 1925 (when the MAC began to phase out its preparatory department), primary pupils outnumbered those in secondary grades by an average of three to two. As the primary grades were discontinued, total school enrolment declined to the point where it was no longer feasible to keep the school open.

Not only was the percentage of Proficiency Certificates earned well below the national average, the average age of MAC pupils was well above average. In 1924, twenty-eight of the thirty students in the primary department (Standards Four, Five, and Six) were above the age of fifteen; similar figures were reported for 1925–29. In 1928, the average age of the school's students was nineteen; the average age of pupils in Standard Six, the final primary year, was eighteen years and four months. In 1929, there were twenty-one students in Standard Six (the only primary form offered that year): one was thirteen years old; thirteen were aged between fifteen

---

63. A. Bell for Director of Education to Principal, Maori Agricultural College, 18 October 1926. This referred only to the registration of the Primary Department, which was compulsory. The Secondary Department was not registered and was not required to be registered at this date.

64. T. B. Strong, Letter to Mr G. M. Henderson, 4 August 1928.

and eighteen; and seven were between nineteen and twenty-two.[65] It is apparent that, although intended as a secondary school for high-school-age pupils, in essence the Maori Agricultural College seems, unfortunately, to have fitted the deprecating statement of early New Zealand Schools Inspector J. E. Gorst that "Native Colleges are an impossibility; they can only become [primary] schools for big boys."[66]

Although its founding rationale was the provision of secondary education for bright young Maori LDS boys who were reported to be proceeding from village primary schools to denominational secondary schools, about half the MAC students were older men who had left school at intervals ranging from one to fourteen years prior to their enrolment at the MAC. In 1928, for example, no fewer than twenty-six of the fifty-five pupils enrolled at inspection time fell into this category. Their average length of time away from school was four years. The oldest student, Samoan John Brunt, was twenty-eight years old and had left school fourteen years before coming to the MAC.[67] It seems clear that American Mormon missionaries in the Polynesian islands were misled by the name "College" attached to the New Zealand institution and were sending men to the MAC with the expectation that they would acquire the equivalent of an American "college education." While some of the younger Islanders were bright and came well-prepared, especially those from the Marist Brothers school in Apia, Western Samoa, Henderson could only describe most of the MAC's overage pupils as "educational misfits from all parts of the North Island of New Zealand and Polynesia." His immediate superior, John Porteous, advised the Director of Education that, in his opinion, in view of the pupils' ages and the poor teaching at the MAC, "it would be better if they were out at work earning their living."[68]

The over-representation of adult and high-school age pupils in the primary department suggests that it may be true that many of these men enrolled to enjoy the music, the football, and the American flavour that

---

65. Compiled from New Zealand Department of Education Inspection Reports.

66. Quoted in R. R. Alexander, *The Story of Te Aute College*, 49.

67. Henderson, Memorandum to Director of Education, 25 September 1928. At least one non-LDS student enrolled (and subsequently baptised) in 1919 was a World War I veteran, and a few Islanders were said to be married men. See John Shaw Welch, Missionary Journal, and Nephi Wharemihihi, in Kenneth Wayne Baldridge, Interviews, 1971.

68. Henderson, Memoranda to Director of Education, 4 October 1926, 25 September 1928; Jno. Porteous, Senior Inspector Native Schools, to Director of Education, 8 January 1929.

accompanied everything at the MAC, rather than to engage in serious academic study. Some MAC "old boys" who had completed their stay at the MAC in the 1920s frankly admitted this motivation when they were interviewed about their experiences at the MAC many years later. In the school's last years, strict enrolment dates were enforced to circumvent this approach; no longer could students arrive at school in late autumn as the teams were chosen and depart as soon as the football season ended.[69] Perhaps the poor qualifications of the staff were somewhat immaterial for these students.

By the 1920s, mission presidents and MAC principals alike were well aware that the MAC was not reaching a satisfactory academic standard; they repeatedly and unsuccessfully begged Church authorities to send more and better-qualified teachers from the United States.

Mission President John E. Magleby recorded in his journal the MAC's failure to obtain funding from the Maori Purpose Fund "because of our low standard and the class of boys we taught," the latter comment referring to the lack of Proficiency Certificates among enrolling students rather than being a disparagement of the social status of Maori pupils. President Magleby realised that if the college wanted recognition as a secondary school entitled to government subsidies, "we must mend our ways."[70] But it was not until it was too late for the MAC that American Church leaders began to comprehend the importance to New Zealand students and their parents of passes in the annual government examinations.

The Final Years

There was improvement under Principal Ariel S. Ballif (1927–30), improvement recognised and commended by the government inspectors. The Education Department made no further threats to deregister the primary department, now greatly reduced in size in any case.[71] But the improved qualifications of the teaching staff and teaching methods were too few and came too late to reverse the image of the MAC among Mormon parents; enrolments continued to plummet. It may also be postulated that, when academic rigour increased and the practice of enrolling for and attending only the winter football season was disallowed, the school became much less attractive to young Mormon Maori males. However, this stricter policy,

---

69. New Zealand Mission, Manuscript History, 12 March 1927.

70. John E. Magleby, Journal, 25 February, 18 July 1929; Ballif, Oral History (Britsch, 1973), 11.

71. Henderson, Memorandum to the Director of Education, 25 September 1928; Ball, Native Schools Inspection Report, Maori Agricultural College, 4 September 1929.

the result of inspectorial complaints that the MAC school year was many weeks shorter than the gazetted New Zealand academic year,[72] also effectively excluded genuine prospective students who needed seasonal work in the shearing sheds in order to finance their MAC attendance.

From the building of the dormitory and chapel in 1912 to its final year, the MAC was a financial drain on the LDS Church and a continual worry to successive mission presidents. By 1929, the annual cost per capita was $US250, of which $174 was subsidised by the Church. "We appreciate that those who attend this institution receive great benefit and that they become leaders in the communities and branches in which they reside. It seems, however, a big expense and effort for the few who attend," wrote the First Presidency to mission president John Magleby in May 1930.[73]

A significant mistake was made very early when the First Presidency was assured that the college could and would become self-supporting. When the farm failed to make a profit and fees could not be collected from indigent Maori parents, the mission presidents became perpetual supplicants trying to justify requests for additional funds. In reality, the amounts sent to the MAC were by no means extravagant when compared with Church funds expended on LDS schools for American students. Amounts spent on U.S. stake academies (Church high schools for day pupils) during the 1911–12 school year, for example, ranged from $US4,200 to $25,000. The sums expended on these academies do not appear to correlate with enrolment figures: several of these day schools with enrolments comparable to those of the MAC received far larger sums than the MAC—and the MAC was a boarding school.[74] The amount spent on the MAC also fades into insignificance when compared with the $US75,000–$90,000 annual losses reported by the Church sugar plantation at Laie, Hawaii.[75]

Rather than consider such comparisons, the First Presidency focused on the staff-student ratio at the MAC, which was 1:5.6 in 1929 and 1:6.8 in 1930; they were reluctant to provide additional salaried teaching staff or to continue to pay those already there unless enrolments increased.[76] The

---

72. Porteous, Senior Inspector of Native Schools, to Director of Education, 8 January 1929.

73. First Presidency, Letter to John E. Magleby, 27 May 1930, in Heber J. Grant Letterbook, as quoted by Kenneth W. Baldridge, "The Maori Agricultural College: An Experience in Rural Education," 40.

74. Osborne J. P. Widtsoe, Report of the Commissioner of Education for the Year Ended 30 June 1913, in "The Schools of the Mormon Church."

75. Magleby, Journal, 17 May 1932, 40.

76. Baldridge, "The Maori Agricultural College," 40. The First Presidency referred to a staff/student ratio of 1:4; it is not clear how they calculated these figures.

situation became a stalemate as Maori parents would not send their sons to the MAC unless more and better-qualified teachers were appointed, and the First Presidency would not appoint sufficient qualified teachers unless increased enrolments justified such a step. When the worldwide Great Depression hit New Zealand, it became more difficult for LDS Maori students to attend as school officers enforced the policy of paying fees in advance. Simultaneously, the Depression made it even more important for New Zealand youth to obtain recognised school-leaving qualifications.

It seems a pity that enough care was not taken in the initial choice of the land; that the Church did not allocate sufficient funds to provide qualified staff; and that the New Zealand school syllabus was not followed in order to prepare students for qualifying examinations. Had these steps been taken, the school might have been more successful. Because these steps were not taken, enrolments continued to decline and the school sank even further into debt. Ironically, at that period, educational theorists and policymakers in New Zealand were again stressing that an agricultural education was the appropriate schooling for Maori youth. Thus, the MAC should have romped home with government grants and aid when the Church now applied for such grants. Instead, government inspectors regretted the MAC's low standard. "The need for a good agricultural college is sufficiently great and we would be glad to be able to recommend [the MAC] if we were sure that it gave the boys a strong interest in and love for agriculture and other forms of farming," wrote Inspector Henderson, who admitted giving "evasive answers" when asked by members of the public for his opinion of the MAC. "So long as the present system prevails of casual class teaching by inexperienced teachers . . . the school can occupy only an inferior position among our educational establishments."[77]

As previously discussed, by 1922, under amendments to the 1914 Education Act, all private primary schools in New Zealand were required to be registered and inspected, and the MAC preparatory department (though not, as has been explained, the secondary department) had been so registered and inspected from 1923. Secondary schools could be registered, and so become subject to inspection, if desired; this was essential for specific government subsidies to be made available. The Maori Purpose Fund Board, founded in 1925 and at first mainly concerned with education,[78] had given some small grants to the MAC, but these were withdrawn when standards failed to reach a desirable level. Additional small grants were made during Ariel S. Ballif's term as principal, and he and mission

---

77. Henderson, Memorandum to Director of Education, 4 October 1926.
78. Michael King, "Between Two Worlds," 289.

president John E. Magleby confidently expected that the MAC secondary department would soon qualify for registration when they announced an impending visit to the MAC by the chief Inspector of Secondary Schools "to arrange for registration."[79]

The inspection duly took place on 2 April 1930; but to the disappointment of all concerned, after receiving the official decision, MAC principal Ballif had to advise President Magleby that once again, the school was not judged of a high enough standard to be registered.[80] Damage to the school buildings during the Napier earthquake the following February spelled the end of the MAC, and its secondary department never did achieve registration.[81]

The MAC was not the only LDS Church school whose continued existence was in doubt. In 1914, Brigham Young University in Provo, Utah, recorded unpaid debts of $185,000; for the next thirty years, its future as a Church school was threatened. During the 1920s, some General Authorities wanted the Church to divest itself, not only of BYU, but also of all other schools (including the MAC) in order to relieve the drain they were becoming on Church finances. "Nothing has worried me more since I became president [of the Church] than the expansion of the appropriation for the church school system," said President Heber J. Grant in the late 1920s.[82] Finally, in 1926, Church leaders decided to withdraw from academic education. Most LDS junior colleges were transferred to the states in which they were situated; Ricks College (now BYU–Idaho) and Brigham Young University (Provo) continued, but under review.[83] The MAC could scarcely remain unthreatened in such a climate. The First Presidency made it clear that the 1931 school year was to be a probationary one for the MAC and would in all likelihood be its last.[84] Its closing was inevitable, only hastened and not caused by the earthquake of February 1931.

The Myth of the MAC

The fame of the Maori Agricultural College has grown since it closed, and the conviction that the MAC was the nursery of the present-day LDS Church in New Zealand became enshrined in the hearts of New Zea-

79. "Nga Whakaaturanga," *Te Karere* 24, no. 3 (19 March 1930): 86.

80. New Zealand Mission, Manuscript History, 15 April 1930.

81. For a fuller discussion of the failure of the MAC to qualify for registration, see Newton, *Tiki and Temple*, 186–87.

82. Gary James Bergera and Ronald Priddis, *Brigham Young University: A House of Faith*, 4–5, 18.

83. Ibid.

84. Magleby, Journal, 19 November 1930, 219.

land LDS Church members and many American missionaries and mission presidents. "The M.A.C. played a great part in the development of the Church in New Zealand and in these Islands," said James Southon in 1971.[85] Southon, born in Samoa, was the son of an English father and Polynesian mother, and graduated from the MAC in 1930. He became a district president in 1958 and the second president of the Hawkes Bay Stake a few years later. "Nearly all the leaders throughout the mission were M.A.C. old boys," said Sidney Crawford, another respected Maori leader and ex-MAC pupil (and Mormon convert), who succeeded Southon as president of the Hawkes Bay Stake, "great leaders, branch presidents, district presidents."[86] "The cadre of Mormon leadership for over four decades was molded at M.A.C.," wrote one historian in the 1970s.[87] Former MAC principal Ariel S. Ballif concurred. "They became tremendous leaders when they finished and had grown up," he said of his former MAC pupils. "[They were] the leading men in the Church in New Zealand when I went back [as mission president] in 1955."[88] Speaking of the evacuation of the American missionaries for the duration of World War II, Ballif said, "These Old Boys who [had] attended the M.A.C. were the ones that carried on."[89] Former MAC student Kelly Harris reiterated that, during the war, "virtually everyone that had a position of any importance in the mission had a link to the College."[90]

Church General Authority Robert L. Simpson reported that, as Church president David O. McKay travelled around New Zealand in 1955, "practically every district president and every branch president, and every leader he came across was wearing a little pin, which was the old M.A.C., the Maori Agricultural College, pin. He was struck by the fact that if it had not been for this school we wouldn't have as many leaders in New Zealand today as we have."[91]

---

85. James Southon, interviewed by Roger Tansley, in Kenneth Wayne Baldridge, Interviews, 1971.

86. Sidney Crawford, in Kenneth Wayne Baldridge, Interviews, 1971. The name of the Hawkes Bay Stake was changed to the Hastings New Zealand Stake in 1974.

87. Baldridge, "The Maori Agricultural College," 52.

88. Ballif, Oral History (Britsch, 1973), 8, 55.

89. Ariel S. Ballif, Oral History, interviewed by Antony I. Bentley, 1981, 7.

90. Kelly Harris, in Kenneth Wayne Baldridge, Interviews, 1971.

91. Robert Leatham Simpson, Oral History, 16. Elder Simpson went on to state that it was seeing this phenomenon that led President McKay to decide to build the Church College of New Zealand; but the new college had been announced nearly seven years earlier and its construction was well under way in January 1955

The assertion that the MAC "old boys" took over as district and branch presidents after the American missionaries were recalled from the South Pacific in October 1940, and that most post-war Church leaders were also MAC alumni, is implicitly believed by Church members and leaders. But as with so much received wisdom about the MAC, close examination of the records does little to confirm the accuracy of this perception. Certainly local New Zealand men, the majority of whom were Maori, were called to serve in district and branch presidencies during World War II; but there is little or no evidence to confirm that most of these were former MAC students. Like many generalisations, those made about the role of the MAC in developing a generation of leaders are somewhat too sweeping; the question of the development of local leadership in the Mormon Church in New Zealand is much more complex than such statements imply.

For several decades after the 1880s, American missionaries were appointed as Mormon district presidents in New Zealand and presided over Maori branch presidents; at some times and in some areas, missionaries also served as branch presidents. When Elder David O. McKay first visited New Zealand in 1921 as a member of the Quorum of the Twelve, he strongly advocated installing local leaders at every level, even if the work was not done perfectly at first; he had confidence in the Maori Saints he met and wanted them to have leadership opportunities. Elder McKay, recollecting what had so nearly happened during the recent Great War, urged the necessity of this step in case the time came (as it did during World War II) when there might be no American missionaries to provide LDS Church leadership in New Zealand.[92]

However, more Maori leaders were not called until John E. Magleby became mission president for the second time in 1928. President Magleby was unaware of the recommendations made seven years earlier by the visiting apostle. To combat the shortage of American missionaries as a result of the Great Depression and in an attempt to win back Maori Latter-day Saints who were defecting to Ratana, President Magleby began placing respected local Maori leaders in district presidencies. While waiting somewhat apprehensively for the First Presidency's reaction to this move, he discovered a copy of Elder McKay's recommendations in the mission office files and recorded his satisfaction that his new policy had authorita-

when President McKay made his first visit to New Zealand since 1921. During his 1955 visit, President McKay decided to enlarge the college already under construction.

92. George Shepard Taylor, Report of Sermons of David O. McKay delivered at the Annual Conference of the New Zealand Mission of the Church of Jesus Christ of Latter-day Saints, held at Huntly, 23–25 April 1921, 14.

tive endorsement.[93] He eventually received congratulations from the First Presidency for his initiative. However, although the MAC had been operating for fifteen years and many of its former students were now mature men, none of the six district presidents that President Magleby installed was an ex-MAC student, and only one of the counsellors was.[94]

There were fourteen districts in the mission when President Magleby was released. A seventh district (Poverty Bay) was given an all-Maori presidency in 1933 by President Magleby's successor, Harold T. Christensen, but missionary elders continued to preside over the remaining eight districts. President Christensen was followed in turn by Rufus K. Hardy (second term), Alvin T. Maugham, and M. Charles Woods. As time passed, President Magleby's hand in the change to Maori presidencies in the most populous Maori districts was forgotten, and Matthew Cowley, who succeeded President Woods, was credited with being the innovator. "We were just getting around to filling the branch and district positions with local leadership when I was there," said Elder Robert L. Simpson, speaking of his first mission (1937–40), some forty years later. "Before that time many of the positions had been filled by proselyting missionaries. But Matthew Cowley especially recognised that if these people were ever going to do what they needed to do in the Church, they had to assume these leadership positions as branch presidents and so on."[95]

However, five of the original six Maori district presidents appointed by President Magleby were still in office when Matthew Cowley became mission president in 1938, and these and another Maori district president were still serving when President Cowley left New Zealand in 1945.[96] The other eight districts were presided over by "Zion elders" until the missionaries were recalled in October 1940. By Easter 1941, when the first wartime Hui Tau was held, the number of districts had been reduced to ten, and local men of necessity presided over all of them; not one was an MAC old boy, though a few counsellors in the various districts were. Two former MAC students, George Watene and Kelly Harris, were sustained at this Hui Tau as mission secretary and editor of Te Karere respectively.

---

93. Magleby, Journal, 14 February 1932.

94. Wilson Paewai, second counsellor in the Hawkes Bay District. Stuart Meha, the other counsellor in the same district presidency, was a Te Aute "Old Boy."

95. Simpson, Oral History, 5. Elder Cowley was Elder Simpson's mission president for most of his first mission.

96. Paora (Paul) Hapi, installed as president of the Mahia District in 1928, died in 1930, and was succeeded by Wi Smith, who in turn died and was succeeded by Sidney Christy. None of the three was an MAC "old boy," though Christy's son (and namesake) attended the MAC for one year.

None of the local men sustained at this conference as mission auxiliary presidents were MAC old boys, though two mission auxiliary counsellors and two auxiliary secretaries were.[97]

It is not possible to check whether most branch presidents during World War 11 were MAC "old boys," partly because not all MAC enrolment records survive and partly because the manuscript history of the New Zealand Mission contains no records whatsoever between August 1940 and July 1945. Thus, the mission paper, *Te Karere*, is the main source of information about leadership changes during World War II. During the war, several branches reported a change of branch president. As far as can be ascertained, only a very few of the men called to serve as branch presidents during World War II were former MAC students. Even without access to complete college records, it is clear that by no means were a majority of war-time branch presidents ex-MAC students.

Three of President Magleby's district presidents (Eriata Nopera, Turi Ruruku, and Henere Pere Wihongi) died between February 1947 and September 1948. Gordon C. Young, who took over as mission president from A. Reed Halversen in July 1948, promptly released the remaining Maori district presidents and installed American missionaries as presidents in all districts. President Young had no confidence in the leadership ability of Maori Saints, though he was willing to have them serve as counsellors in the various district presidencies.[98] He was pleased with the influx of European members. He thought they would make good leaders, "a little different to the Maoris who seem to lack the capacity for sustained leadership."[99] President Young's words and actions do not bear out the legend of a generation of Church leaders nurtured at the MAC. The New Zealanders he released were not educated at the MAC; the men he replaced them with were young American missionaries.

President Young was succeeded by Sidney J. Ottley in 1951. As a young man on his first mission, President Ottley had taught at the MAC. If the legend were true, he could be expected to proudly note the large number of MAC alumni now leading the branches and districts of the mission. Instead, he reflected on the sober reality of affairs in the New Zealand Mission. While mission membership was now over 11,000, not only were American missionaries serving in almost all leadership callings, they were

97. 1941 Hui Tau program, p. [2], inserted in *Te Karere* 35, no. 4 between pp. 626 and 627.

98. Gordon C. Young, Personal Monthly Reports to First Presidency, 30 September, 30 November 1948, in New Zealand Mission, Manuscript History.

99. Gordon C. Young, Letter to the First Presidency, dated Auckland, 23 January 1951.

there by default. In an article in the mission paper, he addressed a question to "530 elders," pointing out that four in every one hundred male Latter-day Saints in New Zealand were ordained elders. "If only half of you were active," he wrote, "it would mean that a president, two counsellors and a clerk could serve each 200 people. . . . What a force of ministers to take care of the needs of the poor and the sick and the aged, with the help of over a thousand others who hold the Aaronic Priesthood, with the authority to officiate in the outward ordinances of the Church." President Ottley made it clear that, while there *should* have been enough local men capable of presiding over every branch in the mission, there were far too few. He challenged the men of the mission to *become* a generation of leaders.[100]

Although Ariel S. Ballif heartily subscribed to the legend of the MAC, as quoted earlier, he also cast doubt on its validity when he stated that the first thing he did when he arrived as mission president in 1955 was "remove all the missionaries from responsibilities in branches or districts. Maoris had had the [Mormon] gospel for over one hundred years and they ought to be prepared and ready to take the responsibility themselves."[101] If President Ballif had to remove American missionaries from executive positions in the branches and districts as late as 1955, the MAC old boys were not the "tremendous leaders" serving in these callings that he said they were. "The training that we gave them for leadership [in his term as mission president from 1955–58] proved very valuable when they changed over to stakes," President Ballif asserted.[102]

Nor, in retrospect, do the actions of Church authorities when the first stakes were organised from 1958 confirm the legend of the MAC as the cradle of Mormon leaders in New Zealand. Americans were called to preside over all early New Zealand stakes. Indeed, it seems certain that organisation of the first three stakes would not have occurred until much later if American building program personnel and Church College faculty members had not been available to fill most of the leadership positions.[103]

---

100. *Te Karere*, February 1952, 48.
101. Ballif, Oral History (Baldridge, 1972), 12; Ballif, Oral History (Britsch, 1973), 38.
102. Ballif, Oral History (Britsch, 1973), 38.
103. William Roberts, Oral History, 43; Simpson, Oral History, 51; Douglas Herbert Strother, Oral History, 13. A parallel situation occurred in Australia, where Americans were called to preside over two of the first three stakes. In New Zealand, the first three stakes were Auckland (1958), Hamilton (1960), and Hawkes Bay (1960). In Australia, the first three stakes were Sydney (March 1960), Brisbane (23 October 1960), and Melbourne (30 October 1960). American stake presidents were called in all three New Zealand stakes and in the Sydney and

Fifteen stakes were organised in New Zealand by November 1981—fifty years after the MAC closed. None of the first presidents of these stakes was an MAC "old boy," although two MAC graduates (James Southon and Sidney Crawford)—served as the second and third presidents respectively of the Hawkes Bay (now Hastings) Stake. The first four presidents of the Auckland South (now Temple View) Stake were American faculty members from the Church College of New Zealand, and it was the fifth president, Herewini Katene, who in 1975 became the first New Zealander to serve as president of this stake. Having been born nearly two years after the MAC closed, President Katene was not an MAC alumnus, though his father was.

While President Ballif claimed that it was he, during his term as mission president in the 1950s, rather than the MAC teachers (presumably including himself during his term as MAC principal), who trained future stake leaders, Erick A. Rosenvall, who built the New Zealand Temple and became its first president, thought that the labour missionary program deserved the credit. "Those people who served as building missionaries are now presidents of stakes, bishops of wards, presidents of Relief Society, etc.," he said.[104] Brother Rosenvall suggested yet another perspective which, if correct, also casts doubt on the legend of the MAC. "A Polynesian is a kind, gentle person. They are not the kind that would seek leadership or domination over anyone," he said. The Pakehas who "have come into the Church . . . are adding their strength and leadership." The Maoris, he said, actually "seem to function better if they have some outside leadership who understands them and treats them properly."[105]

Elder Robert L. Simpson confirmed that "European" Saints (whether Americans or New Zealanders) were called to most Church leadership positions from the late 1950s, when the last MAC students should have been in their prime. Elder Simpson stated that the proportion of Maori Saints perceived to be capable of filling these offices was rising but admitted that "with this Church [in New Zealand] . . . still about 80 percent Polynesian, we have European stake presidents in about three fourths of our stakes. So the leadership breakdown is just the opposite of the Church population ratios."[106]

Parallel developments occurred in Australia, where there was no racial element to confuse the issue and no corps of potential leaders nurtured at the MAC. From the 1890s, American mission presidents in Australia

Melbourne stakes.
104. Erick A. Rosenvall, Oral History, 15.
105. Ibid., 16.
106. Simpson, Oral History, 7.

called local men as branch presidents but did not ordain them to the higher or Melchizedek Priesthood; such ordination was deemed unnecessary because they did not have the opportunity of temple attendance. With a kind of circular logic, within a decade Australian Mission presidents were still staffing all branch and district presidencies with American missionaries *because* the local men did not hold the Melchizedek Priesthood.[107]

It was not until 1929 that the incumbent president of the Australian Mission, Clarence H. Tingey, began ordaining local men to the Melchizedek Priesthood and appointing Australian branch presidents wherever possible; but, unlike President Magleby in New Zealand, President Tingey retained district leadership in the hands of American elders. Like Magleby, President Tingey was undoubtedly motivated to call local men to leadership positions by the shortage of American missionaries as the Great Depression severely reduced the number of new arrivals. As in New Zealand, the appointment of Australian men to leadership positions in the LDS Church during World War II became a necessity when all American elders were evacuated in October 1940. And, as in New Zealand, as soon as the war ended and the "Zion elders" returned, many of these local leaders in Australia were replaced with American elders.[108]

As the Australian parallel illustrates, the fact that some local Mormon men who served in leadership positions in New Zealand after 1928 were Maori, and that a very small percentage of these had been educated at the MAC, seems irrelevant. Of necessity, local leaders had to be called in both countries during World War II from the available membership, and local men would still have been appointed in New Zealand even if the MAC had never existed. Even Maori resentment of the influx of Pakeha converts and their perceived appropriation of leadership roles from the late 1950s was matched by similar resentment in Australia when working-class leaders, who felt they had borne "the heat and burden of the day" during the mission years, found themselves relegated to "lesser" offices when stakes were organised there from 1960. Many stake and ward leadership positions in the new Australian stakes were filled by relatively new converts, usually of middle- or lower-middle-class socio-economic status. It was commonly perceived by the "grass-roots" membership that cars, telephones, and "white collar" occupations were now essential qualifications for leadership callings in the LDS Church in Australia.[109]

---

107. Marjorie Newton, *Southern Cross Saints: The Mormons in Australia*, 180-81.
108. Ibid., 181–85.
109. Leslie F. Bowron, conversation with Marjorie Newton, 27 August 1996, notes in my possession; anecdotal evidence from conversations with several "old timers," names withheld by request.

The Australian experience also discounts implications of racism in leadership choices made in New Zealand. That Americans were appointed to leadership positions in both countries over a long period indicates that they were thought to be both more knowledgeable about Church policies and administration at a local level, and more capable than local candidates, rather than being evidence of specific racial discrimination against Maori.

Still another perspective received attention in 1978 when Elder Robert L. Simpson commented on the Maori affinity with LDS Church teachings about families and family values. "Being a family Church has kept us strong among the Maori. We could write down forty or fifty names of strong original families from forty or fifty years ago, and the offspring of these families would probably represent three-fourths of the Church in New Zealand today," he said.[110] These "strong" families were those who had sent several of their sons to the MAC; surely some credit for the strength of their sons should be given to these Maori parents rather than all honour being ascribed, even by Maori themselves, to the American school and its American teachers.

The legend of the MAC grew with the years. That similar statements had been made to the First Presidency as early as 1930 is evident.[111] In 1940, just nine years after the college closed, the mission paper, *Te Karere*, printed a photograph of the MAC with the following caption:

> Near to the hearts of hundreds of the men of the Church of New Zealand are the memories of their school days spent at the Maori Agricultural College at Korongata, Hastings . . . famous throughout New Zealand for its policy of high ideals and clean living for its students. Agricultural methods and experimentations never before tried in this country were introduced at the College farms with marked success, as well as a system of secondary education that compared favourably with most schools in the country. Thousands mourned its loss as they would that of a true friend when it was destroyed in the Hawkes Bay earthquake of ten years ago.[112]

Novel agricultural methods may have been tried at the MAC but unfortunately not with marked success. And, as has been shown, the contemporary evidence of mission presidents, MAC principals, and government inspectors alike refutes the claim that secondary education at the Mormon college "compared favourably with most schools in the country." Apart from these exaggerated claims, it should be noted that the college was damaged,

---

110. Simpson, Oral History, 7.

111. Baldridge, "The Maori Agricultural College: An Experience in Rural Education," 40.

112. "Photo of the Month," *Te Karere* 34, no. 10 (October 1940): 392.

not destroyed, in the earthquake. The First Presidency refused to consider repair or rebuilding because the MAC was slated for closure anyway.

Also exaggerated in the communal memory of the MAC are both the number of New Zealand men who attended the Church school, and the number of students who graduated from it. Enrolment figures survive for all but two of the eighteen years the college functioned; estimates have been made for the two missing years, gauged from the names of those who were also enrolled in either or both the preceding and following years. This exercise gives a maximum of 480–500 students who attended the MAC between 1913 and 1930. While the exact total enrolment is not known, the number who graduated each year is recorded in either the mission history or the mission paper: only fifty-four students (approximately one in ten) graduated over the life of the MAC. Of the 306 students whose names and years of attendance years are known, 130 attended for only one year and fifty-seven for only two years. Almost all of these were enrolled in the primary or preparatory grades, and so were ineligible for graduation.

President Cowley and the "old boys" of the MAC fostered the legend; but a careful reading of transcripts of two or three dozen interviews conducted in 1971–72 with former MAC students shows that, in several instances, the interviewers put words into the mouths of their subjects. The "old boys" readily agreed that the MAC had produced a generation of Church leaders, but very few volunteered this information.[113] A more realistic assessment was that of former MAC pupil Hixson Hamon, who agreed that the spiritual training received at the MAC was beneficial; the old boys whom he knew, Hamon volunteered, "have all been active [in the Church] right up until the time of their passing."[114] Perhaps this is a more genuine and appropriate tribute to the work and value of the MAC than Matthew Cowley's claim that the MAC had provided not just LDS, but national, Maori leaders, when he stated: "As I went around among the native people, I discovered that the leaders of the natives—of the native race—today are not those who went to the Church of England school or are not those who went to the Catholic schools—the leaders in the native race are the young men who learned at the feet of the Mormon elders at the Maori Agricultural College."[115]

Early Mormon leaders aspired to establish a Mormon Te Aute: even the location chosen for the MAC was as close as possible to that of the presti-

---

113. For example, Kenneth W. Baldridge, interviewing Eruha Kawana: "I heard that quite a lot of good leaders have come out of there." Kawana: "Yes, quite a few good leaders."

114. Hixson Hamon, in Kenneth Wayne Baldridge, Interviews, 1971.

115. Henry A. Smith, *Matthew Cowley: Man of Faith*, 213.

gious Anglican college. The continuing legend of the MAC is that it produced a breed of Mormon Maori leaders comparable to Te Aute's Apirana Ngata, Peter Buck, Maui Pomare, and their renowned associates. That the MAC produced a generation of good men is undeniable, and it is a matter of record that among its graduates were one Maori member of parliament (Steve Watene) and several outstanding LDS leaders (for example, James Southon, James Elkington, and Sidney Crawford). However, in the light of the contemporary evidence cited, to assert that it produced a generation of Church leaders, let alone of leaders of the Maori race, is at the very least debatable.

It seems a pity that inflated claims have been made about both the educational value and the leadership qualities engendered in its pupils by the MAC, when mission presidents, American Church leaders, government school inspectors, and former pupils themselves were unanimous in praising the character training and gospel teaching these young men received there. The testimony of its former pupils indicates that these lessons were beneficial in the later lives of its students and hence, no doubt, affected the progress of the LDS mission in New Zealand for several generations after the school closed. There seems no need for either Mormon leaders, members, or historians to praise the Maori Agricultural College for what did not happen there, instead of for what did happen there. Like the Church College of New Zealand (CCNZ) a generation later, the MAC in its day was the flagship of the Mormon mission in New Zealand.

A New School Proposed

When the MAC opened in 1913, there were no state secondary schools for rural Maori pupils, and very few for Pakeha students either.[116] By 1951, however, only one quarter of the total population of New Zealand lived in isolated rural areas, though about two thirds of the Maori population were still in country districts.[117] Secondary schools were easily accessible for the majority of the population in towns and cities, and more than 100 district high schools had been established in country areas for rural children.[118]Although most Maori students thus lived in reasonable proximity to secondary schools, the proportion of Maori children completing secondary school remained very low. By the mid- to late-1950s, only about one Maori child in twenty (5 percent) left school with a school

---

116. Barrington, "Maori Scholastic Achievement," 9.

117. Pieter H. de Bres, *Religion in Atene: Religious Associations and the Urban Maori, 82.* By 1971, more than 50 percent of Maori were urbanised.

118. Dakin, *Education in New Zealand,* 69.

certificate, compared with 30 percent of European pupils.[119] Even fewer Maori pupils stayed the extra two years to finish sixth form.[120]

Factors other than distance were now the main cause of poor retention of Maori students in secondary schools. Maori families were predominantly from lower-income groups, and most young Maori students left school at the minimum leaving age to work and help boost family income. Cultural disadvantages such as lack of books in the home and lack of family role models and encouragement were also factors in the poor retention rates of Maori youth.[121] Aware of these trends, well evident in New Zealand society in the 1950s, LDS leaders such as Matthew Cowley, Reed Halversen, and Gordon C. Young felt justified in petitioning the First Presidency to establish a new school.

Members of the MAC Old Boys' Association wanted their children to have the opportunity of attending a Church school, and the possibility was frequently discussed.[122] As soon as Matthew Cowley became a General Authority of the Church, he promised the MAC "old boys" that he would do all in his power to get a replacement for the MAC. During his first apostolic visit to New Zealand, Elder Cowley helped mission president A. Reed Halversen compile a report for the First Presidency recommending, among other things, that the Church should build another secondary school for Maori boys, with the possible provision of a girls' school later.[123]

First Presidency approval, when it came, was for a small co-educational boarding school, with "sufficient land and livestock to provide food needs" and with potential for later expansion.[124] As time went by, a modest project became a major enterprise.

Meetings between Elder Cowley, Gordon C. Young (who had succeeded Reed Halversen as mission president) and the MAC Old Boys' Association brought agreement that the new school should be located in the Waikato, thought to be both more central and more fertile than

---

119. The Currie Commission on Education (1962) quoted a figure of 4.8 percent; Dakin suggests 6.1 percent. See Dakin, *Education in New Zealand*, 73, 76.

120. Barrington, "Maori Scholastic Achievement," 10 note 1.

121. Dakin, *Education in New Zealand*, 74–75; see also D. M. Fergusson, M. Lloyd, and L. J. Horwood, "Family Ethnicity, Social Background and Scholastic Achievement: An Eleven-Year Longitudinal Study," 49–63.

122. Matthew Cowley, "The President's Page: M.A.C. Old Boys' Scholarship Fund," *Te Karere* 39, no. 6 (June 1944): 138–39.

123. "Appeal to Old M.A.C. Boys," *Te Karere* 43, no. 2 (February 1948): 56; A. Reed Halversen, Letter to Elder Matthew Cowley, 12 June 1947.

124. "Here and There in the Mission: College for New Zealand," *Te Karere* 43, no. 11 (November 1948): 344.

Hawkes Bay, although both regions contain prime agricultural land. Unfortunately, both areas also include less than ideal farming land; the earlier error was repeated, and a tract containing inferior land was purchased on Tuhikaramea Road, Frankton Junction, a few miles from Hamilton. Extensive reclamation work had to be done to counteract swamp and peat before successful crops could be grown.[125]

Remembering the problems with the MAC, Elder Cowley, President Young and the officers of the Old Boys Association all agreed that the new high school must be of sufficiently high standard to obtain registration. Church leaders were determined that the proposed new school should be registered; it was as well that they were. Within six years of the opening of CCNZ, registration became compulsory for all private secondary schools in New Zealand.[126]

Construction of the first building on the new school site began in 1952. As time went by, concern mounted in Church offices in Salt Lake City when costs of the new college spiralled. President David O. McKay was scheduled to visit New Zealand and Australia early in 1955, and it was planned that, while there, he would review and scale back the project. Instead, after inspecting progress, McKay was so impressed with the possibilities of the school that he announced the construction of two more major buildings, almost doubling the total cost.[127]

In 1957, with new high schools in Tonga and Samoa as well as New Zealand to be administered, the First Presidency appointed a Pacific Board of Education under the chairmanship of Wendell B. Mendenhall,[128] a move that effectually removed the schools from the sole jurisdiction of already overworked mission presidents and thus avoided problems that had surfaced with the MAC. Californian educator Dr. Clifton D. Boyack

---

125. Sidney J. Ottley, Diary, 23 January 1952, 5:13-14. President Ottley recorded sessions with officers of the Waikato Department of Agriculture as he and farm manager Norman Mason learned how to drain and feed swamp land to make it productive.

126. Dakin, *Education in New Zealand*, 82.

127. David W. Cummings, *Mighty Missionary of the Pacific: The Building Program of the Church of Jesus Christ of Latter-day Saints—Its History, Scope, and Significance*, 51. For more information on the building of both the New Zealand Temple and the new school, see Newton, *Tiki and Temple*, ch. 7.

128. "The Board of Education for the South Pacific Islands," 262. On 1 January 1965, the Pacific Board of Education was dissolved, and the Church College of New Zealand became part of the Unified Church Schools System under the direction of Dr Harvey L. Taylor.

was appointed principal of the New Zealand school, which was scheduled to open on 10 February 1958.[129]

As early as 1951, the incumbent mission president, Gordon C. Young, had warned that, with the new school, the Church "must not make the same mistake we did before, in going ahead with our own American ideas."[130] However, after arriving in New Zealand in 1957, Dr. Boyack visited several local high schools and was dismayed by what he considered their out-moded educational methods. Ariel S. Ballif, the last American principal of the old MAC, was serving as mission president in New Zealand when Dr. Boyack arrived. President Ballif knew from experience that, in order to succeed, the new school must prepare students for the New Zealand public examinations so they could obtain worthwhile employment or progress to tertiary institutions. He later reported having experienced misgivings when Dr. Boyack persisted in employing American teaching methods, with comparatively few students passing public examinations.[131]

There was a nationwide shortage of secondary teachers in New Zealand from the late 1950s into the 1970s.[132] Rather than competing for local teach-ers, eighteen American teachers were employed, and arrived in New Zealand with their families on the *Mariposa* on 11 January 1958. In stark contrast to the staff of the MAC, all were fully qualified. In practice, the full staff of twenty-two (which included three or four New Zealanders) was soon found to be inadequate. Because of the teacher shortage and the isolated position of CCNZ, additional permanent and casual teachers were unprocurable, and unqualified or partially qualified faculty spouses were also employed for some years.[133] Two months after the new school opened, President David O. McKay dedicated both the school and the nearby temple in April 1958.

It was not until the arrival of the second principal, Wendell H. Wiser, that due weight was given to preparing students for New Zealand public

---

129. "Headmaster of Our College Has Been Appointed," 268.

130. Gordon C. Young, Letter to Edward O. Anderson, 7 July 1951.

131. Ballif, Oral History (Britsch, 1973), 57; Ballif, Oral History (Baldridge, 1972), 10.

132. Dakin, *Education in New Zealand*, 60–61; Ian S. Ardern, "A Review of the Involvement of the Church of Jesus Christ of Latter-day Saints in New Zealand Education," 43.

133. Ric Morehouse, "The Establishment of Church Education in New Zealand," 34. By 1978, CCNZ had no Americans on its staff, which now included several former students; one, Principal Barney Wihongi, had been the first student body president of CCNZ. See Simpson, Oral History, 25. There was at least one American principal appointed in the 1980s.

examinations.[134] Even then problems continued. The American staff members were totally unused to preparing students for written external examinations. Their four-year contracts disadvantaged the school; just as they began to understand the country, its culture, and its education system, their contracts expired and they returned home, to be replaced by new teachers who had to begin the learning cycle again.[135]

The first year of the Church College of New Zealand (1958) was regarded as successful by Church leaders in spite of its teething problems. Americanisms abounded. The principal was frequently referred to as the "president," again displaying some confusion over whether the school was indeed an American "college"—a tertiary-level institution—or a private New Zealand high school. An elected student-body government replaced the traditional English prefect system.

Despite retrospective statements that no CCNZ students passed the School Certificate examination the first year, or at most three or four,[136] fourteen students obtained School Certificates in 1958, although all seven candidates who sat University Entrance that year failed spectacularly, managing only one single subject pass between them.[137] As at the old MAC, students who completed four years' post-primary work were allowed to "graduate" with or without a school certificate pass. The school became fully registered when it passed its first government inspection late in 1958. While the inspectors made some "constructive criticism," available Church records are silent as to its nature,[138] and gradually most problems were overcome. By the mid-1960s, CCNZ was firmly established. In 1964, another team of seven government inspectors approved the college for all government bursaries.[139] The following year, forty-two of 105 CCNZ candidates passed the rigorous School Certificate examination.

---

134. Ardern, "A Review of the Involvement of the Church of Jesus Christ of Latter-day Saints in New Zealand Education," 59.

135. Ibid., 60.

136. See, for example, Ballif, Oral History (Britsch, 1973), 57; Simpson, Oral History, 25.

137. The CCNZ President's Report for 1958 claimed fifteen School Certificate passes and one University Entrance pass, but CCNZ school records (including an unidentified newspaper clipping listing the names of students who passed the School Certificate examination from each school), show no University Entrance passes and fourteen school certificate passes.

138. "N.Z. College Receives High Rating," *Deseret News,* 20 December 1958, in Journal History, 20 December 1958, 4.

139. Harvey L. Taylor, "The Story of LDS Church Schools," 1:174.

In its first year, 70 percent of students at CCNZ had Maori ancestry.[140] The proportion of Maori students decreased until, of a total enrolment of 662 in 1971, slightly less than half (324 students) were New Zealand Maori. Twelve were Cook Islands Maori; there were eleven Tahitians, nine Samoans, three Tongans, one Fijian, and one Hawaiian, making a total of 361 Polynesian students. The remaining 301 students that year were listed as New Zealand "Europeans" (264), Australians (20), and Americans (17).[141] Even though the percentage of Maori students had dropped, the school population during this period still included six times the proportion of Maori students as in the total high school enrolment for all New Zealand.

Between 1968 and 1976, the school certificate pass rate at CCNZ ranged from 36 percent (1968) to 53 percent (1975) with an average for the nine years of 43.4 percent,[142] 10 percentage points above the national average for those years. In later years, the pass rate climbed to 57 percent in 1990 and 60 percent in 1991,[143] and in 1995, CCNZ ranked sixteenth of forty-one high schools (both private and state) in the Waikato/King Country school districts.[144] Graduation standards rose over the years: by the 1990s, in order to graduate, a student had to accumulate a satisfactory grade point average (50 percent or higher) during four years of secondary schooling, whether or not the pupil passed the actual School Certificate examination.

In line with national retention rates, CCNZ presented fewer candidates each year for the even more rigorous University Entrance examination than for the School Certificate. From 1959 to 1964, an average of eight CCNZ pupils sat for each UE examination, with only one or two students passing each year. The number of UE candidates increased after 1969, when CCNZ became eligible to accredit students for university entrance, clear evidence that government inspection teams found the academic standard at CCNZ satisfactory. Between 1968 and 1976, the number of UE candidates increased from forty-three to 108. Of the 108 UE candidates in 1976, forty-four were accredited and another eight passed the examination, a total of fifty-two, or 48 percent. In the same year, twenty-two students sat for the Seventh Form Bursary examination and seven passed, another good result.[145] Ninety-eight CCNZ students passed Uni-

---

140. Sam Gordon, "General Aims and Methods Employed in the Teaching of Agriculture at the C.C.N.Z.," *Te Karere* 53, no. 7 (July 1959): 300.

141. Morehouse, "The Establishment of Church Education in New Zealand," 26.

142. Hunt, *Zion in New Zealand*, 75.

143. Figures supplied by Principal's Office, CCNZ.

144. "Boys Could Learn Lesson as Girls Grab the Grades," *Waikato Times*, 23 July 1996, 7.

145. Hunt, *Zion in New Zealand*, 75.

versity Entrance in 1990 and seventy-nine in 1991. The ethnicity of these candidates is not available, but it appears that the percentage of Maori and Islander pupils at CCNZ passing both School Certificate and University Entrance was still considerably higher than that in most state schools.

The school's program was gradually enhanced with the addition of advanced secretarial training and farming cadet courses. Another progressive innovation was a pre-apprenticeship auto mechanics course, offered for the first time in 1971 with the backing of the New Zealand Motor Trades and Apprenticeship Boards.[146] The school also earned a formidable reputation in inter-school sporting competitions, repeatedly winning national championships in several sports. Later, the agriculture course was dropped and, following the example of the old MAC, the farm was leased.

A survey conducted in 1970 in preparation for the introduction of the Church's Seminary and Institute program in New Zealand showed that, while CCNZ's academic and sporting results were excellent, the anticipated dividends of strong, committed Mormon young adults were not being obtained. Up to 80 percent of youth educated at CCNZ were classified as "inactive" in the Church within a year of leaving the school. Only 4 percent of male former students were accepting mission calls, and only two in every 100 marriages of New Zealand LDS young adults were being solemnised in the temple.[147] Missions and temple marriages were (and are) the ultimate goals for LDS youth; to be eligible for both requires adherence to strict standards of chastity, tithe-paying, and total abstinence from tea, coffee, alcohol, tobacco, and substance abuse.

Once the seminary program (weekday religious education for LDS high-school-age youth) became available in New Zealand from 1970, Church leaders in Salt Lake City seriously questioned the continuing need for the Church College of New Zealand. They worried about the school's enormous financial drain on the Church, especially if its long-term goals were not being achieved. Boarding fees were highly subsidised. Even though each student was required to work one hour each day in the cafeteria, office, or on the farm, early attempts to fulfil Gordon C. Young's vision of a self-sustaining school, producing its own fruit, vegetables, dairy products, poultry, and meat, foundered as surely as similar ideals at the old MAC had failed and for similar reasons.[148]

---

146. Taylor, "The Story of LDS Church Schools," 1:180.

147. Rhett S. James, "Observations, Recommendations, and Justification as Regards to Expansion of Religious Education Program for NZ Church Youth, 1 Oct 1970," 9, cited in Morehouse, "The Establishment of Church Education in New Zealand," 29.

148. Ottley, Diary, 3 January 1952, 5:13–14. Taylor, "The Story of LDS Church

Apostle Boyd K. Packer presided over a meeting at Temple View on 16 September 1972 during which James's survey of ex-student activity was reviewed with New Zealand Church leaders.[149] As a result of this meeting, several new policies were formulated. From 1973 (for third form) and 1974 (for fourth form), no new boarding students would be accepted for these forms unless there was no high school within reach of a student's home or a student was recommended by his or her bishop because of exceptional home circumstances.[150] Younger students, it was now felt, needed parental guidance during these years, and family ties were being weakened by the boarding system.[151]

Implementation of the new admission policies in 1973–74 caused a drop of one-third in enrolments at CCNZ in the succeeding two years as the school moved to accept mainly day pupils and senior boarders. Thus, while 662 students were enrolled in 1972 and 663 in 1973, only 450 students attended CCNZ in 1974.[152] This dip had been expected, but the cost of running the school escalated sharply as a result. To preserve its independence, the Church would not consider accepting the standard government subsidy for private schools (50 percent of teachers' salaries).[153] For the first time, disposal or closure of the school became a serious option.[154] In 1974, Principal Alton L. Wade, with former student body president Barney Wihongi (by this time a school administrator in Utah and shortly to become CCNZ principal), conducted extensive surveys of Church leaders and

---

Schools," 1:184–85. Dr. Taylor reported that even the provision of large-scale freezing equipment did not make vegetable growing for the school cafeteria feasible as the peak vegetable season coincided with the annual two-month summer vacation, when students were not available to help with the intensive work of harvesting and preserving the crops. The damp climate made poultry raising unsuccessful, and stringent government health standards made it illegal to slaughter farm cattle for school consumption.

149. Alton L. Wade and Barney Wihongi, "The Church College of New Zealand—Past, Present, Future: An Analysis," 1–2.

150. In 1996, there were only eight third-form and eleven fourth-form boarders, compared with 54, 91, and 72 boarding students in forms five, six, and seven respectively. Figures supplied by CCNZ Enrolment Office.

151. Wade and Wihongi, "The Church College of New Zealand," 2.

152. Morehouse, "The Establishment of Church Education in New Zealand," 25.

153. "Growth the Growing Problem for Church," *Auckland Star*, 7 April 1982, 28. The article reported that an unsolicited Education Department cheque for the subsidy sent to CCNZ on one occasion was returned.

154. Another use was found for a portion of the facilities when a Missionary Training Centre was established in 1977.

members, senior students, and New Zealand educators and businessmen in an effort to gain information needed for a well-informed decision.[155]

After analysing the information obtained, Wade and Wihongi recommended retention of the school. Among their detailed suggestions, they proposed that CCNZ concentrate on recruitment for fifth, sixth, seventh and post-seventh forms; that more pre-apprenticeship courses should be offered; that the feasibility of establishing postsecondary certificate classes should be investigated; that supervised board and lodging should be offered to LDS students taking tertiary-level courses at Waikato University, Waikato Technical Institute, Hamilton Teacher Training College, and Waikato Hospital Nurses Training School.[156] Many of these suggestions were adopted.[157] When the Wade and Wihongi survey revealed that to both Latter-day Saints and non-Latter-day Saints in New Zealand, the college, rather than the temple, was the recognised symbol of the LDS Church, leaders felt obliged to maintain it.[158]

The school grew in academic achievement and sporting renown during the 1980s and the two subsequent decades. News items detailing national and district sporting titles won by CCNZ basketball, swimming, hockey, and other teams frequently appeared in issues of the "News of the Church—Australia/New Zealand," inserted in the monthly *Ensign* magazine. The CCNZ Maori culture group performed around the country, winning nine trophies in 1988 alone at a secondary schools' competition at Tauranga. That year, the school basketball team won the national title for the fifth successive year, and other significant achievements were recorded in the *Ensign* insert each year.[159]

It is interesting to note that, by 1997, a table of student ethnicity showed that once again, 484 or 76 percent of a total enrolment of 636 students were Maori, the remainder being classified as European (103) and Polynesian (49).[160] Former principal Ian Ardern, now a General Authority of the Church,[161] felt that CCNZ's greatest contribution from its inception

---

155. Wade and Wihongi, "The Church College of New Zealand," 3.

156. Ibid., 26.

157. By 2006, the enrolment of day students from the Temple View community and nearby areas again brought the total annual enrolment up to around 700 students. Scott C. Esplin, "Closing the Church College of New Zealand: A Case Study in Church Education Policy," 106.

158. Wade and Wihongi, "The Church College of New Zealand," 25.

159. See, for example, "News of the Church: Australia-New Zealand," November 1985, 115; November 1988, 81; September 1989, 83; December 1989, 82; August 1991, 84; October 1994, 82, et al.

160. "Church College of New Zealand—Ethnic Groupings," Table prepared by CCNZ office staff, typescript, copy courtesy CCNZ Office.

161. Elder Ardern was called to the First Quorum of the Seventy in April 2011.

was its success in retaining Maori pupils and that this fact alone justified the continuing existence of CCNZ. Even those superficial American features that persisted, particularly the graduation ceremonies, were worthwhile, Elder Ardern thought, as incentives to keep Maori youth at school until at least completing fourth form (School Certificate level). On a deeper level, Ardern felt that the American model suited Maori needs. "The failure of secondary schools to retain Maori pupils was in part because many of them felt out of place in the typical classrooms which almost universally had adopted quite inflexible streaming practices," he wrote. "The more relaxed, informal atmosphere promised by CCNZ and its less rigid and more imaginative curriculum appealed to Maori students and parents alike."[162] He also reported that, in the 1990s, 60 percent of all missionaries called from New Zealand stakes and missions were from the 10 percent of New Zealand LDS youth who were CCNZ alumni, a considerable improvement on figures reported in 1970.[163]

By the time the Church College of New Zealand opened in 1958, there was little real academic necessity for it, but CCNZ's excellent facilities and its growing reputation for academic success became the very antithesis of the MAC. However, as time went by, the financial drain on the parent Church was enormous. With both free secondary schooling of a very high standard and the LDS seminary program within reach of almost every New Zealand LDS pupil, Church leaders felt that the money needed to upgrade the now aging facilities of CCNZ could be spent more wisely on missionary work and humanitarian aid in other parts of the world.[164] It was only a matter of time before hard economic realities triumphed over sentiment and idealism. The Church College of New Zealand closed its doors at the end of the 2009 academic year, and the LDS Church again withdrew from secular education in New Zealand.

---

162. Ardern, "A Review of the Involvement of the Church of Jesus Christ of Latter-day Saints in New Zealand Education," 58. "Streaming" involved channelling children seen to have potential for high academic achievement into schools, or classes within a school, offering curriculum subjects such as languages, science, and higher mathematics, in order to prepare them for university entrance examinations; those judged to have lesser potential were placed in "vocational" classes with subjects such as woodwork for boys and home science (cooking and needlework) for girls.

163. CCNZ principal Ian Ardern, conversation with Marjorie Newton, 27 February 1997.

164. For a comprehensive discussion of the place of the Church College of New Zealand in the LDS Church Education System, and the factors leading to its closure, see Esplin, "Closing the Church College of New Zealand."

Chapter 3

Mormon Legends in New Zealand

The inflated reputation of the Maori Agricultural College is not the only New Zealand legend of Mormonism that survives. The story of Apostle David O. McKay's visit to the 1921 Hui Tau (mission conference), and the gift of interpretation of tongues bestowed on a large Maori congregation assembled to hear him speak, has become part of the folklore of the international LDS Church. Because of the *de facto* canonisation of this reputed miracle and its occasional inclusion in official lesson manuals, an examination of the story in an historical context seems appropriate in this study.

Two other events are examined in this chapter, each of which has contributed to the legendary status of a former New Zealand mission president. The first story, which involves persecution endured by John Ephraim Magleby, is well known in New Zealand and is an interesting case study of the growth of a legend. The second, which concerns Matthew Cowley and the translation of the Doctrine and Covenants, has also become entrenched as part of the history of the wider Church[1] and, to the extent that it can be shown to be inaccurate, needs correction.

The latter stories will be discussed first. All three legends provide classic case studies of the way religious myths originate, grow, develop, and become entrenched, evidence for which process is rarely available in such detail in any religious community.

John Ephraim Magleby in the Waiapu Valley, 1886

In 1885, Mormon elders attracted converts in a few Ngati Porou villages in the Waiapu valley on the East Coast of New Zealand. The missionaries were opposed by both a local chief, Te Hatiwira Hamakau, and a prominent Maori lay preacher, Mohi Turei, who were dismayed by the

1. See, for example, Robert L. Simpson, "The Church in New Zealand," 3:1014–16.

number of defections from the Church of England. They petitioned the New Zealand government to deport the Mormon elders and threatened local deserters to Mormonism with retribution. The missionaries, Ezra Foss Richards and his companion, a new arrival named John Ephraim Magleby, tried to reassure their flock.[2]

On Thursday, 1 October 1885, a crowd of two to three hundred people assembled at Taumata-o-Tapuhi where Mohi Turei had called on the Mormon elders to debate. "We smelled persecution upon first sight," wrote Elder Magleby. One by one, sixty-three Mormon converts were called on to either repudiate Mormonism or face imprisonment or death—both alternatives probably empty threats, but nevertheless frightening to the Maori converts. Nevertheless, all but two refused to forsake Mormonism.[3]

A few weeks later, Elder Richards learned that their opponents were getting impatient, not having had a reply to their petition to the government. "They did not seem to doubt that the next mail would bring word to have [us] hung," he wrote.[4]

Persecution was so strong in Te Rimu, a village further north, that most of the Latter-day Saints there agreed to leave the Mormon Church; those who would not renounce their new faith were ordered out of the pa (village).[5]

Elder Richards was transferred to Uawa, further south, and Elder Elias Johnson joined Elder Magleby in the trouble spot. A few months later, Johnson and Magleby became protagonists in a small drama that was to be magnified and mythologised by both Maori and Pakeha Latter-day Saints in New Zealand for the next one hundred years.

On Saturday, 6 February 1886, Elder Johnson and Elder Magleby set off on horseback to visit Te Rimu, having to pass through the village of Kawakawa[6] on their way. Here they were halted by a human roadblock as Te Hatiwira and his followers formed a line across the road.[7] After some discussion, the missionaries were allowed to hold Sabbath meetings with their congregation in Te Rimu but were ordered to leave the area on Monday.

As soon as the missionaries left Te Rimu on Monday on their return journey, Te Hati and his men attacked the homes of Latter-day Saints in the village. After throwing the belongings of one family into the street, they proceeded to tear down the house. "We turned [back] to see [so] that we might be witnesses and on our return found the Saints in the street alongside their

---

2. John Ephraim Magleby, Journal, 24 September 1885.

3. Ezra Foss Richards, Journal, 1 October 1885.

4. Ibid., 22 October 1885.

5. Ibid., 2 October 1885.

6. Kawakawa was renamed Te Araroa a few years later.

7. Magleby, Journal, 6 February 1886, 120–21.

things with tears rolling down their cheeks watching their houses being torn down," Elder Magleby wrote.[8] The two missionaries decided to ride to the nearest town to seek help from law enforcement authorities.

By the time they reached the nearest police officer on Tuesday, 9 February, they heard that houses of the Saints at Kawakawa had been burned, that some of the Saints were tied up, and that others were wandering homeless in the bush. The police constable agreed to go to Kawakawa himself, so the two elders decided it would be safe for them to return and do what they could to help. They left on horseback on Thursday morning.[9]

About a mile out of Kawakawa, Johnson and Magleby were ambushed by Te Hati and several of his men, who demanded to know where they were going. The missionaries claimed the right of "free born Americans" to decline to answer unless shown the chief's authority for the question. Te Hati grabbed their horses' bits to prevent them from proceeding, so the missionaries backed up in opposite directions, hoping Te Hati would have to let go. However, Te Hati hung on "like a lion," according to Elder Magleby, and called for his men to come. The elders were forcibly dismounted, and the ropes they were using as reins were used to tie their hands and feet and fasten them to a nearby fence while their assailants conferred about what to do next.

Shortly afterwards, Te Hati returned and rifled through the missionaries' saddle bags, eventually finding a small notebook of Elder Magleby's and demanding that the two elders write and sign a statement that they would leave the area permanently. "We wouldn't promise any such thing," Magleby recorded in his journal, "hence we were left in our tied position for about an hour when he loosed us." They were taken to the pa, and although threatened with the whare herehere (prison), were simply held in a whare karakia where they were fed and allowed to participate in karakia (prayers) before being given flax mats on which to sleep and blankets for covering.[10]

Next day, the missionaries were disappointed to hear that the police were not coming, "not thinking it was a big enough affair to worry about which gave the Chief more courage to persecute us and said he wouldn't let us go unless we signed a note stating we would never come back or teach or preach." They held out for another twenty-four hours; then Te Hati accepted a signed note dated Kawakawa, 13 February 1886, stating "We hereby testify or witness that we will not come & endeavor to preach the

---

8. Ibid., 8 February 1886, 124.
9. Ibid., 11 February 1886, 126.
10. Ibid., 11 February 1886, 127–28.

doctrine which we proclaim to be the word of God to Te Hati or any of his people who reject us or don't want to hear us."[11]

The elders left immediately and arrived back at their base pa in the early hours of Sunday morning only to have their noses "almost rubbed off" by the local Maori Saints who were very relieved to have them safely back after having heard they had been captured. "I must say we appreciated their love," Magleby wrote.[12]

After consulting mission president William T. Stewart, Johnson and Magleby took out summonses for assault on Te Hatiwira and Hore Mahue.[13] The court hearing took place at quarter sessions on 9 March 1886. The assault charges were dismissed on the grounds that no bodily injury was incurred by the plaintiffs.[14] The two Mormon elders decided to ask for help from the Hon. John Ballance (Member of Parliament and Cabinet Minister for Native Affairs), who was due shortly at the nearby town of Waiomatatini.

Considerable numbers of Maori converged on Waiomatatini, including about one hundred Mormon converts—men, women and children. Ballance listened to speeches from both sides, then made it clear to the assembled Maori that the government "would sustain all churches under the Law; that the Mormons had as much right as the English church."[15] He warned their opponents that they must not take the law into their own hands and that the Mormons must not be harmed. "You must not persecute them," he told the assembled crowd. "If you do, the Government will punish you."[16]

While Ballance helped settle the atmosphere somewhat for the Mormons in the Waiapu Valley, his warning did nothing specific to help either the missionaries' appeal in their assault charges or a second summons regarding the houses that were destroyed. Both cases were mentioned in court on 31 May 1886 and adjourned till September, when they were finally dismissed.

11. Ibid., 13 February 1886, 131.

12. Ibid., 14 February 1886, 132. Elder Magleby referred to the Maori custom of ceremonial greeting with a hongi, or pressing noses together.

13. Richards, Journal, 19 February 1886.

14. Ibid., 13 March 1886.

15. Sondra Sanders Jr., Journal, 11 April 1886, 200–201.

16. "Correspondence: Elders Arrested by Maories, Progress of the Work, Curious Customs [Edward Cliff, Letter to the Editor, dated 15 July 1886, Hastings, Hawkes Bay]," *Deseret Evening News*, 12 August 1886, [2]; New Zealand Mission, Manuscript History, 7 April 1886.

John E. Magleby could speak very little Maori when he and Ezra Foss Richards had their first confrontation with Te Hatiwira. He had been in New Zealand less than two months; and just two weeks before the "debate" with Turei at Taumata-o-Tapuhi, he had recorded in his journal that the Maori Saints could not understand him when he spoke to them.[17] But he soon mastered te reo and was reputed to be the best Maori speaker of any Mormon missionary who ever served in New Zealand. He was much beloved. His initial mission lasted from July 1885 to February 1889, and in later years he twice served as mission president (1900-1902 and 1928-32). As his reputation grew, the story of his 1886 kidnapping became the stuff of legend.

Exaggeration began almost at once. Elder Magleby recorded in his journal that he and Elder Johnson were tied to the fence for an hour.[18] A month later, Elder Ezra Foss Richards recorded the story of the court case, as he had heard it, in his journal and stated that Elder Johnson had testified to being tied up for an hour and a half.[19] This may have included the time involved as Te Hati conferred with his men. When the story appeared in the Deseret News a few months later, it had become three hours; in 1915 the same newspaper told its readers that, in February 1886, "Elder Elias Johnson and John E. Magleby were taken from their horses, their Bibles taken, and they were bound with cords and tied to a fence; in this condition they were left for three days and two nights."[20]

Gradually, Elder Johnson was omitted from the story altogether and Magleby, the junior companion, was featured. In 1974, American Ariel S. Ballif, whose late 1920s term as principal of the Maori Agricultural College overlapped John E. Magleby's second term as mission president, paid tribute to Magleby. "Ephraim Magleby was possibly the greatest Maori speaker that the Church has ever had. You could put him in a room with other Maoris and Maoris outside couldn't detect that he was an English man speaking Maori. . . . Just as a sideline," Ballif continued, "on his first mission, he was tied up by the Maoris while they were fixing the big pot to cook him. He didn't know for a little while whether he would ever get out of there or not but it worked [out] all right. They didn't boil him."[21]

---

17. Magleby, Journal, 15 September 1885.

18. Ibid., 11 February 1886.

19. Richards, Journal, 13 March 1886.

20. "Correspondence: Elders Arrested by Maories," [2]; "The New Zealand Mission," Deseret Evening News, 20 November 1915 in Journal History, 20 November 1915, 3.

21. Ariel S. Ballif, Oral History, interviewed by R. Lanier Britsch, 1973, 19.

Also in 1974, Pakeha convert and long-term district president in Auckland, William R. Perrott, recounted the story as he knew it. "He [Magleby] was at Taupo, he was preaching around there when he was on his mission and they tied him up to a tree and were going to burn him. But they tied him up to the tree and left him there overnight. And an old Maori woman came along and released him. And the next morning he goes right on to the marae and was there and told them that they were a wicked lot and the mountain would blow up and come down and kill the lot of them. And I heard that this happened, too, that the mountain blew up, Mt Turararo [Tarawera], and covered cities. . . . Buried cities. They're uncovering some of them now. It killed thousands, or at least hundreds. I don't know about thousands but hundreds were killed. And that's President Magleby for you."[22]

Mount Tarawera, near Rotorua, erupted during the early morning hours of 10 June 1886, some four months after the missionaries experienced their confrontation with Te Hatiwira many miles away on the East Coast. The eruption caused great destruction to the picturesque area and engulfed several Maori villages, causing the loss of more than one hundred lives.[23] However, there is no record that Te Hatiwira or any of his tribe were anywhere near the scene of the disaster; and there is no contemporary record that Elder Magleby ever made any such prophecy.

Both Ballif and Perrott knew President Magleby well during his 1928–32 term as mission president. There is no record that Magleby himself ever contributed to the inflated versions of the story; he was, in fact, somewhat disconcerted when he arrived back in New Zealand in 1928 and discovered the legendary status the episode had attained. In a letter to his friend Louis G. Hoagland (another former president of the mission), written from New Zealand on 8 January 1929, Magleby referred to the incident. "My being tied by Ngati Porou [Te Hatiwira's tribe] has been so much spoken of in N[ew] Z[ealand] and so magnified that I am bashful about saying anything about it. When home again, you and I alone, I may tell the story." Magleby was planning a conference visit to the Waiapu district the following month. "I am looking forward with fear and trembling to our going in there," he told Hoagland. President Magleby found it difficult to publicly correct influential leaders, either Maori or Pakeha, who

---

22. William Rosser Perrott, Oral History, 9.

23. The official death toll was 153, but this is currently thought to have been inaccurate and that there were probably no more than 120 deaths.

told and re-told the story, but he was distinctly embarrassed and uncomfortable about the fame he had acquired.[24]

Matthew Cowley and the Translation of the Doctrine and Covenants

Like John E. Magleby, Matthew Cowley also became a much beloved mission president in New Zealand. Also like President Magleby, he learned to speak Maori fluently during his first mission to New Zealand, where he arrived on 23 November 1914 at the age of seventeen. After having shown exceptional leadership ability and fluency in the Maori language, Elder Cowley was sustained as both president of the Mahia District and as mission Sunday School superintendent at Hui Tau in April 1917.[25] When the New Zealand government refused to grant visas to more American missionaries to replace those departing,[26] Elder Cowley, whose three-year missionary term would normally have been completed in November 1917, agreed to stay another year. He was eventually released in April 1919 and sailed from Wellington on 14 May 1919, then returned to New Zealand as mission president from February 1938 to July 1945. He also made several apostolic visits to New Zealand between his call to the Quorum of the Twelve in October 1945 and his premature death in 1953.

According to Elder Cowley, he spent the final two years of his extended mission revising the existing Maori edition of the Book of Mormon (a process which, he said, involved changing some 2,500 verses) and translating the Doctrine and Covenants and Pearl of Great Price into Maori.[27] At Hui Tau in early April 1918, Elder Cowley was released as a district president but continued serving as mission Sunday School superintendent. He also received two new assignments—as a "special traveling elder" (in which capacity he assisted mission president James N. Lambert and accompanied him on many of his journeys around the mission) and as a member of a four-man

---

24. John E. Magleby, Letter to Louis G. Hoagland, 8 January 1929.

25. New Zealand Mission, Manuscript History, 8 April 1917.

26. For the full story of this wartime measure, see Marjorie Newton, *Tiki and Temple: The Mormon Mission in New Zealand, 1854–1958*, 142–45.

27. Matthew Cowley, Letter to Mrs. Laura Brossard (his sister), dated Salt Lake City, 30 October 1932. According to President James N. Lambert's journal and the mission history, the revision of the 1889 edition of the Book of Mormon was actually begun in June 1916 and was the work of several elders and local members, including President Lambert himself, and Elders Roundy, Banks, and Thomas, plus Stuart Meha. In April 1917, Elder Cowley's assignment was to revise their work and prepare it for the printer. The second Maori edition of the Book of Mormon was published in 1918.

"Committee on Translating the Doctrine and Covenants and Pearl of Great Price."[28] Shortly after Hui Tau, Elder Cowley wrote to his parents about his new assignments, concluding "Last but not least, I was appointed in company with Brothers William Takana [Duncan] and Tuati [Stuart] Meha to translate the Doctrine and Covenants and Pearl of Great Price in the Maori language, a work which has never before been attempted."[29]

Despite Matthew Cowley's statement that this work had never before been attempted, and contemporary references to his work as translation,[30] this was not the first translation of the Doctrine and Covenants into Maori. Nor does it seem that Elder Cowley's work on the Doctrine and Covenants should be termed a "translation" at all. A more accurate description would be a revision, yet both he and his mission president repeatedly referred to it as a translation, and Elder Cowley continues to be credited with translating the Doctrine and Covenants to this day.[31]

Six years before young Elder Cowley arrived in New Zealand, the incumbent mission president, Rufus K. Hardy, decided to publish the Doctrine and Covenants in Maori, section by section, in the mission paper *Te Karere.* The Maori translation of Section 1 appeared in *Te Karere* on 26 February 1908, and further sections followed in most issues. President Hardy had the work typeset as it was translated; as soon as four pages were typeset, they were printed in the mission paper and the type was saved. "By the time the translation is completed the book will be ready for binding at very little extra expense," the mission clerk of the time recorded.[32] One missionary who worked on the translation was Elder William H. Dickson,[33] but many others whose names are unknown must have been

---

28. New Zealand Mission, Manuscript History, 7 April 1918.

29. Matthew Cowley, Letter to his parents, 18 April 1918, quoted in Henry A. Smith, *Matthew Cowley: Man of Faith*, 57. The fourth member of the translation team was mission president James N. Lambert, *ex officio.*

30. For example, see James Needham Lambert, Journal, 11 July 1918, 565.

31. See, for example, R. Lanier Britsch, *Unto the Islands of the Sea: A History of the Latter-day Saints in the Pacific*, 298-99; Smith, *Matthew Cowley*, 53; Brian W. Hunt, *Zion in New Zealand: A History of the Church of Jesus Christ of Latter-day Saints in New Zealand, 1854-1977*, 25; Elva T. Cowley, Autobiography, 148; Stanley M. Barrett, "Matthew Cowley, President of the Pacific Mission;" Suzanne Willis and Jo Ann Seely, "Register of the Matthew Cowley Collection," 1; Simpson, "The Church in New Zealand."

32. New Zealand Mission, Manuscript History, 5 February 1908.

33. Ibid., 7 July 1909. Hunt noted that Elder Dickson had translated several sections of the Doctrine and Covenants by 1909 but was apparently unaware of the continuing translation, as he still credited Elder Cowley with the first Maori translation of this volume of LDS scripture. Hunt, *Zion in New Zealand*, 25.

involved, as translation and publication of the Doctrine and Covenants continued under succeeding mission presidents George Bowles (1909–11), Orson D. Romney (1911–13), and William Gardner (1913–16), long after Elder Dickson's release and return home.

Additional pages of the translation appeared in most—but not all—fortnightly issues of *Te Karere* over a period of almost eight years from 1908. Perhaps reflecting a decreasing number of competent Maori speakers among the missionaries, the pace of translation and publication slowed as the years passed; only eleven sections (Sections 112–122) were published in 1914 and seven sections (Sections 123–129) in 1915. On 22 December 1915, the last issue for that year, Section 129 was published, together with the first seven verses of Section 130, with the notation "*Taria te roanga*" (to be continued) appended after verse seven.

Church archives files of Volume 10 (1916) of the Maori edition of *Te Karere* are incomplete. The first three issues are among those that are missing, so it is not known whether the last sixteen verses of Section 130 or any of the six remaining sections were published in these issues. At the beginning of 1916, then, there remained to be translated and published only sixteen verses of Section 130 and Sections 131–136. This initial translation project may never have been completed, as no part of the missing sections appears in the odd issues of Volume 10 that survive. It is possible that the project was discontinued when the First Presidency became aware that an unauthorised version of the Doctrine and Covenants was being published in New Zealand, and that Matthew Cowley's was therefore the first *authorised* translation.

Young Elder Cowley must have been well aware of the earlier translation; it was still being published section by section in the Maori edition of the mission paper (though not in every issue) during the first thirteen months of his mission, while William Gardner was mission president. A short article written by Matiu Kauri (the Maori transliteration of "Matthew Cowley") appeared on page 185 (a right-hand page) of the Maori edition of *Te Karere* dated 4 August 1915. The left-hand page (page 184), opposite Elder Cowley's article, contains the last four lines of the Maori translation of Doctrine and Covenants 127, while Sections 125, 126, and the first nine verses of Section 127 are printed on previous pages of the same issue (pp. 181–83).[34]

So although in April 1918 Cowley was assigned by mission president James N. Lambert to translate the Doctrine and Covenants and Pearl of Great Price into Maori, and this translation was authorised by cable from

34. Matiu Kauri, "He Ratapuki Ki Wairoa," *Te Karere* 9, no. 16 (4 August 1915): 184–85.

the First Presidency,[35] it appears that Matthew Cowley did not produce a new translation of the Doctrine and Covenants but simply revised the version previously published in *Te Karere*. For the remainder of his life, he referred to his work on the Maori Book of Mormon as "revision." Thus, there seems no logical explanation of why he invariably spoke of his work on the Doctrine and Covenants as translation, rather than revision.

Careful examination of the entire volume should be made by competent Maori scholars to confirm exactly how much of the 1919 edition of the Doctrine and Covenants was the work of Cowley; or whether it was, as it appears, simply a revision of *Te Karere* translation. In the meantime, a comparison of several sections strongly suggests that the work was a revision. For this comparison, the first ten verses (or the complete section, where a section contains fewer than ten verses) of Sections 1, 2, 3, 10, 20, 30, 40, 90, and 100 were examined,[36] with the following results:

Of eighty-six verses and the introductory matter to all nine sections, that is, of ninety-five discrete pieces of text (all hereafter referred to as "verses"), twenty-five are identical in both versions. The text of another thirty-one verses is identical, but punctuation has been altered and some vowels lengthened or shortened ("maatua" to "matua," or vice versa). Another thirty-one verses have minor textual differences: typographical or grammatical errors have been corrected (or possibly made) and transliterations bettered (for example, "Peterika" [Frederick] in the *Te Karere* version is replaced by "Pererika" in the Cowley version). In only fourteen of ninety-five verses did Cowley substitute a different word for the word in *Te Karere* text. There is no instance at all of a completely different translation: in none of these ninety-five verses was more than one word altered.

It does not seem possible that Elder Cowley could have produced a new and independent translation that so closely duplicated the work of several other men. Those who might see this as the result of inspiration should consider Matthew Cowley's own account of the differences in the versions produced by Wi Duncan and Stuart Meha and himself. Both Duncan and Meha, like Elder Cowley, had been set apart for the work and so were also entitled to inspiration.[37] The original translators of the Book of

35. New Zealand Mission, Manuscript History, 30 March 1918.

36. Translations of these sections appeared in the following issues of *Te Karere*: Sec.1 in vol. 2, no. 3 (26 February 1908): 25–27; Secs. 2–3, in vol. 2, no. 4 (11 March 1908): 37–39; Sec.10, in vol. 2, no. 8 (6 May 1908): 85–88; Sec. 20, in vol. 2, no. 15 (12 August 1908): 169–71; Sec. 30, in vol. 2, no. 23 (2 December 1908): 266–67; Sec. 40, in vol. 3, no. 1 (10 February 1909): 2-3; Sec. 90, in vol. 5, no. 13 (26 July 1911): 145–47; Sec. 100, in vol. 6, no. 13 (24 July 1912): 146–47.

37. "The three of us would read a verse in the English then each of us would

Mormon, Elders Sondra Sanders Jr. and Ezra Foss Richards, experienced similar disagreements in the 1880s. The latter men, both officially called and set apart for the work, finally had to divide the text as they could not agree on translation when working together verse by verse.[38]

Also puzzling is an entry in the mission records dated 12 July 1918. On that date, the mission secretary recorded that "the translation of the Doctrine and Covenants by Elders Matthew Cowley, Wiremu Duncan and Stuart Meha is progressing very nicely. Considerable difficulty, however, was [sic] being experienced in translating the Lectures on Faith."[39] Unlike most of the Doctrine and Covenants, the Lectures on Faith (included with the Doctrine and Covenants until 1921) had never previously been translated into Maori, and it appears that Elder Cowley and his helpers were not finding it easy to do this without reference to an earlier version. Elder Cowley's revision of the Doctrine and Covenants and his translation of the Pearl of Great Price were eventually published in 1919 without the Lectures on Faith.

Although Matthew Cowley did translate the Pearl of Great Price into Maori for the first time (no small undertaking), it is remarkable that no one has ever questioned his claim to have made the first Maori translation of the Doctrine and Covenants. There must have been literally hundreds of people who knew of the *Te Karere* version. Matthew Cowley was human enough to exaggerate, and his trade-mark humour was frequently based on exaggeration. But a tendency to exaggerate scarcely equates with claiming credit for other men's work. There does not appear to be anything in Matthew Cowley's well-documented life to make such a proceeding credible, and the matter remains inexplicable.

David O. McKay and the Gift of Interpretation of Tongues

Towards the end of 1920, just eighteen months after Matthew Cowley left New Zealand at the close of his first mission, the First Presidency announced that the following year Apostle David O. McKay, accompanied

---

make our own translation into Maori. We would then read the three translations and select the best. We continued this method for two or three weeks and then due to the fact that my translation was the one invariably that was chosen, my two friends left me to it and I spent two years translating these two books." Cowley to Brossard, 30 October 1932.

38. Richards, Journal, 30 June 1887, 5 January 1888.

39. New Zealand Mission, Manuscript History, 12 July 1918. Mission president James N. Lambert's journal contains a similar entry for the same date. Lambert, Journal, 12 July 1918, 566.

by Hugh J. Cannon, president of Salt Lake City's Liberty Stake, would tour LDS missions throughout the world. Elder McKay, age forty-seven, had been a professional educator before his call to the Quorum of the Twelve in 1906. Among other assignments, he had been Church Commissioner of Education since 1918 and so was responsible for the Maori Agricultural College in New Zealand as well as all other Church schools. Hugh J. Cannon, age fifty-one, was a son of George Q. Cannon, one of the early Mormon missionaries in the Sandwich Isles (Hawaii). George Q. Cannon had served as a counsellor to four Church presidents (Brigham Young, John Taylor, Wilford Woodruff, and Lorenzo Snow). In 1919, his son Hugh J. Cannon was serving concurrently as the president of the Liberty Stake in Salt Lake City and as a member of the general board of LDS Sunday Schools.

The annual Hui Tau or New Zealand mission conference, which would normally have been held at Easter (the last weekend of March in 1921) was rescheduled so that it would take place while McKay and Cannon were in New Zealand. The events of this visit were well documented in several contemporary sources.[40]

What Happened at Hui Tau, 1921

Mission president George S. Taylor met the travellers at the wharf in Wellington on Thursday, 21 April 1921, and escorted them on a sixteen-hour overnight train journey to Huntly, in the Waikato, to attend Hui Tau. Through the night, Maori Saints and missionaries travelling to Hui Tau joined the train at various stops along the way. Next morning, after alighting from the train, the guests of honour were driven to the Maori village of Puketapu, just outside Huntly, where two huge tents—each, as Cannon recorded, the size of a three-ring circus tent in the United States—and several smaller ones had been erected on a property belonging to a local Latter-day Saint woman. Conference meetings were held in one of the largest tents. This tent became a communal dormitory each night, with the bedding doing double duty as seating for the conference sessions by day. The other large tent was the dining room. It was furnished with eight tables, each seating forty people, so that 320 visitors could be served at each of several sittings for

---

40. These include, but are not limited to, McKay and Cannon's personal travel journals; McKay's frequent letters home to his wife; the personal journal of New Zealand mission president George Shepard Taylor; the minutes of each Hui Tau session, recorded at the time by the mission secretary and added to the New Zealand mission history; transcriptions of Elder McKay's sermons, taken down in shorthand and then transcribed by Elder Graham H. Doxey; and the journals of various American missionaries and MAC faculty members present at the 1921 Hui Tau.

every meal over the five-day conference. Ceremonial Maori welcomes were extended to the eminent visitors and were repeated, according to Maori custom, for each arriving party as the Saints assembled for the most momentous Hui Tau in the history of the New Zealand Mission.

Among the arrivals during the afternoon were two missionaries of the Reorganized Church of Jesus Christ of Latter Day Saints,[41] a Mr. Savage and a Mr. A. L. Loving. They received a welcome from LDS mission president George S. Taylor, who hospitably invited them to stay for dinner. He would not, however, agree to their request to speak at the priesthood meeting scheduled for Saturday evening or for an hour in any meeting in which to present their views. "[I] told them they could not have one minute," President Taylor wrote. He went further and prohibited their discussing doctrinal matters or passing out their literature on the grounds, which were, after all, private property. When they ignored this and his subsequent request for them to leave, "[the] owner of the place, Sister Raiha, ordered them off and as they still refused to go, Brother James Elkington [one of the Hui Tau "policemen" or security guards] picked one of them up and dropped him over the fence into the road and others drove his companion out," President Taylor continued. "They stated they will return tomorrow and attend our Conference."[42]

Next morning (Saturday, 23 April 1921), the first conference session began at 10:00 a.m. in the big tent. A table served as pulpit, and chairs were provided for Elder McKay and Brother Cannon, President Taylor, mission secretary Elder Fred W. Schwendiman (who recorded the minutes), and Elder Graham H. Doxey, a competent shorthand writer, who recorded all Elder McKay's Hui Tau sermons and later transcribed and typed them. Also seated at the table were Stuart Meha, who interpreted the sermons given in English into Maori; Sid Christy (Hirini Whaanga's grandson, raised in Utah), who was seated beside Elder McKay, and Elder Gordon C. Young, who was next to Brother Cannon. Christy and Young were each assigned to interpret those remarks made in Maori to one of the visiting dignitaries.

Elder McKay, of course, was the main speaker. He began with a moving and memorable promise. "O, how I wish I could speak to you in your own language," he began, "to tell you what is in my heart, but since I cannot I am going to pray that while I speak in my own tongue, you may have the gift of interpretation and discernment. While you may not understand the words, the spirit of the Lord will bear witness to you of the words that I give to you under the inspiration of the Lord."

41. Now Community of Christ.
42. George Shepard Taylor, Private Journal, 22 April 1921, 2:125–26.

The main thrust of Elder McKay's first sermon was the necessity of unity. "We have met here not as representatives from various tribes. We have met here as one body; members of the body of Christ," he said. "We do not meet here as 'pakeha' or as Maori; we meet as brethren and sisters in the brotherhood of Christ. Let us forget our nationalities; let us forget our tribal superiorities. . . . [L]et us drive from our midst every spirit of dissension."[43] The mission clerk recorded: "He gave a wonderful sermon. The Spirit of the Lord was present and we certainly heard words of inspiration. Every one was so touched by the Spirit present that there was scarcely a dry eye in the assembly. . . . Elder Stuart Meha then interpreted in Maori the main points of the sermon."[44]

Hugh J. Cannon was scheduled to be the main speaker at the second general session of the conference that began at 2:00 p.m. and was attended by the Reorganized Church missionaries. Conscious of their presence, Brother Cannon preached on succession in the presidency of the Church, testifying that Brigham Young's call to succeed Joseph Smith was from God. Elder McKay had not intended to speak at this session but rose and said he "felt constrained in the spirit" to do so. He then related a sacred experience on the island of Maui two months earlier, when he and Hugh J. Cannon and three other brethren—Hawaiian Mission president E. Wesley Smith, American missionary Samuel Harris Hurst, and Hawaiian missionary David Keola Kailimai—bowed in prayer at Pulehu, where the earliest branch of the Church was organised in Hawaii. During the prayer, Elder McKay said, David Kailimai saw a vision of two men shaking hands. Elder McKay told the Hui Tau congregation that after the prayer, he had said, "'Brother Keola, I don't know the full significance of your vision, but I do know that the veil between us and God and the brethren on the other side was very thin.' Then Brother Cannon, with tears in his eyes said, 'There was no veil,' and the testimony of his vision is too sacred to give. But let me tell you my beloved brethren and sisters, his father, George Q. Cannon and Joseph F. Smith, nephew of the Prophet Joseph . . . let me tell you that they live, and these men gave approval of the work now known as Mormonism, which you, brethren and sisters, have embraced."[45]

---

43. George Shepard Taylor, "Report of Sermons of David O. McKay Delivered at the Annual Conference of the New Zealand Mission of the Church of Jesus Christ of Latter-day Saints, held at Huntly, 23-25 April 1921." Elder McKay's sermons, as stated, were recorded by Elder Graham H. Doxey but have been catalogued in the LDS Church History Library under President Taylor's name.

44. New Zealand Mission, Manuscript History, 23 April 1921.

45. Taylor, "Report of the Sermons of David O. McKay," 4. In the early 1850s, Joseph F. Smith was, like George Q. Cannon, one of the earliest LDS missionar-

Just as Elder McKay finished, Loving loudly called out a comment but was quieted by missionaries seated nearby. "This [sermon] was also interpreted to the Saints by Stuart Meha," records the mission history. Immediately after the benediction, Loving headed for Elder McKay, wanting to argue the succession question, but was completely disarmed when McKay simply took his hand and smiled at him. Obviously affected by Elder McKay's charismatic personality, Loving became tearful and almost incoherent, and could only stammer out his hope that "Zion would soon be built" whether by the LDS or RLDS Church. Elder McKay patted him on the back and advised him to build up his own house and not tear down other people's and then, perhaps, "he would . . . be able to assist in building up Zion."[46]

At the 10:00 a.m. Sunday School session next morning, (Sunday, 24 April), the sacrament was administered to the large congregation. Elder McKay invited all the children to come forward and sit on the ground in front of the packed congregation. The American elder serving as mission Sunday School superintendent then spoke to the children. He was followed by Brother Cannon (a member of the Sunday School General Board) and Elder McKay (general superintendent of the Church's Sunday Schools worldwide), who told the children a story, after which Stuart Meha briefly interpreted his words.[47]

The Sunday afternoon session began with the business of the conference, as Church and mission leaders were sustained. Following this, Principal F. Earl Stott gave the annual report of the Maori Agricultural College. After a musical item, Elder McKay rose to speak again. He was feeling "bilious" and suffering from a toothache and a cold, which was causing him to lose his voice. Some seven or eight hundred people had crammed into the tent; the flaps were raised, and the remainder of the large congregation, estimated at 2,000, sat or stood around outside. When it was Elder McKay's turn to speak, he apologised for his hoarseness and confessed that he doubted the wisdom of trying to address them at all. However, as he continued to speak, his laryngitis abated. As soon as he began to testify of the mission of Joseph Smith, Loving, who had apparently recovered from his discomposure of the previous day, appeared in one of the open

ies in Hawaii. In 1901, Joseph F. Smith became the sixth president of the LDS Church and had died just over two years before McKay and Cannon's spiritual experience at Pulehu.

46. New Zealand Mission, Manuscript History, 23 April 1921; Taylor, Journal, 23 April 1921, 2:128–29; David O. McKay, "Journal of World Mission Tour, 1921," 23 April 1921.

47. New Zealand Mission, Manuscript History, 24 April 1921.

flaps of the tent and shouted, "Joseph Smith never did teach polygamy! I challenge you to prove it."[48] He was forcibly removed by indignant Maori Saints, while Elder McKay calmed the congregation, reminding them that, at the Council in Heaven "when the sons and daughters of God met, the devil came also," drawing instant laughter from the large crowd.[49] "I want to tell you that when you find a man that is attacking others, that likes to live upon slander, on vilification, you will find a man that is not prompted by the spirit of Christ," he said.

In spite of his laryngitis, Elder McKay held the crowd enthralled as he preached what many felt was the most outstanding sermon of the conference. His sermon was once again, according to the minutes, interpreted by Stuart Meha. As the session concluded, the RLDS missionaries could be seen outside arguing with the group that had ejected them. Elder McKay urged the Saints not to get involved but to go and get their dinners, telling them that "it [the Reorganized Church] is just a boil on the body of the Church and when you rub it, it gets sore so let us not rub it but just attend to our own business."[50] He found the whole episode distasteful. "We have treated them courteously, and kindly as our guests, and they have violated every principle of good conduct. . . .The whole affair tended to convince me that our best policy is to treat them with absolute indifference. In the future they are not invited to any meeting I attend," he wrote.[51]

Elder McKay did not speak at the Sunday night Mutual Improvement Association session; and at the Monday morning (Anzac Day) session,[52] he turned the meeting over to those who had served or who had lost loved ones in the recent Great War to speak and to testify. However, he was once again the main speaker in the Monday afternoon session. Speaking of Anzac Day, he told the congregation how he had shed tears when, some months earlier, he had read an account of the bravery of the Maori soldiers at Gallipoli.[53] He then spoke on life beyond the grave, dwelling on

48. Taylor, "Report of the Sermons of David O. McKay," 7.
49. Ibid.; David O. McKay, "Journal of World Mission Tour," 24 April 1921.
50. Taylor, "Report of the Sermons of David O. McKay," 9.
51. David O. McKay, "Journal of World Mission Tour," 24 April 1921.
52. Anzac Day commemorates the landing of the Australian and New Zealand Army Corps on the Gallipoli peninsula in the Dardanelles on 25 April 1915. A military bungle and tactical disaster, the ensuing battle resulted in enormous losses for the colonial troops, who showed outstanding gallantry both on the day of the initial landing and in the following months until the survivors were evacuated.
53. Historian Keith Sinclair states that over 100,000 New Zealanders served overseas in World War I (more than 10 percent of the population) and that "nearly 17,000 men—one in sixty-five of the population—did not return from battle. This

the Mormon doctrine of vicarious ordinances, and prophesied that there would be a temple in New Zealand as soon as the people were ready for it and could keep it busy. "I have no doubt in my heart but what you will get a Temple," he concluded. "You must be ready for it, however."[54] The minutes reported, "Stuart Meha then interpreted the major points of the sermon in order to make them more clear to some of the Native Saints."[55]

A final public session was held that evening (Monday night), and both the visitors spoke. Next morning, a missionary meeting was held. Elder McKay told the elders that they were in New Zealand to do missionary work, and accordingly, local men should be ordained to the priesthood and serve as branch presidents. "It should be a violation of the rules that any elder do anything a native brother or sister can do. . . . He may not be able to do it so well as you, but help him. A time may come," he prophesied, "when there will be no elders from Zion."[56]

Tuesday afternoon was devoted to sports and recreation, including the haka and the poi dance, which Elder McKay thought one of the most beautiful dances in the world. The conference concluded with a concert, the tent being crammed and several hundred people standing round the open sides. Next day, Saints and missionaries dispersed, and the visiting authorities and the Taylor family travelled to the mission home in Auckland. That evening, President Taylor recorded, "all the household were glad of a toast and hot milk supper after our five days on Maori food."[57] Elder McKay and Brother Cannon sailed from Auckland on the *Tofua* the following Saturday; two months later, after visiting Tonga and Samoa, they returned briefly to tour the New Zealand Mission before sailing on to Australia and from thence to India and Europe.

What Is Believed to Have Happened at Hui Tau, 1921

The fame of the 1921 Hui Tau lives on in the collective memory of New Zealand Mormons, and has been celebrated in the wider Church, but perhaps for the wrong reasons. Half a century after the event, Gordon C. Young, who was not only present but was seated between David O. McKay and Hugh J. Cannon in each conference session, gave form to the story in the way it is generally repeated today:

---

death-roll was greater than that of Belgium, which had six times the population and was a battlefield." Keith Sinclair, *A History of New Zealand*, 227.

54. Taylor, "Report of Sermons of David O. McKay," 12.
55. New Zealand Mission, Manuscript History, 25 April 1921.
56. Taylor, "Report of Sermons of David O. McKay," 14.
57. Taylor, Journal, 27 April 1921, 2:135.

I was sitting right there. President McKay was speaking when that marvelous miracle occurred; that mass interpretation of tongues. . . . It was Sunday afternoon and the Europeans and the Maoris were all there. . . . President
McKay got up to speak. It was Anzac Day . . . . He spoke several sentences
and then Stuart [Meha] would interpret into Maori. Then he'd make another statement in English and Stuart would interpret. All at once everything
was quiet, and all over the congregation the Maoris—not the Europeans but
the Maoris—called out, "Stuart, sit down, don't interpret; we can understand
what the Apostle is saying." They didn't speak English and they didn't understand anything President McKay was saying before, but now they were calling
out to Stuart to sit down. He was rather disconcerted; people calling out all
over the audience, right out in the meeting. President McKay didn't know, but
he sensed evidently that something was happening. Stuart didn't know what
to do so he started to interpret again. The calls came again, "Stuart, sit down.
Don't interpret." So Stuart just sat down, and President McKay went on and
gave one of the most beautiful talks I have ever heard in my life and those
people all understood what he was saying. This is, of course, recorded. That's
a miracle of record.[58]

Unfortunately, it is not a miracle of record. There does not appear to
be any contemporary record of this miracle whatsoever; rather, there does
not appear to be any *genuine* contemporary record. A careful examination
of the diary of one American missionary who was present, Elder Warren
S. Tonks, suggests that, nearly forty years later, he adjusted his journal to
include an account of the miracle he was supposed to have witnessed.

Elder Tonks's surviving mission diary consists of carbon copies of entries in a duplicate book; like many missionaries of the period, he tore out
the original pages and posted them home as letters, keeping the book of
carbon copies as his journal. His version of the miracle story has been written in ink, in a more mature handwriting, on the back of the relevant page
of his carbon-copy record.[59] The carbon copy of his original report on the
Hui Tau begins:

Saturday Apr 23rd 1921 The Hui Tau began today and we certainly had a
great spiritual feast. Elder McKay and Cannon spoke very fine.
Sunday Apr 24th 1921 This morning Sunday School for the little kiddies
was held. . . . In the afternoon Elder McKay was giving a powerful discourse
and two Josephites who were in the audience arose and challenged Apostle
McKay to prove that Joseph the Prophet had more than one wife. The Spirit
of the Lord and the spirit of the Devil were there. The two Josephites were
taken out, and Elder McKay, calm as a summer day, asked the people to sit

58. Gordon Claridge Young, Oral History, 9–10.
59. Warren S. Tonks, Missionary Diary, notes interpolated on back of page containing carbon copy record of 24 April 1921.

still and he continued one of the most powerful discourses I ever have heard and the Devils' [sic] plan to break up the meeting was thwarted.

Monday Apr 25th 1921 The Hui Tau continued and [new page] the morning session was turned over to the people in honor of their holiday called Anzac Day. Elder McKay has surely gotten the love and support of the people here and they shall never forget him.

On the back of the carbon copy entry for Sunday, 24th April, the following is written in ink:

At the beginning of this Sunday afternoon meeting the Maori interpreter Stuart Meha turned to Elder McKay and said, "Elder McKay, the power of interpretation of tongues has been given to this audience. They understand what you are saying as you speak. You do not need an interpreter." So Brother Meha sat down and Elder David O. McKay gave a powerful sermon to the wonderful people. The gift of interpretation of tongues was manifest just like on the Day of Penticost [sic] as told in the Bible.

An arrow is drawn to show where this passage is meant to fit in the original manuscript. This is the only account found to date that even pretends to be contemporary. Nowhere in Elder Tonks's journal, except in this ink interpolation, is there any suggestion of a miracle; the sensational event that rated a mention by Tonks at the time was the interruption by, and subsequent ejection of, the RLDS missionaries.

Not one of the contemporary or near-contemporary accounts of the 1921 Hui Tau records such a miracle. It is not mentioned in the mission history, which contains detailed minutes of each conference session. There is no mention of it in the mission paper, *Te Karere*.[60] Elder McKay did not record it in his travel diary nor, apparently, did Brother Cannon in his.[61] Elder McKay's first published account of the Hui Tau was written on board the *Tofua* en route to Tonga, just a few days after the conference. It was published in the *Improvement Era* three months later; the manuscript draft is preserved in his scrapbooks in the Church archives, and, like the published article, does not refer to the reputed miracle.[62]

---

60. *Te Karere* was not published on 27 April 1921, the scheduled date. The first issue after the mission conference was that of 11 May 1921. Elder McKay's sermons were translated into Maori and published in the next few issues.

61. McKay kept a pocket-size looseleaf diary during the journey, which was later typed onto quarto (A4) pages. Cannon's original travel diary, kept in shorthand, has not survived. However, he prepared the manuscript for publication but died in 1931 before completing the project; the manuscript, transcribed by his wife, has been published. See Hugh J. Cannon, *To the Peripheries of Mormondom: The Apostolic Around-the-World Journey of David O. McKay, 1920–1921*, 68–75.

62. David O. McKay, Scrapbooks, 1928-70, Vol. 128, reel 53; David O. McKay,

It seems unlikely that Elder McKay would forget to mention such an occurrence. More importantly, Elder Graham H. Doxey, keeping a shorthand record of Elder McKay's sermons, did not report any such sentence-by-sentence interpretation by Stuart Meha or any reported calling to Meha by members of the congregation during Elder McKay's talks, yet he faithfully recorded the interjections of the RLDS missionaries and Elder McKay's asides with regard to them. Neither did mission president George S. Taylor record the miracle in his private journal or mention it in his report given at the October 1923 general conference in Salt Lake City, although in his general conference address he spoke of the Tuesday missionary meeting as one which nobody present would ever forget.[63]

Other surviving missionary journals, such as that of Ernest A. Ottley and Jonathan Royal Bennett, also fail to mention the miracle. Elder Ottley recorded the RLDS disturbance but, like President Taylor, reserved his highest praise for the Tuesday missionary meeting, which was, he wrote, "the best meeting I ever attended without exception."[64] While it is perhaps possible that Elder Ottley found the missionary meeting more inspirational than one in which a great mass miracle had occurred, it is difficult to believe that he did not find the miracle worthy of mention. Elder McKay, in a letter to his wife written on board the *Tofua* on 4 May, just ten days later, echoed both Taylor and Ottley, telling "Ray" that the missionary meeting was "one of the most inspirational meetings I've ever attended!"[65] He did not mention the miracle of interpretation of tongues even to his wife.

It might be assumed that Elder McKay felt the miracle was too sacred to mention even in his diary or in his letter to his wife; yet he had had no hesitation in telling the Hui Tau throng the story of his and Brother Cannon's experience on the island of Maui just two months earlier. This experience was far more intimate, personal, and sacred, especially to Brother Cannon, who might justifiably have desired Elder McKay to preserve privacy about a manifestation that apparently involved his dead father. Elder McKay did, in fact, refrain from going into details about Brother Cannon's testimony of what actually happened but felt quite at liberty to tell the story.

That Elder McKay, as far as can be ascertained, never told the story of this miracle of interpretation of tongues until December 1934, suggests that for thirteen years he was unaware of the reputed miracle, until repeat-

"Hui Tau," *Improvement Era* 24, no. 9 (July 1921): 769–77.

63. The Church of Jesus Christ of Latter-day Saints, *Proceedings of Ninety-fourth Semi-Annual General Conference, 5–7 October 1923*, 132–34.

64. Ernest A. Ottley, Diary, 26 April 1921; Jonathon Royal Bennett, Journals, 1921–23, 26 April 1921.

65. Quoted in David Lawrence McKay, *My Father, David O. McKay*, 130.

ed telling by Maori Saints and New Zealand missionaries had established it as part of the folk history of the New Zealand Mission.

Birth of a Miracle Story

The story was first drawn to Elder McKay's attention by Rufus K. Hardy during his second term as New Zealand Mission president (1933-34). President Hardy wrote to Elder McKay from Auckland on 3 August 1934. He wrote of talking to Maori Saints who

> always refer to the Hui Tau ... [when] the mercy of God ... permitted them to fully understand and interpret literally your speech which you delivered on Sunday of this conference; notwithstanding you spoke in the European tongue which was foreign to the majority of the great audience, they understood it perfectly. In fact, many of them have referred to it as a demonstration of the Spirit of God unto them, which was equal to that given to the Ancients on that memorable day of Pentecost.[66]

President Hardy enclosed written testimonies from four Maori Saints who had been present at that conference session in 1921: Stuart Meha, Wi Smith, Sidney Christy, and Karena W. Takoro.[67] All four retrospective accounts, together with Hardy's covering letter, were later pasted into Elder McKay's scrapbooks by his long-time secretary, Clare Middlemiss, and may be examined in the LDS Church History Library.[68]

Stuart Meha's typescript testimony, titled "A Wonderful Manifestation of the Gift of Interpretation of Tongues," is dated 17 May 1934. His account confirms that Elder McKay and Brother Cannon both, at their own request, gave their complete addresses *without* sentence-by-sentence interpretation, and that he, Meha, merely gave a summary at the end of each talk. Meha wrote:

> Hui Tau, 1921, was the most outstanding, the most wonderful ever held. Each of its sessions was attended by a rich outpouring of the spirit of God, the presence of the two distinguished visitors contributing to that spirituality. It would be idle to designate one meeting of that Hui Tau from the others as

---

66. Rufus K. Hardy, Letter to David O. McKay, Auckland, 3 August 1934.

67. Ibid. Although Elder McKay later stated that President Hardy had these accounts notarised, there is no evidence for this in Hardy's letter nor on the original documents. McKay also said (incorrectly) that Hardy collected these accounts during his 1938 visit to New Zealand with Apostle George Albert Smith. See David O. McKay, *Gospel Ideals: Selections from the Discourses of David O. McKay, Ninth President of the Church of Jesus Christ of Latter-day Saints,* 552.

68. David O. McKay, Scrapbooks, 1928–70, vol. 128.

being the most spiritual, for they were all alike—wonderful, soul-satisfying, faith promoting.

I will now come to what I have in mind, and relate an instance which occurred at that Hui Tau, and which to me was a wonderful manifestation of the Gift of Interpretation of Tongues. I remember Elder McKay spoke to me that they would like to speak in the meetings first, then I would interpret afterwards and give the message as best I could. The brethren had decided that they would speak as the Spirit gave them utterance, and not be hampered and diverted in thought by having me interpret sentence by sentence. I acquiesced.

Elder David O McKay, in the majesty of his office, stood up to speak in the Sunday morning general session. He commenced by saying—"I wish, oh how I wish, I had the power to speak in your own tongue and tell you what is in my heart, but since I have not the gift, I pray, and I ask you to pray, that you might have the spirit of interpretation, of discernment, that you may understand at least the Spirit while I am speaking and then you will get the thought in the words when Bro. Meha interprets."

Then followed a remarkable kauwhau [sermon] lasting some forty minutes or more. The spirit of God that was in that great audience, for the hearts of men and women melted—men and women whom I knew did not understand English, shed tears with those who did understand. They understood the message Elder McKay gave in that meeting. I remember after the meeting Bro. Christy came up and said: "Bro. McKay the people understood you even before Bro. Meha interpreted."

The second document was handwritten in the form of a personal letter to President Hardy from Wi Smith, dated Nuhaka, 14 May 1934:

> This is to certify that I, Wi Smith, President of the Mahia District . . . did personally witness and heard Apostle David O. McKay offer up a prayer asking the Lord to enlighten the Maori congregation during his sermon . . . without the aid of a Maori interpreter.
>
> And I testify that this eventually happened, all the Maoris, young and old enjoyed his sermon.
>
> Furthermore, while he was speaking two men members of the Josephite Creed started interrupting him by passing unnecessary remarks. Finally one of the men with uplifted hand rushed up to strike Apostle McKay. Within striking distance the Apostle raised his right hand and instantly the Josephite cowered down in a kneeling position whimpering and mourning before the Apostle who without ["any" crossed out] stopping in his discourse or showing by facial expression signs of fear continued his sermon. He was not disturbed again till he finished speaking then turning he raised up the Josephite.
>
> I state in all sincerity and truthfulness that this actually took place in view of hundreds present at said Hui Tau. [Signed] Wi Smith.

The third account was handwritten by Sidney Christy. This document is untitled and is not addressed. After writing that his statement was absolutely true, Christy also referred to Elder McKay's fervent desire for the Spirit to bear witness to the congregation:

> Here I, Sidney Christy, do testify that after he had spoken for a few minutes the Apostle had the whole congregation in tears, and when the old Maori people who did not understand English were approached after the service, they stated that they ~~had under~~ knew every word uttered by the Apostle.
>
> During this Conference, there were two Josephites who were doing their level best to make trouble. After one of the meetings in which they interrupted the speakers several times, one of them approached Apostle McKay and in a sarcastic manner, said to him, "I would like to shake hands with an Apostle of the Church of Jesus Christ of Latter-day Saints, for I have never seen one before."
>
> He then extended his hand and as soon as it came in contact with the Apostle's he shivered as with an ague and collapsed at the Apostle's feet and sobbed . . . .
>
> This was witnessed by scores of people and it is common knowledge throughout the New Zealand Mission.
>
> [Signed] Sidney Christy. May 18, 1934.

The fourth, handwritten by Karena W. Takoro in Maori, was translated into English by President Hardy:

> Puketapu, Waahi, Huntly West, New Zealand. July 26, 1934.
> To Rufus K. Hardy . . .
> As the Apostle was speaking, the Great Good Spirit descended upon the entire assemblage. It was plain to see that all the old men and all the old women, in fact, all present, were crying and shedding tears, although they did not know how to listen intelligently or how to interpret or understand the European Language. Nevertheless the Spirit of God gave unto them the true spirit of interpretation. They all said, "Notwithstanding many of their ancestors had been called home to paradise, it was as though they that day stood before them, and for this reason they desired to continuously hear the Apostle speak."

The time-frame is compelling. Elder McKay apparently knew nothing of the reputed miracle until he received these accounts with President Hardy's covering letter in late August or early September 1934. Three months later, Elder McKay (sustained as a counsellor in the First Presidency in October 1934) told the story in public for the first time when he gave an illustrated lecture on his 1921 world tour of LDS missions. A typescript of his notes for the relevant part of this lecture is preserved in the LDS Church History Library. This version was used when the story was published for the first time the following year.[69]

---

69. Jeremiah Stokes, *Modern Miracles: Authenticated Testimonies of Living Wit-*

Compared with Gordon C. Young's 1972 account, President McKay's was cautious:

> One of the most important events on my world tour of the missions of the Church was the gift of interpretation of the English tongue given to the Saints of New Zealand, at a session of their conference, held on the 23d [sic] day of April, 1921, at Puketapu, Huntly, Waikato . . .
>
> In other missions I had spoken through an interpreter but, able as all interpreters were, I, nevertheless, felt hampered, in fact, somewhat inhibited, in presenting my message . . .
>
> When I arrose [sic] to give my address, I said to Brother Stuart Meha, our interpreter, that I would speak without his translating sentence by sentence what I said and then, to the audience I continued:
>
> "I wish, oh how I wish, I had the power to speak to you in your own tongue, that I might tell you what is in my heart; but since I have not the gift, I pray, and I ask you to pray, that you might have the spirit of interpretation, of discernment, that you may understand at least the spirit while I am speaking, and then, you will get the words and the thought when Brother Meha interprets."
>
> My sermon lasted 40 minutes and I have never addressed a more attentive, a more respectful audience. My listeners were in perfect rapport—this I knew when I saw tears in their eyes ["in their eyes" substituted in pencil for "streaming down their cheeks," which has been crossed out]. Some of them at least, perhaps most of them, who did not understand English, had the gift of interpretation.
>
> Brother Sidney Christie [sic], a native New Zealander, who had been a student at the Brigham Young University, at the close of my address, whispered to me "Brother McKay, they got your message."
>
> "Yes," I replied. "I think so, but for the benefit of some who may not have understood, we will have Bro Meha give a synopsis of it in Maori."
>
> During the translation, some of the Maoris corrected him on some points, showing that they had a clear conception of what had been said in English.[70]

Anatomy of a Myth

As with the manifestation on Maui, there are discrepancies in the different accounts of the miracle. While not necessarily invalidating the story, they invite consideration.

The inventive elaborations with regard to the Josephite incident in two of the four retrospective Maori accounts, both solemnly attested as truth,

---

nesses, 97–106.

70. David O. McKay, "Gift of Interpretation of Tongues Bestowed: Testimony of President David O. McKay, Given in an Illustrated Lecture on His World Tour of the Missions of the Church at Salt Lake City, Utah, 25 December 1934."

make it difficult for the reader to accept other passages of these documents uncritically. And it is interesting to note that Christy specifically and expressly changed his mind about testifying that the "old Maori people" understood every word, and replaced "understood" with "knew."

There is no consensus about the day and session in which the miracle was stated to have occurred. President McKay's 1934 account placed the miracle on Saturday, 23 April, in the morning session of the conference. Gordon C. Young, whose account reflects popular belief, stated that the miracle occurred on Anzac Day during the Sunday afternoon session of conference; but Anzac Day (25 April) fell on Monday in 1921. Warren S. Tonks pinpointed the Sunday afternoon session, but his diary interpolation was almost certainly made after he had heard Gordon C. Young's story in April 1958, when many former New Zealand missionaries travelled to New Zealand for the dedication of the New Zealand Temple. David O. McKay (by then Church president and prophet), Young and Tonks were all there, as well as Stuart Meha and others who had been at the 1921 Hui Tau.[71] The story was undoubtedly repeated many times that week; and it was probably after this visit that Tonks adjusted his mission diary to include an account of the miracle he had inexplicably failed to notice at the time.

In President McKay's earliest version of the story (1934, published 1935, by which time, as stated, he was a counsellor in the First Presidency), he simply dates the event at 23 April 1921 (Saturday) and refers to his sermon in the morning session. In a later version (published in the *Church News* in 1952 and included in a collection of his sermons published in 1955, after he had become Church president), he did not specify a date. Rufus K. Hardy's letter named a Sunday session; Stuart Meha designated the Sunday morning session, Sid Christy the opening session on Saturday; neither Wi Smith nor Brother Takoro specified either a day or session.

There are other discrepancies in the story. President McKay's 1934 version has Christy whispering to him, "Brother McKay, they got your message." Twenty years later, President McKay recalled Sid Christy rushing up to him afterwards. The first version is by far the most likely; Christy was actually seated at the table beside Elder McKay during each conference session, interpreting the Maori sermons for him, while Young was assigned to do the same for Brother Cannon. It is not a matter of great moment and simply illustrates that even the best memories are somewhat

---

71. President McKay also dedicated the Church College of New Zealand on this occasion.

unreliable. The actual manner of the reputed miracle's occurrence is of more importance.

Young states that Meha translated Elder McKay's remarks as he went along; but Elder McKay states that he felt hampered by an interpreter, and asked Meha to give a synopsis of his sermons when he had finished, which Meha's 1934 letter confirms. That this was the method of interpretation used, though not the only reason for it, is borne out by at least three contemporary sources: the mission history, McKay's diary of his travels, and the transcript of Elder McKay's speeches as reported by Graham H. Doxey and submitted to the Church History Department by his mission president, George S. Taylor, and catalogued under Taylor's name.

The conference minutes explicitly state that Meha interpreted the sermons, not only of Elder McKay, but of Cannon, Taylor, and MAC principal F. Earl Stott, *after* each speaker had concluded his address. The minutes of the first (10:00 a.m.) session on Saturday, 23 April, contain the following passage:

> Elder David O. McKay then took up the time. He gave a wonderful sermon. The spirit of the Lord was present and we certainly heard words of inspiration. Everyone was so touched by the Spirit present that there was scarcely a dry eye in the assembly. (See copy of sermon, attached, as reported by Elder G. H. Doxey.)
>
> Elder Stuart Meha then interpreted in Maori the main points of the sermon.

The mission history continues with minutes of the 2:00 p.m. session on Saturday, 23 April:

> Elder McKay occupied a few minutes. Stated it was not his intention at first to speak but he gave a wonderful testimony of the divinity of Brigham Young's calling and also his successors. (See report of remarks attached.)
>
> This was also interpreted to the Saints by Stuart Meha after which President Taylor made a few announcements.

The same procedure was specifically noted at every subsequent session in which Elder McKay spoke. Meha's 1934 account confirms this procedure. This evidence contradicts Young's account of sentence-by-sentence interpretation and fails to substantiate his story of the suddenly comprehending Maori calling out to Meha that his continuing interpretation was unnecessary. It is quite possible that some Maori Saints corrected Meha as he made his end-of-sermon translations; but neither Doxey nor the mission clerk recorded this happening, though they recorded other interjections.

An Unnecessary Miracle

More than thirteen years after the event, President McKay intimated that the reason he asked Stuart Meha not to interpret as he went along but rather to wait until the end of his sermon, was because he "felt hampered" and even "inhibited" by the former procedure. This may well have been so. Certainly Meha suggests this reason, and McKay had read Meha's account just before he first told the story in 1934. However, Elder McKay's travel journal, written at the time, gives a different, or at least additional, and very significant reason for the adoption of this procedure. "Elder Stewart [sic] Meha is interpreting our addresses," he wrote. "*As a number of the hundreds in attendance understand English very well,* we speak continuously until the address is finished, then Bro. Meha repeats. The efficiency and fluency with which he does this is simply marvelous. It seems to me he betters our speeches, and he scarcely misses a word, not to say a thought."[72]

This statement of Elder McKay's is confirmed by another significant sentence in the minutes of the Monday afternoon session: "Stuart Meha then interpreted the major points of the sermon in order to make them more clear to *some of the Native Saints.*"[73] The fact that McKay's aside about the devil evoked instant laughter from the large congregation is evidence that the majority understood it.

As early as 1884, Mormon missionaries reported that many Maori understood English. "There were two Europeans present the rest were all Maoris, but the most of them could understand english," wrote William Gardner of a meeting in the Waikato district in 1884.[74] This statement, of course, referred to one particular group of Maori in one particular area; it certainly was not true of all areas of New Zealand at that date. At the same period, Elder Charles Anderson reported that missionaries must be able to speak Maori in order to operate successfully amongst them.[75] However, just a year later, Elder Gardner, still in the Waikato, held a service in a Wesleyan chapel. After hymns and a prayer, Gardner invited his newly arrived companion to speak. "I then told the Natives my Brother would speak to them in English which he did many of them would understand him," he wrote.[76]

---

72. David O. McKay, "Journal of World Mission Tour, 1921," 23 April 1921; emphasis mine.

73. New Zealand Mission, Manuscript History, 25 April 1921; emphasis mine.

74. William Gardner, Diary, 29 June 1884.

75. "New Zealand Mission," *Deseret News,* 9 February 1885 in Journal History, 3 January 1885, 5.

76. Gardner, Diary, 17 May 1885.

Elder John E. Magleby was in Colac Bay in 1900. "[The] Maori down here only seems half natural as, the people are english speaking nearly all together, being also half cast in reallity by birth," he recorded. Magleby, a fluent Maori speaker, gave a lantern lecture at a Maori village three miles from Kaiapoi, near Christchurch, on 16 August 1900, noting that he spoke in English "as the maoris understand it as well as maori."[77] In 1901, Elder John W. Gardner decided it would be very difficult to learn Maori in the Hawkes Bay and Wairarapa Valley. "The Maoris here are mostly half-casts [sic] and talk very good European language," he wrote, commenting that the local Maori seldom spoke Maori themselves.[78]

Similar reports from various parts of the mission are scattered throughout surviving missionary journals and correspondence. From Whangarae in 1906, sister missionary Esther Linford wrote to her mission president, Louis G. Hoagland, that if he wanted her to learn Maori, he would have to send her "to the Kings Country [sic] or some where else where the people talk Maori. These people all talk English." She did add that they seemed to become lost when the missionaries preached in English. She was pleased when another missionary wife arrived in New Zealand. "I hope this Sister can have better success with Maori than I have had," she wrote to President Hoagland. "I never hear Maori except on Sunday and as soon as the amen is said, everybody begins talking English."[79] "There are two thirds, also, of the young Maori that can read English," wrote mission president Louis G. Hoagland in 1906, speaking of the mission as a whole while campaigning for establishment of the mission paper.[80] John Johnson, first principal of the Maori Agricultural College, spoke in a church service at Kohunui on 26 January 1913. "I spoke in English at all the meetings, and had no interpreter," he recorded. "Nearly all of the natives could understand all that I said."[81]

There is little doubt that by 1921 the great majority of Maori Latter-day Saints understood English reasonably well. So competent were they that by 1916, many new missionaries could not see any point in learning the Maori language.[82] By no standards could it be said, as Rufus K. Hardy

---

77. Magleby, Journal, 8, 16 August 1900; original spelling and punctuation.

78. Eldon J. and Alice Gardner, eds., *Day Journal of John W. Gardner in New Zealand LDS Mission,* 15 August 1901, 14.

79. Esther Linford, Letters to Louis G. Hoagland, dated Whangarae, 26 February, 30 October 1906.

80. Louis G. Hoagland, Letter to W. Frank Atkin, dated Auckland, 18 August 1906, in W. Frank Atkin, Papers, fd 10.

81. John Johnson, Journal, 26 January 1913.

82. Lambert, Journal, 18 June 1916.

assured David O. McKay in 1934, that the "English tongue was foreign to the majority of the great audience" assembled at Hui Tau in 1921.[83]

At the 1922 Hui Tau, just twelve months after the reputed miracle, the Sunday afternoon session was, according to a report published in the *Deseret News*, presented wholly in English "on account of the great number of Europeans present and *so many of the natives being able to understand the English language*."[84] It seems highly unlikely that they had learned English in one year; neither is there any suggestion that the gift reported to have been miraculously given a year earlier had stayed with them permanently. The conclusion seems warranted that, if a majority of the Maori Saints understood both David O. McKay's 1921 sermons and this 1922 Hui Tau session, it was because most of them could already understand English when Elder McKay arrived in New Zealand.

Just nine years after McKay's visit, in 1930, Auckland newspapers reported that the Maori language seemed to be dying out, despite the fact that it was now being taught in schools throughout the Dominion. John E. Magleby, in New Zealand again for his second term as mission president, commented on these newspaper reports, stating that few missionaries now bothered to learn te reo, "nor does it seem possible for them to do so." Pure Maori was no longer heard; even the old Maori people, President Magleby reported, were "half-casting" their language, that is, using a combination of English and Maori. "It does look like the Maori language will in a very few years become practically extinct as far as the living races are concerned," he wrote.[85]

Fortunately, there has been a resurgence of interest in Maori language and culture, and these dire newspaper predictions were unfulfilled; but the situation President Magleby reported did not appear overnight in 1930. It is an inescapable conclusion that most (though not all) Maori both understood and spoke English a decade earlier. The exceptions were the minority of "old Maori people" to whom Sid Christy referred as "knowing," rather than understanding, Elder McKay's words.

Implications for the Church

What, then, can be made of an apostle, later president of the LDS Church, promoting a story that was, it appears, at worst fabricated, at best exaggerated? How relevant are the inconsistent and differing accounts of

---

83. Hardy, Letter to David O. McKay, 3 August 1934.

84. "Missionaries and Saints of New Zealand, 'Hui Tau' at Annual Conference at Otiria," *Deseret News*, 2 June 1922, in Journal History, 17 April 1922, 4; emphasis mine.

85. John E. Magleby, Letter to Louis G. Hoagland, 19 September 1930.

the vision or manifestation in Hawaii, which also involved David O. Mc-Kay, a few weeks before the miracle at Hui Tau?

There seems to be strong evidence that something outside normal experience occurred to the small group of Latter-day Saint elders bowed in prayer in Hawaii just weeks earlier. While individual accounts differ in detail and interpretation, several participants wrote contemporary or near-contemporary accounts of their experience; David O. McKay himself told this story at Hui Tau in New Zealand just two months after it occurred.[86] There is no contemporary or even near-contemporary report of the reputed miracle in New Zealand. The first accounts were written in 1934, and the first published version is dated 1935.

Mormon congregations are commonly deeply moved by the Spirit when listening to men whom they revere as apostles and prophets. The longed-for visit of an apostle to the South Pacific missions in 1921—a visit for which they had begged since the turn of the century—brought congregations filled with anticipation and open to the witness of the Spirit. Elder McKay obviously spoke with great power and moved everyone who heard him. The Maori are a deeply spiritual people and also a very emotional people; they are more quickly and easily moved to tears than similar congregations in Australia or England might be. There is nothing implausible or even unusual in Elder McKay noting tears streaming down their cheeks, according to the unedited wording in his 1934 account. Given the Maori ability to tangi, with what Elder McKay himself in his travel journal testified were genuine tears, this observation was credible and much more likely than the edited version of "tears in their eyes."

It is inconceivable that Elder McKay neither recorded such a miracle at the time nor referred to it when he wrote to the Maori Saints one year later.[87] From the organisation of the LDS Church in 1830, Mormon leaders and missionaries were expected to record miraculous events and faith-promoting incidents, and David O. McKay faithfully kept detailed journals of his life experiences and travels. All Mormon missionaries were encouraged to do the same, and to report faith-promoting incidents to their mission president. These were duly included in the regular mission reports. At the 1922 Hui Tau, just one year after the alleged miracle, the assembled American missionaries were reminded by their mission president that they should "send in a write up of remarkable happenings and

86. Lavina Fielding Anderson, "Prayer under a Pepper Tree: Sixteen Accounts of a Spiritual Manifestation," 55–78.

87. New Zealand Mission, Manuscript History, 24 December 1922; David O. McKay, "Ki nga Hunga Tapu o te Mihana o Niu Tirini e Noho huihui ana ki te Hui Tau ki Porirua," dated 8 November 1922.

healings."[88] Yet this same mission president himself had neither recorded the miracle at Hui Tau a year earlier nor reminded his missionaries to do the same. The only possible conclusion to be drawn is that President Taylor was also unaware that a miracle had taken place.

The fact that Elder McKay *did* report the manifestation in Hawaii and did not report the gift of interpretation of tongues bestowed on a congregation of approximately two thousand just weeks later in New Zealand, strongly suggests that he was unaware that there *was* such an incident in New Zealand until thirteen years later. When he was told what was by then believed to have happened, he immediately wrote an account and deposited it in the Historical Department Archives. But unless documentary evidence not yet available comes to light, it seems that President McKay can be accused of nothing more than guilelessness—which is, after all, a virtue. He was led to believe that something had happened at Hui Tau 1921 of which he was unaware at the time; he trustingly believed what he was told had happened and, accordingly, began to recount the miracle at Hui Tau as a faith-promoting story.

An Uncelebrated Miracle

David O. McKay *did* experience a miracle, and the congregation witnessed it, during Hui Tau 1921—a smaller and less dramatic miracle, but one that Elder McKay recorded at the time and which has been overlooked by historians writing about the New Zealand Mission and by most of Elder McKay's biographers. Elder McKay arrived in New Zealand suffering from severe toothache, pyorrhoea, and a respiratory infection.[89] By Sunday, 24 April, the cold that he had first recorded on 15 April, while still on board the *Marama*, was worse; when he awoke this Sunday morning, Elder McKay felt he had aggravated his condition by getting his feet wet the day before. He was so hoarse that he could scarcely speak. Auckland Branch president Charles Spencer, a pharmacist, gave him something for his hoarseness. "I managed to tell the children a story, but my voice was very husky," he wrote in his diary, adding, in a letter to his wife, "Faith and works took us through."[90]

In the afternoon meeting, Elder McKay arose to speak, feeling somewhat apprehensive. "My voice was husky [a statement borne out by Graham Doxey's shorthand notes], and the tent large, and people standing in

88. New Zealand Mission, Manuscript History, 17 April 1922.

89. David Lawrence McKay, *My Father, David O. McKay*, 129.

90. Ibid., 129; David O. McKay, "Journal of World Mission Tour, 1921," 24 April 1921.

circles on the outside!"[91] To address such a huge crowd without any form of microphone or public address system while suffering from laryngitis must have seemed a daunting prospect. He began his sermon; this was the session in which he was interrupted by the RLDS interjectors some five minutes after he began to speak. Elder McKay made his quip about the devil attending what in Mormon theology is called the Council in Heaven, and continued his sermon. "Then happened what has never happened to me before," he wrote in his journal. "I entered upon my discourse with all the earnestness and vehemence I could command, spoke as loud as possible, and when 30 or 40 minutes later, I concluded, my voice was clearer and stronger than when I began!"[92] Both Elder McKay and Brother Cannon freely acknowledged divine help, Cannon humorously admitting that his prayers for Elder McKay were the more urgent out of fear that he might have to substitute.[93] That Elder McKay could speak for so long, and be heard by so many, while his voice improved rather than deteriorated as would be natural under such conditions, was a remarkable, but largely unremarked, occurrence.

"Many wonderful things happened during the [1921] Hui Tau," wrote one respected LDS historian, introducing his account of the miracle of interpretation of tongues.[94] Wonderful things *did* happen when David O. McKay visited the LDS New Zealand Mission conference in 1921, even without a mass Pentecostal miracle. During this conference, Elder McKay developed a great love for the Maori people, a love that bore fruit during his presidency of the Church. He promised that a temple would be built in New Zealand as soon as the Saints were ready for it. He reached the hearts of a people still wearied and saddened by the sacrifices of four long years of war by showing great understanding of the Anzac story and appreciation of the courage of the Maori contingent at Gallipoli. He and all present experienced a miracle when his laryngitis disappeared.

History or Myth?

The stories discussed in this chapter fit the category of myth rather than history. The popular conception of "myth" equates the word with either fiction or falsehood, depending on the context. However, most LDS scholars agree with other historians that a myth is something more than either. "Myths are narrative vehicles which convey to the community the

---

91. Quoted in David Lawrence McKay, *My Father, David O. McKay*, 129.
92. David O. McKay, "Journal of World Mission Tour, 1921," 24 April 1921.
93. David Lawrence McKay, *My Father, David O. McKay*, 130.
94. Britsch, *Unto the Islands of the Sea*, 304.

values it collectively holds," wrote LDS anthropologist David Knowlton.[95] It is difficult, if not impossible, to recreate past events with absolute integrity. "The past is never fully recoverable—either by sober historians or by common people recounting events from their own lives," wrote Mormon folklorist and English professor William A. Wilson. "Any attempt to reconstruct that past will be governed by what the person doing the reconstruction considers important and will of necessity require highlighting some details, leaving some in shadow, and dropping some completely—otherwise, the telling of the event would take as long as the event itself. . . . When we tell stories of the past we do not add or drop details in a random fashion. We remember and recount the past in terms meaningful to us in the present."[96]

"Our memories reshape events in our mind to make them conform to our emotional impressions and interpretations," says former *Sunstone* editor Elbert Eugene Peck, in a statement that could have been tailor-made for the "miracle" at Hui Tau. "Undoubtedly, all our stories go through such a refining process in their retelling, whether to our own mind or to an external audience, before they are permanently recorded." Peck warns that "faith-promoting stories," beloved in the Mormon Church, can do more harm than good when similar outcomes do not automatically follow in the lives of believers. When the past is either consciously or subconsciously altered to build faith, there is always danger that the house built on sand might fall. "As much as we need stories to live, we also need historians and journalists to keep our storytelling in touch with the world of fact and experience, to keep it honest."[97]

The late Richard Poll also discussed the role of myth in the LDS Church: "The creation of historical myths—idealized versions of important past experiences—is an inevitable process which contributes to the pursuit of righteousness to the extent that it provides role models and motivating traditions which are consistent with truth. . . . Historians, with their documents, contribute to the pursuit of righteousness when they check the myth-making capability to generate and perpetuate untruth and half-truth."[98]

Those who prefer that mythic faith-promoting stories should be left uncorrected might well ponder the words of the late missiologist Eric J. Sharpe, who reminds us that there is still "that uncomfortable command-

---

95. David C. Knowlton, "Belief, Metaphor, and Rhetoric: The Mormon Practice of Testimony Bearing," 24.

96. William A. Wilson, "The Spinners of Tales," 51.

97. Elbert Eugene Peck, "Casting Out the Spell," 13.

98. Richard D. Poll, *History & Faith: Reflections of a Mormon Historian*, 123–24.

ment (not by the way a suggestion) which forbids you from bearing false witness against your neighbour. . . . I believe that history written for propaganda purposes (and I do not care who writes it) is bad history. There is no easier way to bear false witness than to misrepresent those who are no longer in a position to defend themselves, merely in order to comfort the true believers."[99]

---

99. Eric J. Sharpe, "Manning Clark Revisited," 29 August 1993.

Chapter 4

Mormon Leaders and Maori Culture[1]

As the number of Maori converts to Mormonism rapidly increased from the early 1880s, the question of the compatibility of some aspects of Maori culture with gospel teachings began to exercise the minds of successive LDS missionaries and mission presidents. During the next one hundred years, several specific aspects of Maori culture particularly offended some Mormon leaders at different times and for differing reasons.

Mormonism and Maori Marriage Customs

Tribal and regional variations are important and must be kept in mind, but some generalisations about Maori social and marriage customs in the pre- and early post-European period can be drawn. Although Maori placed a high value on marriage, children, and family life, the first Christian, and later Mormon, missionaries, were often deeply worried by the apparent immorality of the Maori people. However, Maori tribal society before European contact had its own standards of sexual behaviour and specific sanctions for their violation. Many of these attitudes carried over into the European era.

Only daughters of high rangatira, who were often puhi (ceremonially dedicated) or taumau (betrothed, often in childhood), were expected to remain chaste until marriage. For the remainder, premarital sex was regarded as normal, but this convention changed after marriage.[2] "Sexual intercourse

---

1. A version of the section of this chapter on Maori marriage customs was published as "From Tolerance to 'House Cleaning': LDS Leadership Response to Maori Marriage Customs, 1890-1990," *Journal of Mormon History* 22 (Fall 1996): 72–91.

2. While Margaret Mead's account of adolescent sexual freedom in Samoa (*Coming of Age in Samoa: A Study of Adolescence and Sex in Primitive Societies*) has been challenged by Derek Freeman in *Margaret Mead and Samoa: The Making and*

was not a sin, though it was often a social offence when it occurred between the wrong persons," writes anthropologist Bruce Biggs. "The freedom allowed to women however ceased abruptly on marriage, and adultery involving a married woman was a serious crime."[3]

Maori marriage customs were less formal and ritualistic than those of the Christian churches. Matches were arranged through discussions between the extended families, though prompting from the interested parties was common. However, there does not appear to have been any kind of formal marriage service before European contact. "The endeavour to demonstrate an elaborate marriage ritual for the Maori, even when the couple were of the highest rank, seems to have failed for lack of corroboration," Biggs asserts.[4]

Once a marriage was agreed upon, the bride was either escorted to her husband's home and formally given into his care, or the young couple simply began life together. In the former case, the families exchanged gifts and then celebrated together with an elaborate feast. The social customs were important. As Biggs points out, "The fact that such observance did not consist of a sacrament or other ritual ceremony need not have lessened its effectiveness as a symbol of the marriage contract."[5]

Dissolution of a marriage was correspondingly simple and cheap. As no legal documents or ritual were involved and there was no dowry to be returned, marriages could end by mutual agreement. The most common grounds seem to have been childlessness (because children were highly valued and desired), adultery, or desertion. In the case of adultery or desertion, the family of the injured party would extract compensation (utu,

---

Unmaking of an Anthropological Myth, Freeman makes it clear that his objections are to Mead's methodology and to her attribution of customs of Eastern Polynesia (specifically, Tahiti and the Cook Islands) to Western Polynesia (see pp. 227, 234, 284). New Zealand Maori culture is acknowledged to be Eastern rather than Western Polynesian. Statements by other anthropologists about Maori adolescent sexual freedom (see, for example, Bruce Biggs, *Maori Marriage: An Essay in Reconstruction* and Joan Metge, *The Maoris of New Zealand: Rautahi*) are corroborated by numerous journal entries written by Mormon missionaries in the 1880s and 1890s. Unlike Mead in Samoa, the Mormon missionaries lived with the Maori people and many of them learned to speak Maori fluently.

3. Biggs, *Maori Marriage*, 15.

4. Ibid., 41. Biggs traces all references to Maori marriage rites to a paper on Maori marriage customs given to the Auckland Institute in 1903 by noted anthropologist Elsdon Best. Biggs points out that Best never suggested that formal rites characterised any but marriages of high-born couples and concludes that Best's informants were telling him of post-Christian contact customs.

5. Ibid., 42.

satisfaction or payment) from the other family by a forceful act of muru (plunder). "This effectively dissolved the union, leaving both free to make other matches," writes anthropologist Joan Metge.[6] Even in the late nineteenth century, polygyny was still practised by many Maori chiefs, who often married up to four wives.

Church of England (1814), Wesleyan (1823), and Roman Catholic (1838) missions had converted large numbers of Maori during the decades before the Mormon missionaries in New Zealand turned their attention to the native race. Several tribes initially accepted Christianity enthusiastically; but, as discussed briefly in Chapter 1, after the Land Wars of the 1860s left many tribes deprived of their land, there was extensive Maori dissatisfaction because most of the Christian missionaries had aided the British regiments during the conflict.[7] Several Maori churches, usually millennial and centred on a Maori prophet, developed in succeeding decades. As is common in such situations, syncretism resulted and elements of Christian doctrine and Maori tradition were blended to the satisfaction of the Maori.[8] The Latter-day Saint doctrine of celestial marriage simply added another element to the amalgam.

Because the original Christian missionaries encouraged Christian marriage services, many Maori couples were married by either European or Maori Christian ministers. The government allowed but did not require Maori couples to be married in Christian ceremonies, and Maori marriages were not even registered until 1911.[9] Thus Maori were free to marry either by tribal law and custom or with Christian marriage ceremonies, and were also free to combine elements of both Christian and Maori culture.

---

6. Metge, *The Maoris of New Zealand*, 21.

7. The conflicts of the 1860s are frequently referred to as the "Land Wars." Sorrenson feels that this term "imposes a monocausal explanation on a complex process of interaction that degenerated into war," and lists deeper causes. M. K. P. Sorrenson, "Maori and Pakeha," 148.

8. Bronwyn Elsmore, *Like Them That Dream: The Maori and the Old Testament* and *Mana from Heaven: A Century of Maori Prophets in New Zealand*; Tony Swain and Garry Trompf, *The Religions of Oceania*, 174; Michael Hill and Wiebe Zwaga, "Religion," 282.

9. Maori marriages were registered from 1911 but were registered separately from Pakeha marriages until 1952. From 1911, Maori could be married legally under either the Maori Land Act or under the Marriage Act. Civil registration of Maori births and deaths was not compulsory until 1913. Registration of births and deaths of European settlers began in 1848, marriages from 1854. Some church records exist for the period before civil registration began.

In the 1880s, the Mormon missionaries expressed no concerns about Maori polygyny. "Brother [X] was baptized at Taonoke [in April 1884], also his two wives and other persons," reads one account of early missionary work. As plural marriage was both a recognised doctrine and current practice of Mormonism, this reference to the plural wives of the convert is almost casual in its tone of acceptance.[10] Nevertheless, many Mormon missionaries were concerned about the lack of a formal, Christian marriage ceremony, and some began to excommunicate those Maori Saints who married "Maori fashion."

On Sunday, 8 July 1888, two young women from Tamaki requested rebaptism. Both had been baptised earlier but were now living in Maori marriages. "Most of the Maories are," commented Elder Nelson S. Bishop ruefully. The women were not excommunicated, but the missionaries taught them that they were committing the sin of adultery.[11] Elder Bishop visited their non-Mormon husbands and explained to the men that

> in order to be rebaptized [their wives] would have to be married. But the men refused, saying they preferd to live as they were. I told them that when maories had no law from God, they was justified by doing as they did, but now they had the law of God, and would be judged by that law and by that law they was living in sin, but they still refused to be married by our Church, I then told them they could be married by their minister, or the law of the land.

The men still refused, placing the women in a difficult situation. Bishop asked one of the women what she would do if the mission president, William Paxman, ruled that she should be "cut off" from the Church. "She said she was not able to leave hur husband," he recorded sadly.[12]

The situation was further complicated because the Mormon missionaries were not registered marriage celebrants in New Zealand before 1903. "Elder E. F. Richards received a letter from the [mission] president, concerning the law of marriage in this country," wrote John Ephraim Magleby

10. R. H. Manihera, "Account of Missionary Work in New Zealand: A Copy of an Unsigned, Handwritten Manuscript given to Louis G. Hoagland in Papawai, Wairarapa, in August 1918." Names of individual Latter-day Saints have been withheld to preserve the privacy of living descendants.

11. In most Christian churches, the sacrament of baptism is administered once only. During the nineteenth century, the LDS Church administered the ordinance of rebaptism for various reasons such as renewal of covenants, uncertainty about the validity of an earlier baptism, and cleansing before attending the temple or before receiving an "administration" or health blessing. Today, rebaptism is administered only after excommunication.

12. Nelson Spicer Bishop, New Zealand Mission Diaries, 8 July 1888, 338. Original spelling and punctuation in all quotations.

in his journal in August 1886. "We the Elders are allowed to marry maories only, as there is a strict law regarding half casts [sic] and Europeans."[13]
"Half casts" were numerous, given that intermarriage, or at least miscegenation, had been common in New Zealand since the 1830s.[14] Thus many
Maori converts to Mormonism had some Pakeha ancestry.[15] "The Maories
wanted me to baptize and marry a couple. but I didn't," wrote Elder Bishop
in December 1886. "In the first place he was a half cast and the law of the
land wont alow us to marry anyone but Maories. And in the second place
he had been cut of [sic] from the church for Adultery And I wouldent do
it without the consent of the president of the district."[16]

Nearly eighteen months later, at a mission conference in April 1888,
the missionaries met in council "to consider the marriage question," wrote
Elder Bishop. "And we thought it best to allow the [native] pres[idents]
of Branches to do all of the marrying on account of our not being able to
marry half cast &c (the law of the land would not allow us to marry any
white blood)."[17] As the Maori branch presidents were not legal marriage
celebrants either, this decision did nothing more than shield American elders from the perceived threat of prosecution for inadvertently performing
marriages for individuals of mixed Maori and Pakeha ancestry.

Thus, by the turn of the century, the situation was proving confusing
for missionary and convert alike. The conflict of Maori tradition with the
Mormon missionaries' firm belief in the necessity of a Western marriage
ceremony and their ineligibility to perform such a ceremony for most of
their converts, together with the Church's official retreat from polygamy,
proved a considerable headache for the puzzled mission presidents.

Elder Ezra Foss Richards from Farmington, Utah, served his first mission among the Maori from November 1884 to April 1888; during this
mission, he helped translate the Book of Mormon into the Maori language. A son of Apostle Franklin D. Richards, he returned to New Zea-

13. Magleby, Journal, 12 August 1886, 50.

14. As the European settlers assumed that the Maori race would eventually be
"amalgamated" or absorbed by intermarriage, little social stigma attached to children
of mixed race. Sorrenson, "Maori and Pakeha," 142, and M. P. K. Sorrenson, "How
to Civilize Savages: Some 'Answers' from Nineteenth-Century New Zealand," 97–
103. Keith Sinclair suggests other perspectives in "Why Are Race Relations in New
Zealand Better Than in South Africa, South Australia or South Dakota?" 121–27.
No statistics on the number of half-castes were kept until 1886.

15. Eldon J. Gardner and Alice Gardner, eds., "Day Journal of John W. Gardner in
New Zealand LDS Mission, 17 July 1901 to 23 January 1904," 15 August 1901, [n.p.].

16. Bishop, Diaries, 11 December 1886, 34.

17. Ibid., 8 April 1888, 282.

land ten years later as the last president (September 1896-January 1898) of the original Australasian Mission.[18] Disturbed by the marriage problem, President Richards finally wrote to the First Presidency (Wilford Woodruff, George Q. Cannon, and Joseph F. Smith), outlining Maori marriage customs and requesting a ruling on whether Maori customary marriages were acceptable or whether those living in them should be subjected to Church discipline. The First Presidency's reply was dated 19 March 1897:

> Where couples living together as man and wife have observed the requirment [sic] of their people, tribe or nation, their union should be respected by our brethren. Where the Maori saints have observed the national custom so far as marriage is concerned but have not been united by any Christian Church, they should not be excommunicated because they have not done so. The Elders should be instructed to counsel them in kindness to have an Elder perform the ceremony so that there may be no cloud on their union; the advantages of doing this should be explained to them, but if they cannot understand the necessity for such a course, and are keeping the covenants they have already made, no farther [sic] action should be taken.[19]

These instructions were clear as far as they went, and seem remarkably free from prejudice or a paternalistic desire to impose "higher" laws on the Maori. But even Maori Saints who had taken part in western marriage ceremonies had no qualms about dissolving them at will according to tribal custom. The First Presidency's counsel was far too simple to cope with the realities of Maori "divorce" and the subsequent apparently casual entrance into new unions. Were those following this native custom also to be tolerated, or were they to be seen as not "keeping the covenants they [had] already made" and subjected to Church discipline?

A few months after receiving the First Presidency's reply, President Richards wrote again, describing the "peculiar case" of Brother [Y] and asking for counsel.[20] A very active and highly respected LDS rangatira, Brother [Y] had taken a second wife at the suggestion of his first wife, whose health apparently precluded her from bearing further children.[21]

---

18. In October 1897 (effective 1 January 1898), the First Presidency announced the division of the Australasian Mission into the Australian and New Zealand Missions.

19. George F. Reynolds for First Presidency, Letter dated Salt Lake City, 19 March 1897, received in New Zealand Mission office on 1 May 1897 but added to New Zealand Mission, Manuscript History under date of 8 April 1897.

20. Ezra F. Richards, Letter to Wilford Woodruff, dated Poverty Bay, 13 September 1897, copy in Ezra Foss Richards, Journal, 13 September 1897.

21. Ibid. In Maori culture, "barrenness was considered grounds for divorce or taking a second wife." The family of a woman who died or who proved to be barren felt obligated to offer the husband a younger kinswoman as a second wife. Metge,

Previous mission authorities had regarded this situation, not as Maori polygamy, but as adultery, and had excommunicated Brother [Y]. His first
wife took their children to Utah in 1894. "In as much as he has two women
and has a family by each—one being in Zion and the other here—and the
maoris not counseled to gather at present and he and his legal wife not
having been legally seperated [sic], what disposition would you suggest
my making of the case?" pleaded President Richards. He omitted the additional complication that the man had not been "legally" married to his
first wife either.

The First Presidency's reply was cautious. "Regarding Bro.[Y]'s case,
the brethern [sic] feel that great care will have to be used lest the suscep-
tibilities of the natives be hurt. Inasmuch as his wife is here, could he not
obtain a divorce from her on the ground of desertion; and if so would that
be the best and wisest course to pursue[?]"[22] President Richards approved.
"I have felt since first hearing of the [Y] case that the manner [you have]
suggested would be the most likely way out, and that the best results would
be reached," he replied, "and I think perhaps it can be brought about if outside relatives don't intercept it but there are many feeders to these Maori
matches it will have to be worked with great care."[23] President Richards's
diary does not describe the resolution of this complex story. We get another glimpse of the no doubt confused but still loyal Brother Y a few years
later when John E. Magleby, serving as New Zealand Mission president
from February 1900 to August 1902, recorded in his journal: "Thursday.
Aug 29/01 last night I took up a labor with Brother [Y] as to his being
baptized. . . . For some time he has been wanting to come [back] into the
church but [was] refused on the ground that he was not married but from
the fact that his former wife has left and again that he has never been
married to his first wife neither to this one with whom he is now living."
Magleby indicated that he also had written to the First Presidency about
this case. "No answer coming," he continued his journal entry, "we have
worked on our own jud[g]ment, thus he and his wife were both baptized."[24]

President Magleby had a genuine love for the Maori people and great
understanding of and sympathy with their culture. Two faithful women,
daughters of an outstanding Maori leader, had been excommunicated under a previous regime for leaving their husbands. Magleby rebaptised both.

The Maoris of New Zealand, 21–22, and "The Maori Family," 113. A barren woman
was often the one to suggest a second marriage. Biggs, *Maori Marriage*, 58, 73.

22. George Reynolds, Letter to Ezra F. Richards, 6 November 1897, copied into
Richards, Journal, 6 December 1897.

23. Richards, Letter to Woodruff, copy in Richards, Journal, 17 December 1897.

24. Magleby, Journal, 29 August 1901.

"We have determined not to ask them to consent to return [to their former husbands] . . . having no love for them," he wrote.[25] Nevertheless, President Magleby preached strong sermons on virtue, cleanliness, and chastity.[26]

However, such case-by-case decisions did not resolve the larger marriage problem. President Magleby tried to explain the complexities of Maori marriage customs to the First Presidency:

> First, a couple are married properly with general consent. . . . In a year or such . . . they divorce themselves, in Maori style, are given in marriage to another, remember without a divorce; which by the way is hard to get legally. Now in cases like this, where the law neither speaks for or against, could we in the eyes of the Church sustain the mode of living and retain them as members or would it be considered a case of adultery? We would not dare to remarry them as a Church nor can they be remarried by any Church or law without a divorce save the Maori tradition and . . . a [European] divorce is almost out of reach of most Maoris.
>
> Again, we as a Church make a union. Time proves it to be no union at all, only a mere form of ceremony as parties often separate. In other cases, parents interfere, being dissatisfied, thus causing a separation. Here is the question. Can we either by Church or Maori law dissolve the union and give them to another in marriage? Heretofore, such cases have been disfellowshipped and most cases cut off while their hearts are with the work. . . .
>
> These questions may seem simple but we have them to deal with frequently and I am not clear upon them hence the reason for making inquiries.[27]

By the end of 1903 there were 4,548 Maori Latter-day Saints,[28] and there were still no clear-cut guidelines for dealing with the large percentage of couples who were not legally married according to LDS beliefs. President Magleby's successor was Charles B. Bartlett (1902–5) from Vernal, Utah, who, like President Magleby, had served a prior mission in New Zealand in the 1880s. During President Bartlett's tenure, the Church's nominated representatives were officially authorised as marriage celebrants (1903), but this fact had little effect nor, apparently, did governmental attempts to regulate Maori marriages in order to simplify the work of the land courts.[29]

---

25. Ibid., 13 October 1900.

26. Gardner and Gardner, "Day Journal of John W. Gardner," 18 August 1901, 15.

27. John E. Magleby, Letter to George F. Reynolds, New Zealand Mission, Minutes, 16 April 1900.

28. Charles B. Bartlett, "The New Zealand Mission," *Millennial Star* 66, no. 32 (11 August 1904): 499. Bartlett gave the total mission membership "at the time of writing" as 4,823 "of whom 275 are Europeans," giving a total Maori membership of 4,548.

29. Formal marriages made it easier for the Native Land Court (established

Without firm guidance from Salt Lake City, individual mission presidents in New Zealand reacted to Maori marriage customs according to their own perceptions of Maori morality. During the three-year presidency of Rufus K. Hardy (1907–9), only one Maori was excommunicated for adultery, while President Hardy's successors (George Bowles, Orson D. Romney, and William Gardner), excommunicated a total of 220 Maori Saints for sexual sin, usually adultery—an average of thirty-six each year between 1909 and 1915. From 1916 to 1921, under James N. Lambert and Fred W. Schwendiman, only fifteen of ninety-two excommunications (an average of 2.5 per year) were for adultery or other sexual transgressions; the most common reason given for the remaining seventy-seven was apostasy, usually manifested by joining another church.[30]

As these figures show, some mission presidents developed a resigned and reluctant acceptance of the realities of Maori marriages. President James N. Lambert (1916–20) recorded having a long talk with an active Latter-day Saint who had left his first wife and was living with another woman. "The truth of the matter is," President Lambert recorded in his diary in 1917, "when he was married first, his marriage was a Maori one which was [by] consent of all parties concerned. While this is binding to the extent that all children born are his heirs, he can marry according to the law of the land another woman and she will be his legal wife. Brother [C] knows this. He don't [sic] want to repudiate his first wife and the one whom the Church recognizes for after all the marriage ceremony of the Maoris is just as binding in the sight of the Almighty as that of the white man's."[31] President George S. Taylor (1920–23) also took the situation somewhat for granted. "Brother [D] and his wife . . . have been living

---

1865) to determine inheritance rights and legal ownership of land, an extremely complicated problem in New Zealand where most tribal land was jointly owned. The Native Land Court converted Maori communal and customary ownership to title derived from the Crown. Paper title deeds were easily negotiable; this made it easier for British settlers to obtain, by purchase or lease, such land as the Maori retained after widespread land confiscation following their defeat in the Wars of the 1860s. Seduced by the easy money obtainable by selling land to Pakeha, many Maori sought to have their claims to land validated; unless their claim had been cleared by the Land Court, they could neither sell nor lease. The peripatetic land court hearings became occasions for large tribal gatherings often accompanied by feasting and drunkenness. The Mormon missionaries (like ministers of other denominations) not infrequently took advantage of land court sittings to preach to large assemblies of potential converts.

30. Annual Statistical Reports for the New Zealand Mission, 1907–1921, Form EE.
31. James Needham Lambert, Journal, 15 January 1917, 156.

together for 5 months, Maori fashion," he wrote, "and were desirous of being married legally, Saturday they secured a lisence [sic] and this afternoon I performed the Marriage Ceremony."[32]

Although not all couples co-operated so willingly with Church teachings, many did. Elder Julian R. Stephens and his companion were instructed by the mission office in 1925 to survey all the families in their district, ascertain their marital status "and marry, baptize, bless as necessary." Stephens reported performing several weddings where grandchildren were present at the ceremony.[33]

The opening of the Hawaii Temple in 1919 caused further problems for the Mormon mission presidents. Quite a few Maori couples desired to visit the temple and had the means to do so. President John E. Magleby, during his third mission to New Zealand and his second term as mission president (1928–32), worked tirelessly on the organisational details and government red tape involved in sending groups of Maori Saints to Hawaii. But some problems were harder to resolve. "Wrote a letter to [Hawaii Mission and Temple] Prest Wm. M. Waddoups—with reference to Temple marriages, for our young people—whether they should carry a licence or can they get one in [Hawaii]," he recorded in his journal shortly before Christmas 1928. Concerned about established couples whose marriages had been arranged "Maori fashion" many years before, he asked if such couples could have their marriages sealed in the temple despite the lack of a formal marriage certificate. "The Marriage question in N.Z. is complicated," he told President Waddoups.[34]

President Waddoups's reply was uncompromising. Young people could get their licence in Honolulu and be married in the temple. People living with each other but not married by a civil or religious ceremony would not be allowed in the temple. President Magleby accepted this verdict reluctantly. "This [policy] rather works a hard ship on this mission—as there are so many who have been married and left each other and have chosen another pardner [sic] outside the marriage vow," he wrote.[35]

The previous November, President Magleby had written to Church President Heber J. Grant asking "whether or not we may baptize one man who has been and one who now is living in plural marriage."[36] President Grant's reply was also unequivocal. "No man living with more than one

---

32. George Shepard Taylor, Private Journal, 16 May 1921, 149.

33. Julian Rackham Stephens, "My Life's History or a Reasonable Facsimile of It," 22.

34. Magleby, Journal, 6 December 1928, 117.

35. Ibid., 26 February 1929.

36. Ibid., 2 November 1928.

wife can be baptized into the Church. But those who have heretofore lived so and will now discontinue doing so and will live with none but their legal wives [legal, presumably, according to European law] would be fit subjects for baptism." However, President Grant added, "if the man [living in plural marriage] has proven himself worthy during his life he can have his work done in the Temple after he has passed away, and his wives can also be sealed to him & his children."[37]

By World War II, little had changed. Although both churches and government now expected Maori couples to formalise their marriages, either by religious or civil rites, a significant number of unions remained informal. Few Maori, LDS or not, bothered with formal divorce, which was both difficult to obtain and extremely costly,[38] before entering a new union. Census statistics show that legal divorce rates among Maori were considerably lower than among Pakeha couples in New Zealand; sociologists feel that these statistics were probably influenced as much by economic factors and by the fact that many Maori marriages were *de facto* in the first place (and therefore not subject to legal dissolution) as by casual Maori attitudes.[39] President Matthew Cowley (later an apostle) administered the mission virtually single-handed during the World War II years when the "Zion elders" were evacuated for the duration. He had neither time, manpower, nor inclination to insist that Maori members abandon their traditional ways and does not appear to have made any attempt to impose Church discipline on his native flock, now numbering some 8,000. His successor, President A. Reed Halversen (1945–48), found his time fully occupied reorganising the branches and reclaiming scattered members after six long years of war.

President Gordon Claridge Young (1948–51), like most of his predecessors a former New Zealand missionary, arrived in Auckland in 1948 with his wife and two youngest children. After becoming acquainted with current conditions in the mission, President Young embarked on a program of what he referred to as "cleaning house." Writing in May 1950 to David O. McKay, then a counsellor in the First Presidency, President

---

37. Heber J. Grant, Letter to Magleby in reply to Magleby's letter of 2 November 1928, copied in Magleby, Journal, 26 December 1928, 125.

38. Alan Holden, *Family Law and You*, 7. Legal divorces were financially beyond the reach of many Pakeha as well as most Maori; only thirty-three divorces were finalised in New Zealand in 1897. Amendments to the Divorce Act in 1920 made divorces more easily obtainable but no less expensive; there were still only 614 divorces in New Zealand in 1926 among a population of nearly 1.5 million. See Erik Olssen, "Towards a New Society," 280.

39. Roderick Phillips, *Divorce in New Zealand: A Social History*, 96.

Young confessed himself "disappointed" at the condition of the mission. "To find adultery rampant among our people to the extent of about 70% of our members made me feel the necessity of drastic action being taken," he wrote. Like most New Zealand mission presidents, President Young had previously served among the Maori and was almost as well acquainted as John E. Magleby and Matthew Cowley with their habits, beliefs, and customs. Unlike Magleby and Cowley, President Young did not recognise Maori cultural practices as having any legitimacy, and embarked on a series of warnings, threats, and ultimately Church court actions. "I could not feel that these people after some of them being the fifth Generation in the Church should be allowed the leeway of at any time leaving their wives and husbands and living with other men and women," he explained to President McKay, justifying what he himself referred to as his "crusade."[40]

In later years, President Young said he had "straightened out" some 168 couples, though, he said, only a small number were actually excommunicated. "I only had to do about three before they stopped," he stated.[41] He saw himself as something of a martyr because of his high standards. "I wasn't liked," he recalled twenty years later. "It would be very foolish to say that I was loved because I wasn't, I was disliked and in many cases hated because I cracked down on immorality."[42]

With hindsight, President Young claimed that his actions were a necessary preparation for the New Zealand Temple and ultimate stakehood. "To progress and have stakes and a temple there meant that these practices had to stop.... I just didn't let this adultery situation go on."[43] He treasured a few letters in which some leading Maori Saints acknowledged the necessity for his actions, one even asserting that President Young had done more for the New Zealand Mission than any other president, including the legendary Matthew Cowley.[44]

The New Zealand Temple was dedicated in 1958 during the presidency of Ariel S. Ballif (1955–58), brother-in-law of Apostle Marion G. Romney and a former principal of the Maori Agricultural College. Despite President Young's claims to have "cleaned house," President Ballif found many members still living in "Maori marriages." "I performed many marriages for Maori families who had been married Maori style for as long as twenty-five years," he said in an interview recorded in 1973.

---

40. Gordon Claridge Young, Letter to David O. McKay, dated Auckland, 12 May 1950.

41. Gordon Claridge Young, Oral History, 21.

42. Ibid., 20.

43. Ibid., 21.

44. Ibid., 52.

"The Government said they couldn't have their claims to their property validated unless they were legally married. So many of them had the marriage ceremonies performed." Apparently land court requirements finally accomplished what threats of excommunication had failed to do. Those who were recalcitrant were excommunicated. "We had to excommunicate quite a number of people . . . because they couldn't justifiably be permitted to remain on the Church records with the things that they were doing," President Ballif explained.[45]

Even in the 1990s, President Young and, to a much lesser extent, President Ballif were regarded with ambivalence by some Maori Saints. Fostered somewhat by his own statements, President Young's reputation for having prepared the mission for stakehood and a temple lived on simultaneously with deep pain at his disciplinary actions. Maori Latter-day Saints who had chosen to forsake or give less emphasis to their "Maoriness" fully accepted the necessity of Young's and Ballif's actions. Others, particularly since the nation-wide revitalisation of interest in Maori culture that burgeoned from the 1970s, struggled with mixed feelings as they attempted to reconcile Maori practice with gospel teachings. A few of these Saints looked back on the Young era with mixed feelings. While acknowledging, accepting, and living the gospel principles involved,[46] and even crediting President Young with preparing New Zealand for stakehood and a temple, they nevertheless deplored his harsh treatment of Maori marriage customs, including what they sometimes described as "serial polygamy." Implicit in their feelings—and occasionally articulated—was a quite accurate awareness that the *principle* of plural marriage, unlike its practice, has never been repudiated by the LDS Church.[47]

The observations of anthropologist Joan Metge still seem valid many decades after they were written: The Maori of New Zealand, she wrote, "accept legal registration, by authorized persons in the presence of witnesses, as

---

45. Ariel S. Ballif, Oral History, interviewed by R. Lanier Britsch, 1973, 38-39, 47. President Ballif did not completely resolve the problem either. Five years after his term as mission president ended, a Pakeha (European) couple was assigned to work with unmarried Maori couples; where necessary, they even helped them raise money for divorce proceedings in order to make legal marriage possible. Quarterly Historical Report of the New Zealand Mission, 31 March 1963.

46. For example, William Roberts reported that, in his ten years as president of the Auckland Stake (1960–70), he was never called on to complete the dissolution of a temple marriage for either Maori or non-Maori Latter-day Saints. William Roberts, Oral History, 43.

47. Maori LDS high priest (name withheld) interviewed by Marjorie Newton, 13 October 1993; notes in my possession.

the normal and proper way to establish a marriage. At the same time, they neither condemn nor ostracize couples who are not legally married. . . . Maoris argue that if Pakehas had not introduced registration, de facto unions would be valid by Maori standards."[48] Metge noted that the term "Maori marriage" was reserved in New Zealand law for de facto unions "established by mutual consent between persons not already married." By 1976, when Metge was writing, such marriages were valid only for purposes of succession and if contracted before 1952. She pointed out that, in everyday usage, Maori themselves apply the term "Maori marriage" to unions involving at least one partner who is legally married to someone else.

While the great majority of New Zealand Maori Latter-day Saints conformed to Church and government requirements by at least the 1970s, LDS indigenous members in the Cook Islands District of the New Zealand Mission experienced a similar "house-cleaning" in 1989. "There are many members of the Church who have been living in a de facto relationship which is nothing more than cohabitation," wrote mission president Herschel N. Pedersen (1987–90). "They have been living this way for many, many years. The Cook Islands Government does not recognize it as a marriage, in my own mind I consider it as immorality. Therefore we have proceeded to hold courts." Feeling that it was his responsibility to "cleanse the inner vessel first," President Pedersen proceeded to hold 113 disciplinary courts during 1988–89, some couples proceeding through the stages of probation and disfellowshipment to excommunication.[49] "Most came back to the Church," he reported.[50] But at least some Cook Islands Latter-day Saints have a different perception. "We were shocked," said a Rarotongan member who served a mission in Australia and later returned to Australia to live. "Some of my friends were excommunicated for adultery when President Pedersen was there. But they were married our way. Our Government *does* recognise our marriages," she insisted. "We were shocked," she repeated. "My friends don't come to Church any more."[51]

For more than one hundred years, then, the marriage question among the Maori people of the New Zealand Mission perturbed, puzzled, and

48. Metge, *The Maoris of New Zealand*, 139.

49. New Zealand Auckland Mission, Annual Reports for 1988 and 1989 in New Zealand Mission, Manuscript History and Historical Reports. Probation is more or less a suspended sentence; the next step in Mormon discipline is disfellowshipment, which stops short of formal excommunication but temporarily debars offenders from taking the sacrament and silences them in Church meetings.

50. Ibid.

51. Cook Islands Maori Latter-day Saint interviewed by Marjorie Newton, 5 December 1993, name withheld; notes in my possession.

worried successive LDS mission presidents. After World War II, Church leaders took an increasingly firm line with traditional Maori marriage forms, and by the 1990s strict obedience to Church standards was required of Maori Saints.

The reconciliation of deeply ingrained cultural *mores* with LDS teachings is never easy for Mormon leaders to achieve among their converts; neither is it a simple matter for converts of any background to relinquish their traditional ways where these conflict with what Church leaders teach are universal gospel laws. The marriage question is a difficult one. Few Latter-day Saints would argue that there should be special exemptions or different laws for particular ethnic groups, but perhaps the transition among the Maori could have been made more sympathetically. For example, long-standing Maori marriages might have been accepted for live temple endowments and sealings when the Hawaii Temple opened in 1919, at least until 1952, the date from which the Maori Land Court ceased recognising new Maori customary marriages.[52]

Mormonism and Maori Funeral Customs

While doctrinal problems with Maori marriage customs began to surface within a decade of large-scale Maori conversion to Mormonism, it was not until the 1950s that there was any concerted attempt by Mormon leaders to wean Maori Latter-day Saints from their traditional tangihanga (funeral and mourning customs). The early missionaries soon began to graft elements of American Mormon funerals onto Maori practice, which had already incorporated much of the Christian burial service.[53]

Early Mormon missionaries seldom failed to describe a tangihanga in their journals or in their letters home, usually showing little awareness of the cultural significance involved. "Took a walk . . . and on our way back we stopped at a grave of a Maori," wrote Elder Nelson S. Bishop in November 1886. "There was a house built over the grave and fence around it with geraniums planted all around which made it look quite nice but on looking in we saw a second-hand store. They had everything that he owned in the clothes line there even to his bed. . . . There was some half dozen shirts, two or three pairs of britches, shoes etc."[54] Two years later, Elder Bishop still had little understanding that these items were tapu (sacred, under cer-

52. Alan Ward, "Law and Law Enforcement on the New Zealand Frontier, 1840–1893," 133 note 20.

53. Harry Dansey, "A View of Death," 106; James Irwin, *An Introduction to Maori Religion: Its Character before European Contact and Its Survival in Contemporary Maori and New Zealand Culture,* 58.

54. Bishop, Diary, 21 November 1886, 27.

emonial religious restriction). "We went to a funeral and dedicated the grave," he wrote, adding that the body was lowered and then, "according to custom," his clothes were buried with him. "I would have been pleased to have changed shoes with him," he commented. "The Maoris said they would rather go naked before they would wear anything belonging to one who was dead and they could not bare [sic] to see others wearing their clothes or even have them around."[55]

Even such a friend of the Maori as President John E. Magleby had little comprehension of tapu. After dedicating the grave at a funeral conducted by a Protestant minister at Dannevirke in 1928, he recorded with some degree of satisfaction, "I also hindered them from throwing his old clothes on the coffin."[56] To thrifty American Mormons, raised from pioneer stock whose philosophy was expressed in their often-quoted adage "Use it up, wear it out, make it do, or do without," the idea that the belongings of the deceased were tapu appeared a luxury that Maori, especially those living in relative poverty, could ill afford. The spiritual dimensions of the Maori custom do not appear to have touched the American observers at all.

In 1883, Elders Alma Greenwood and Ira N. Hinckley conducted a short Mormon funeral service for the small grandchild of their two rangatira converts, Ihaia and Manihera. Greenwood then dedicated a little grave on Ihaia's land, as Masterton cemetery authorities refused permission to bury the child because it had been blessed by the Mormon missionaries instead of receiving baptism at the hands of the local Church of England minister, the Rev. W. E. Paige. "The proceedings apparently pleased the natives," reported Elder Greenwood. "It was a great change from the manner in which some of the Maori burials were conducted as they sometimes would purchase a large quantity of grog and all hands got jolly and drunk."[57]

As well as barriers to Mormon funerals, whether Maori or Pakeha, caused by prejudice and doctrinal disagreements with other churches, legal requirements also prevented early Mormon missionaries from conducting funerals for members of their flock. When Paora Hoperi died at Huntly in 1905, the American elders reported to the mission president that the Church of England minister had to conduct the funeral service and certify the burial so a death certificate could be issued. Without this certificate, the family could not claim Hoperi's insurance policy.[58] However, few min-

---

55. Ibid., 18 February 1889, 439.
56. Magleby, Journal, 26 June 1928, 53.
57. Alma Greenwood, Diary and Scrapbook, 1882-88, 29, 30, 31 July 1883, 164–65.
58. W. D. Walton, Letter to L. G. Hoagland, dated Huntly, 3 September 1905.

isters objected to the Mormon custom of dedicating graves, and this soon became the main Mormon input into Maori funerary customs.

A tangihanga often lasted a full week and involved much more than a funeral service and burial. The same basic protocols were followed among different tribes, although some procedural differences could occur even between different marae of the same tribe.[59] The body of the deceased lay in state in an open casket on the marae. Once photography was introduced into New Zealand, it became customary to display photographs of the deceased and other departed family members. The chief mourners were women whose hair was wreathed in greenery and who sat beside the coffin, greeting the arrival of each party of manuhiri (guests, visitors) with formal wailing. Speeches were made to the deceased and to surviving relatives, then, to remove tapu, the visitors were fed before they were free to join prior arrivals and greet subsequent arrivals.[60]

On the third or fourth day, the corpse was buried, along with his or her clothing and personal possessions. After burial, specific rites were conducted in the deceased's home to remove tapu, and an elaborate haakari (funeral feast) took place. Another ceremony was held when the memorial gravestone was unveiled a year later, a ceremony that had replaced the pre-European contact custom of exhumation and reburial.[61] Another pre-European mourning custom, face-laceration, was seldom practised by the time the Mormons began proselytising among the Maori.

Sometimes the work involved in preparing the haakari prevented observance of LDS religious duties. "This morning there was three men to prayer but no women," wrote Elder Bishop after a death in one village in 1888. "The women is [sic] too busy cooking . . . to come to karakia." Bishop was not happy about this, and reprimanded both men and women.[62] President Magleby was annoyed when he had to postpone a conference at Muriwai in 1901 because the entire congregation went away to a tangi.[63] Half a century later, according to Elder Robert L. Simpson, the proclivity of paid Maori workmen to walk off the job to attend tangi was one of the

---

59. Cleve Barlow, *Tikanga Whakaaro: Key Concepts in Māori Culture*, 122.

60. Food is noa (ordinary, commonplace) and contact with food nullifies the tapu of death as well as any tapu inadvertently brought on to the marae by the manuhiri.

61. For a fuller discussion of both pre- and post-European Maori death customs, see Barlow, *Tikanga Whakaaro*, 14, 16, 120; Metge, *The Maoris of New Zealand*, 27–28, 261–64; Irwin, *An Introduction to Maori Religion*, 49–59.

62. Bishop, Diary, 16 August 1888, 352.

63. Magleby, Journal, 31 August 1901.

factors leading to the establishment of the volunteer "labour missionary" chapel construction program in New Zealand.[64]

Financial burdens of the tangihanga also worried the missionaries. "What I hate worst about it is they will eat our good Saints here out of house and home," Elder John W. Gardner commented in 1902 when writing about an extended tangihanga at Hiona.[65] Many years later, mission president Ariel S. Ballif experienced similar concerns about the expense of the tangihanga.[66]

The missionaries soon became somewhat cynical about the presence of some mourners at local tangi, especially if the deceased was a noted rangatira. "Of course all that comes expects to receive of the good things of this life as far as kai [food] goes," noted Elder Nelson S. Bishop, "and there is a goodly number that travels around to these gatherings just for the kai and to hear the news."[67] Non-Mormon observers have made similar allegations, but there is little doubt that kinship means far more to Maori than to most Europeans. "The death of a relation, even one whom I know little, if at all, affects me deeply, just because of relationship," wrote Harry Dansey. "To many Maori, and certainly to me, it is enough that we were related, enough to give me reason to mourn. . . . My relation and I are part of the same tree, we share the same ancestry and the claims of that ancestry are very real."[68]

Most Mormon missionaries accepted that the tears shed at tangi were genuine. Elder Jonathan R. Bennett described the cries and observed the tears running down the cheeks of the mourners. "It is no[t] put on it comes right from the heart," he wrote.[69] On the other hand, in the 1950s, mission president Gordon C. Young referred disparagingly to the "crocodile tears" shed at Maori tangi.[70] Young wrote of his gratification that no tangi was held for Henry Davies, who died suddenly after visiting Salt Lake City; he was "doubly happy" that the decision not to hold a tangi was made when he himself was out of town and could not be blamed for this departure from tradition.[71]

---

64. Robert Leatham Simpson, Oral History, 24.

65. Gardner and Gardner, "Day Journal of John W. Gardner," 17 March 1902, 100.

66. Ballif, Oral History (Britsch, 1973), 49.

67. Bishop, Diary, 25 June 1887, 112.

68. Dansey, "A View of Death," 109.

69. Jonathan Royal Bennett, Journal, 19 August 1921, 109.

70. Gordon C. Young, Letter to Matthew Cowley, 6 February 1951.

71. Gordon C. Young, Journal, 1 February 1951. Young stated that Davies had used the term "crocodile tears" about Maori tangihanga to him before his death.

Ariel S. Ballif, speaking of his term as mission president in the late 1950s, made it clear that "the Church" frowned on the tangi at that period; but the reasons he gave were ethnocentric rather than doctrinal. "Even today in some areas they hold a tangi," he said in 1973:

> The Church tried to discourage it and we tried extra hard to discourage it while we were there. At the tangi they would place the dead person's body in an open coffin out in front of the whare—that is a big house or chapel—and then on the marae . . . [which] is always a green or open space around the meeting house. The people would come from all over the country and they would tangi. Cries would go on for days and you could hear them for miles. There were professional criers, too. Someone would always be crying and pressing noses with the members of the family of the deceased. The family sits beside the casket with a picture of the deceased and all the relatives and mourners pass by.

According to President Ballif, the Church discouraged the tangihanga for two reasons. In addition to the burden of expense for the bereaved family, he said, "the ritualistic part of it was no good. We believe in proper burial and proper ceremonies and then burying people and going to your home." He admitted that even Americans provided post-funeral refreshments for the immediate family and friends, "but there [in New Zealand] it was everybody."[72]

Mormons, of course, were not the only Europeans who failed to understand Maori attitudes to death and who consequently criticised the tangihanga.[73] But to Maori, Maori ways *are* the "proper" ways. Harry Dansey explained:

> The dead are to be cared for, cherished, mourned, spoken to, honoured in a way which others might consider to be over-emotional and over-demonstrative. . . . The Maori—and I am sure this still applies to most Maori—want to see their dead, to have them with them until that ultimate committal to the earth. . . . Very few Maori families have their dead taken from the hospital mortuary to the undertaker's chapel until the funeral, away from sight in a closed casket. The dead in most cases go home to a house or meeting house or tent on a marae where, round the open casket, surrounded by pictures of others who have died before, the family gathers to mourn and to greet those who come to mourn with them. . . . For me this is still my way of farewelling the dead and comforting the living. It is proper, satisfying, comforting, leaving me when all is over with no more tears to shed and fit to take up the business

72. Ballif, Oral History (Britsch, 1973), 48–49.
73. Dansey, "A View of Death," 110.

of life once again. In a strange way, I feel emotionally drained and at the same time emotionally refreshed.[74]

There was some correspondence between Maori and Mormon attitudes to death and the dead. Both believed that death is a separation of body and spirit. Like Latter-day Saints, Maori continued to prefer burial over cremation after the latter option became available in New Zealand. The physical body was committed to earth; Maori believed that the spirit journeyed to Cape Reinga and from thence to a nether region beneath the ocean,[75] while Mormons taught that the spirits of all human beings wait for judgement and resurrection in a spirit world, a place which is paradise for the righteous but a spirit prison for the wicked.[76] Both Mormons and Maori believed in multiple gods and in multiple "heavens." Io, the supreme god who dwells in the highest of twelve heavens,[77] was easily identified as a Maori version of the Mormon Elohim, with whom righteous Mormons aspire to dwell in the afterlife in the highest of three kingdoms of glory.[78] Maori preservation of whakapapa (oral recitation of ancestry) resonated well with the Mormon emphasis on collecting genealogical records and tracing one's family back as far as possible.

Because early Mormon missionaries stressed superficial similarities only (for example, there was no concept of divine judgement with concomitant postmortal rewards or punishment in pre-European-contact Maori cosmology),[79] it was not until Maori Saints began visiting Latter-day Saint temples in Hawaii and the United States that major doubts were voiced about the traditional tangi. The matter became of more acute concern to American Church leaders when the New Zealand Temple opened in 1958. Early in 1960, a meeting was held between the presidents of both North and South Missions (Robert L. Simpson and Alexander P. Anderson respectively), plus temple president Erick A. Rosenvall and Auckland Stake president George R. Biesinger, "to consider the proper instructions to give to the Maori Saints relative to their funerals, particularly those who have been to the Temple and are buried in their Temple clothes."[80] From today's perspective, it could be seen to have been somewhat insensitive that such

---

74. Ibid., 108.

75. Irwin, *An Introduction to Maori Religion*, 51.

76. Bruce R. McConkie, *Mormon Doctrine*, 761-62.

77. Irwin, *An Introduction to Maori Religion*, 34; Swain and Trompf, *The Religions of Oceania*, 126.

78. Doctrine and Covenants, Section 76; McConkie, *Mormon Doctrine*, 115–17, 224, 420.

79. Irwin, *An Introduction to Maori Religion*, 20.

80. New Zealand South Mission, Quarterly Historical Report, March 31, 1960.

a policy-making meeting should have been conducted by four American leaders, with no Maori participating. Their decisions were not recorded in any document accessible to researchers.

New Zealand-born Pakeha convert Douglas H. Strother and his Maori wife, Mihi, were leaders in the Dannevirke Branch in the late 1950s and early 1960s. "Everything in New Zealand [Mormonism] at that time was a combination of Maori customs and the gospel of Jesus Christ," Strother told historian R. Lanier Britsch in 1974. He recalled conducting a funeral for one Maori member, "a Temple man," who had stipulated that he did not want a tangi. "They speak to the dead and sort of send him off on his way. On this particular case I had to choose something that was half way between a temple funeral and a Maori funeral," said Strother. The compromise involved a family service in the chapel where the body was kept so there could be no liquor on the premises, but Maori friends were permitted to visit and speak at a separate meeting the night before the funeral.[81] According to Strother, there had been an earlier conflict between an American missionary appointed as district president and some local Maori when the American tried to insist that family and friends leave the graveside of another deceased member before the actual interment, a Utah custom wholly foreign to the Maori, for whom witnessing the interment is a vital part of the grieving process.[82]

Elder Robert L. Simpson, interviewed soon after his release as Area Supervisor of the LDS Church in the South Pacific, was quite specific in stating that the tangihanga was the main reason why the Church began to "wean" the Maori Saints from their traditions. "It became rather a touchy thing," said Elder Simpson. "It was the custom for visitors who came from great distances ... as they came on to the village square where the body was held in state to make actual physical contact with the body, pressing noses, for example . . . and fondl[ing] the body as they cry and weep and wail. Of course we just couldn't visualize this happening to someone dressed in their temple robes." Elder Simpson explained that the problem became acute after the widespread administration of the Mormon endowment ordinance from the opening of the New Zealand Temple in 1958.[83]

To prevent non-LDS relatives from the deceased's birthplace claiming a body dressed in temple clothing, New Zealand Church leaders had older members sign a statement requesting that their funeral arrangements should be handled by the Church of Jesus Christ of Latter-day Saints. "And in order

---

81. Douglas H. Strother, Oral History, 8.
82. Dansey, "A View of Death," 108, 112.
83. Simpson, Oral History, 27.

to overcome the fondling of the temple robes and contact with the body, we finally put clear plastic right over the coffin so that they could see but they couldn't touch," said Elder Simpson,[84] a concession from an earlier edict, bitterly opposed by Maori Saints, that the coffin lid was to be closed.[85]

This meant, of course, that hongi with the dead was effectively prohibited. Maori (and Mormon) anthropologist Cleve Barlow explains that the hongi is symbolic of shared breath, "symbol[ising] the action of the gods in breathing into humans the breath of life." A hongi between the living demonstrates the desire for unity, peace, and harmony. "The hongi signifies that life comes from the gods," writes Barlow. "[To hongi the deceased is] a token of life, that is to say, even though the body is consigned to Mother Earth, the spirit lives on and returns to the world of the gods."[86] As the hongi has such deep spiritual meaning to Maori, it is not surprising that prohibition of hongi with the dead led to some disquiet and disaffection among Maori Church members. Feelings ran high even among the expatriate Maori community in Sydney, Australia, where traditional Maori funerary customs were prohibited by local Church leaders. There are still a few Australian Latter-day Saints who remember the 1960s "hi-jacking" of a coffin containing a Maori corpse from the Mormon chapel in the Sydney suburb of Greenwich so that traditional rites could be observed elsewhere.[87]

The observations of anthropologist Erik Schwimmer agree with Elder Simpson's statement that the tangihanga was a significant source of Mormon/Maori cultural conflict. In his study of the Maori villages of the Whangaruru district on the eastern coast of New Zealand's Northland, he noted that the Maori inhabitants "always had two systems to choose from, perceived by them as being 'old-time' and 'Mormon.'" Contradictions arose, Schwimmer noted, "most notably in the conducting of funerals."[88] Major elements of the tangi were so institutionalised in Maori culture that, although most of the religious life of the Maori villages of Whangaruru followed the Mormon pattern, funeral customs were still distinctly Maori in the early 1960s.[89] On the other hand, Harry Dansey felt that, by 1975, although the Church of England, Methodist, and Roman Catholic churches allowed their Maori members to retain elements of Maori death customs, leading to sub-

84. Ibid., 28.

85. Erik G. Schwimmer, "The Cognitive Aspect of Culture Change," 163.

86. Barlow, *Tikanga Whakaaro*, 27–28.

87. LDS ecclesiastical leader in Sydney, Australia, interviewed by Marjorie Newton, June 1994; name withheld by request.

88. Erik G. Schwimmer, "Mormonism in a Maori Village: A Study in Social Change," 6–7.

89. Ibid., 96–97.

tle differences of praxis between Maori and Pakeha congregations of these churches, this was not so with the Mormons. "It is likely that a Maori member of the Church of Jesus Christ of the Latter Day Saints [sic] will have much the same attitude to death as a Mormon anywhere else," he wrote, "provided he is well schooled in the principles of his faith."[90]

Despite Dansey's observation and the efforts of LDS Church leaders (including some Maori leaders) to eradicate some funeral practices, elements of the traditional tangi, such as talking to the deceased, linger in some LDS Maori funerals today. Perhaps, as James Irwin observed, the "underlying beliefs of pre-European Maori religion are still present in the very warp and woof of contemporary Maori society."[91]

From the time the town of Temple View was built in the 1950s, Maori Saints wanted a marae there. For thirty years there was consistent lobbying and some agitation for a marae, particularly desired by the Maori Saints for funerals. As real estate values in Temple View escalated, fewer Maori could afford to live there (this in itself making some Maori Latter-day Saints feel marginalised),[92] but there were always some who kept petitioning Church leaders for a marae.

Successive Area Presidencies in the 1980s made it clear that the Church would not countenance a marae on Church land "in the shadow of the Temple" but that there would be no objection to a marae a little farther away. Accordingly, Maori leaders considered buying a site two miles south of the temple but could not raise the $2–$3 million required. Elder Glen L. Rudd, Area President from 1989–91, suggested a compromise; and accordingly, a large, commodious building on Church College land was refurbished as a kai house, the work paid for wholly out of the CCNZ budget. This meant that the building was totally Church-owned and under Church control.[93] The new facility, named Te Rau Aroha, was dedicated by a later Area President, Elder Rulon G. Craven, on 4 March 1994.

Both area authorities were adamant that the Church was not opposed to Maori culture. At the dedication of Te Rau Aroha, President Craven, like Sir James Carroll a generation earlier, specifically urged Maori to "cling onto" Maoritanga.[94] Despite popular application of the word "marae"

---

90. Dansey, "A View of Death," 106.

91. Irwin, *An Introduction to Maori Religion*, vii.

92. Maori LDS high priest interviewed by Marjorie Newton, 13 October 1993; name withheld; notes in my possession.

93. Former New Zealand priesthood leaders, conversation with Marjorie Newton, 13 June 1995; notes in my possession.

94. Quoted in Ian G. Barber and David Gilgen, "Between Covenant and Treaty: The LDS Future in New Zealand," 218.

to the new facility,[95] Church leaders insist that it is not a marae because there is no traditional carved house there, a carved meetinghouse being an essential feature of the traditional marae complex. In this regard, Te Rau Aroha is similar to some multi-tribal community facilities built in urban areas by other churches or with government aid.[96] However, many Maori Saints regard the nearby Beisinger Hall, built by labour missionaries in 1960 as a tribute to building supervisor George R. Beisinger, as satisfying the requirement for a meeting house, as it has Maori carvings decorating the entrance, thus qualifying the immediate area as a marae. Nevertheless, Church leaders prefer Te Rau Aroha to be called simply a "kai house."

Te Rau Aroha has been well used and has become a highly valued facility in the Temple View community, but the closing of the Church College of New Zealand in 2009 also affected the future of both the kai house and the George R. Biesinger Hall. Extensive discussions were held between Church authorities, local government officers, and community members about the future of the site and the various buildings on it. While some buildings have been and others will be demolished, both Te Rau Aroha and the George R. Biesinger Hall will be renovated and preserved.[97]

Directions from the Pacific Area Presidency (1992) restated official worldwide Church policy that bishops should preside over and keep control of funeral services. Some concession to Maoritanga was, however, made by the Area authorities: Maori may be spoken at funerals (though not, as a general rule, in other Church services); when a funeral is held on a marae, Maori protocol is to be respected; and if local ecclesiastical leaders do not understand such protocol, a Maori spokesman should be consulted; the casket may either remain open or closed during the viewing, depending on the wishes of the family.[98]

"The tangihanga or funeral ceremony is one of the few surviving institutions in Māori culture," writes Barlow. "There are many customs and traditions associated with the tangihanga, and many important concepts con-

---

95. For example, Barber and Gilgen repeatedly refer to the facility as a marae. Ibid., 218, 221.

96. Ranginui J. Walker, "Marae: A Place to Stand," 27-32; Robert Macdonald, *The Fifth Wind: New Zealand and the Legacy of a Turbulent Past*, 265.

97. See www.lds.org, Local Content, NewZealand/Pacific, Temple View for updated information.

98. Office of the Pacific Area Presidency (Douglas J. Martin, Robert E. Sackley, and Rulon G. Craven), Church of Jesus Christ of Latter-day Saints, To: Regional Representatives, Stake, Mission & District Presidents, Bishops and Branch Presidents in N.Z., Memorandum: Guidelines Re: Language and Cultural Values in New Zealand, 25 May 1992, photocopy in my possession.

cerning both the physical and metaphysical world are revealed here. Also, many of the profound philosophies and ideas concerning Māori cultural values and practices are talked about and performed on these occasions."[99] Dansey expressed similar views. "The tangihanga is the major Maori ceremonial occasion. Within its orbit is drawn virtually every phase of Maori custom and belief that exists today. Its strength is such that in spite of Pakeha opposition, criticism and derision for more than a century, it has survived and continues, with many adaptations and changes in form, with the same purpose and spirit as in the past."[100] Barber and Gilgen reiterate that "this interactive community ritual, and its associated hui [gatherings] are . . . central to the cultural identity and mana . . . of tangata whenua [people of the land]."[101] "Within the ritual of the *tangihanga* we retain the sanctity, the awe, and aura that identify us as Maori," wrote Matiu Te Hau.[102] As stated earlier, Schwimmer reported that Mormon leadership directions regarding tangihanga resulted in some bitterness in the 1960s; this bitterness still lingered in various Mormon/Maori communities in northern New Zealand until at least the turn of the twenty-first century.[103]

Ambivalent Attitudes to the Haka

While often described as a war dance, the posture dances known as haka are far more complex than this term implies and are an integral feature of Maori ceremonial gatherings such as welcomes to distinguished visitors and tangihanga.[104] Like tangihanga, haka had also been criticised by nineteenth-century Pakeha society, long before Mormon proselytising began among the Maori. One early commentator regarded it as "an *exposé* of the evil which really lies at the root of their present prostrate condition, an exhibition of . . . utter immorality, depravity, and obscenity."[105]

The early Mormon missionaries found haka somewhat bizarre and recorded their often negative impressions in their letters home and in their missionary journals. Elder John T. Smellie (1887-90), wrote that "the one who can come nearest to making his tongue touch his ear, his eyes jump from their sockets and shout the loudest is considered the leading man. . . .

---

99. Barlow, *Tikanga Whakaaro*, 122.

100. Dansey, "A View of Death," 110.

101. Barber and Gilgen, "Between Covenant and Treaty," 219.

102. Quoted in Thomas K. Fitzgerald, *Education and Identity: A Study of the New Zealand Maori Graduate*, Appendix 6: Maoritanga; Section B, Matiu Te Hau, 167.

103. Barber and Gilgen, "Between Covenant and Treaty," 219.

104. Metge, *The Maoris of New Zealand*, 251; Macdonald, *The Fifth Wind*, 99–105.

105. "The Great Native Meeting at Wairoa," *Wellington Independent*, 20 April 1867, 6.

They also cause their bodies to twist and take peculiar shapes evidently with the intention of frightening people away rather than bid them welcome."[106]

The haka was one of the main competitive events of the annual Hui Tau, and a number of American missionaries learned one version or another; these were occasionally performed at missionary reunions at home in the United States.[107] Not all American missionaries or their leaders were comfortable with haka, however; and some mission presidents tried, without success, to discourage the haka by prohibiting or limiting performances. Reasons for Mormon doubts about the propriety of the haka varied from simple culture shock to antagonism in the latter half of the twentieth century because participants removed their temple undergarments in order to wear the traditional piupiu for the performance.[108]

Despite his well-documented love for the Maori people and his almost limitless patience with most of their cultural customs, John E. Magleby disapproved of the haka, which, he wrote in his journal, was "a rude affair at the best [and] rather tending to vice and evil."[109] Magleby tried to limit its performance during his first term as mission president (1900–1902). Efforts by the mission presidents who succeeded him to have haka omitted from Church conferences were apparently successful for a time, as a report of the 1907 Hui Tau in the mission paper praised the Saints for the different competitions held as part of the conference, especially for "the absence of the offensive Maori haka."[110]

It soon reappeared by popular demand, and mission president Orson D. Romney felt it necessary to again prohibit the haka, this time from the 1913 Hui Tau at Korongata during which the MAC was dedicated. "This enangered [angered, enraged] the natives," wrote MAC principal John Johnson, "and some strong language was used on both sides. . . . It was finally decided that [haka] should be discouraged everywhere, and put entirely down at all conferences where the Saints are in charge."[111]

President Romney and his successors found it impossible to enforce the ban. "It is a pretty bad dance," commented Elder Jonathan R. Ben-

---

106. John T. Smellie, Letter to the Editor, dated Taunoke [sic], 15 April 1889, in *Deseret News*, 17 May 1889, copy pasted in New Zealand Mission, Manuscript History, under date of 6 April 1889.

107. See, for example, "New Zealand Missionaries Hold 'Hui Nui' in Hollywood: Elder Matthew Cowley Attends," 5.

108. There does not seem to have been any contemporary record of similar concern about missionaries or lay members removing their temple garments to play basketball.

109. Magleby, Journal, 18 June 1902.

110. "General [Mission] Conference," *Te Karere* 1, no. 6 (15 April 1907): 56.

111. John Johnson, Journal, 20-21 March, 5 April 1913.

nett after watching some children practise a haka some years later, "and is discouraged all the time but it is hard to get them to stop it."[112] Elder Bennett was in New Zealand when Apostle David O. McKay and his companion, Hugh J. Cannon, attended Hui Tau in the Waikato in 1921. The formal, ceremonial greeting (mihi) to the visitors featured both haka and poi dances. So pleased was President McKay by the poi dances that they were repeated next day at his request. Although less ecstatic about the haka, he found it exciting and neither voiced nor recorded any disapproval, though he jokingly wrote that he was somewhat apprehensive in case he should be expected to reciprocate in kind.[113]

In 1938, Elder George Albert Smith became the second Mormon apostle to visit New Zealand; and according to his travelling companion, Rufus K. Hardy, he enjoyed the welcome haka.[114] However, post-World War II mission president Gordon C. Young prohibited performance of the haka, not only by missionaries but also by all endowed members, thus increasing his unpopularity with the Maori Saints.[115]

In 1953, Rangi Davies, a Maori woman who had been endowed in the Cardston, Alberta, temple in 1950, hinted at doctrinal reasons necessitating total prohibition of the posture dance. She begged Sidney J. Ottley, Gordon C. Young's successor, not to relax President Young's ban on the haka. "[I] pointed out to him what we [presumably she and her now deceased husband] discovered at the temple," she reported in a letter to Young in Utah, "and if he was to undo all that President Young had straightened out it will be more or less abominable in the eyes of the Lord and added that Pres. Young was the only one who was game enough to prevent all that terrible thing (sic) to do for anyone who has entered the House of the Lord as well as being on a mission."[116] Nothing more explicit is recorded in their correspondence, and no other indications of any possible doctrinal reasons for disapproval of haka performances have been found.

A few years later, a haka was featured on the program presented to welcome President David O. McKay when he returned to New Zealand in 1958 to dedicate the newly completed temple and the Church College of New Zealand. Two years later, Apostle Spencer W. Kimball was also welcomed by a program which included both haka and poi dances when he visited New Zealand to organise the Hamilton and Hawkes Bay stakes.

112. Bennett, Journal, 21 September 1921.

113. David O. McKay, "Hui Tau," 770-71, 774.

114. Rufus K. Hardy, "With Church Leaders in New Zealand," *Deseret News*, 25 June 1938, in Journal History, 25 June 1938, 8.

115. Young, Journal, 27 March 1951.

116. Rangi Davies, Letter to Gordon C. Young, dated Auckland, 11 January 1953.

President Kimball was obviously delighted with the graceful, intricate poi dances of the women but, unlike President McKay, was displeased by the haka. He recommended that the Maori Saints should keep their "wild war dances" for an annual festival devoted to perpetuating their traditional culture but "substitute their peaceful, beautiful dances for more frequent use at Church entertainments."[117] Such ingenuous suggestions, of course, however well meant, completely overlooked the important role of the haka in Maori welcomes and other ceremonial occasions.

At present there does not seem to be any general prohibition of performances of haka by Maori Latter-day Saints, endowed or otherwise, although in the last few years, occasional (and unsuccessful) attempts by individual presiding officers to ban it from specific occasions have been noted.

Moko (Tattooing) and Tohunga Healing

Although the reactions of Mormon leaders to Maori marriage and funerary customs and to the ceremonial haka varied according to the understanding, inclinations, and perceptions of individual mission (and Church) presidents, two elements of Maori culture earned the united disapprobation of all Mormon missionaries and their leaders. These were the custom of face-tattooing in ancient patterns (moko), particularly for women, and the practice of and/or belief in tohunga healing. Mainstream Christian missionaries had condemned both practices since the 1820s.

There was a resurgence of tattooing during the Land Wars of the 1860s, but tattooing of Maori men had almost disappeared by the 1870s. Tattooing of Maori women's chins and lips continued for much longer[118] and was still practised in a small way in the 1950s, though seldom for traditional reasons. Usually thought to have been a representation of hereditary rank, in later years it was more a celebration of traditional arts and crafts, or an affirmation of Maoritanga. By 1970, fewer than one hundred traditionally tattooed women survived; these few older women were accorded great mana (prestige) and took prominent places in formal ceremonies.[119]

Less is recorded about Mormon missionary response to moko than to other customs, but surviving accounts make it clear that new tattoos were grounds for Church discipline. "There is some trouble here about one of

117. Edward L. Kimball and Andrew E. Kimball Jr., *Spencer W. Kimball: Twelfth President of the Church of Jesus Christ of Latter-day Saints*, 327.

118. Sir Peter Buck (Te Rangi Hiroa), *The Coming of the Maori*, 300; Michael King, *Moko: Maori Tattooing in the 20th Century*, [6].

119. King, *Moko: Maori Tattooing in the 20th Century* , [2, 24–25, 28]. King discusses in some depth the complex reasons for women taking the moko. See also his *Maori: A Photographic and Social History*, 18.

our young women tattooing her chin," wrote Elder Nelson S. Bishop from Awapuni in 1887. "Several wanted it. Brother Stevenson found it out and talked to some of them and they obeyed him [but] there was one self-willed woman that had her chin tattooed for all that was said." Her Maori branch president threatened to excommunicate her and was disappointed when Elder Bishop, as presiding elder, settled for a public confession of disobedience and a request for forgiveness.[120]

A few years later, Elder William Douglass reported having "two women up for tattooing." In this instance, the women were required to ask the congregation for forgiveness and were then rebaptised.[121] Another missionary, Elder Ray Gudmansen, wrote that he was "embarrassed" to find the "intelligent and beloved Relief Society president" of Nuhaka "wearing a newly-inflicted tattoo upon her mouth in spite of all that has been said and demonstrated by the Elders in the past." Several other women were about to visit the local tohunga for the same purpose, "feeling themselves licensed from her doing," wrote Elder Gudmansen. Gudmansen felt that the situation was "perilous" and lectured the women severely. The Relief Society president was repentant and sorrowful, especially when Elder Gudmansen stripped her of office, "for it almost appears that she deliberately did that, contemplating a gentle forgiveness thereafter," he continued, adding, with a note of genuine sympathy, "We cried together."[122] There seems to be little further mention of moko in Mormon records. Buck suggests that the practice died out more from lack of qualified tohunga practitioners than as a direct result of Christian prohibition,[123] though Michael King questions this explanation and suggests that the disappearance of practising tohunga-te-moko was "an effect rather than the cause of the decline."[124]

A much greater worry to Mormon leaders was the widespread popularity of Maori tohunga as healers. The early Mormon missionaries usually translated the word "tohunga" as "sorcerer" or "witch doctor," but one basic meaning of the term is simply "expert." In this sense, it was applied to skilled craftsmen as well as priests. The term originally had deep religious significance and usually combined the ideas of skill and expertise, especially in ritual and healing, with priestly, mediatorial function, though it often included an element of magic. By 1900, the ancient art was dying,

120. Bishop, Diary, 23 October 1887, 173.

121. William Douglass Jr., "Journal Notes of William Douglas Jr., while on a Mission to New Zealand," 19 July 1891.

122. Ray Gudmansen, Letter to Louis G. Hoagland, dated Nuhaka, 3 July 1906.

123. Buck, *The Coming of the Maori*, 300.

124. King, *Moko*, [28].

and many practising tohunga Maori, both male and female, were perceived as charlatans by both press and public.[125]

Like members of other Christian denominations, sick Mormon converts were actively discouraged from consulting tohunga Maori. Instead, Mormon converts were taught to request the LDS ordinance of administration.[126] This consists of elders anointing the patient with oil, laying their hands on the patient's head, and pronouncing a blessing that includes healing or at least amelioration of symptoms if it is God's will. Those Latter-day Saints who persisted in practising as tohunga Maori were excommunicated.[127]

The Mormon ordinance of administration was not quite a simple substitution of one method of faith-healing for another. Despite a fundamentalist strain that led some early Utah Mormons to avoid doctors and rely on folk remedies, there was no general suspicion of medical practitioners among Mormons such as some of them exhibited towards lawyers. A physician, Dr. Willard Richards, had been a member of the Church's First Presidency from 1847 to 1854, and Utah men and women travelled east to qualify in medical schools in the later decades of the nineteenth century. There was no prohibition against Latter-day Saints consulting qualified doctors, though they were encouraged to exercise faith and seek healing blessings through the laying on of hands as well.

In New Zealand, sick missionaries consulted qualified physicians, surgeons, and dentists whenever necessary, as did their European and well-to-do Maori converts. Only one record has been found of a missionary rebuking a Maori member for consulting a doctor. In 1887, Hawaiian elder John Kauleinamoku refused the ordinance of administration to Arapata Meha because Meha had already consulted a Western-trained doctor. When Arapata did not improve, Elder Kauleinamoku's companion, Nelson S. Bishop, gave him the desired blessing anyway.[128]

Few of the early Maori Saints lived within reach of, or could afford to pay, European doctors,[129] so sick Maori Mormons could choose only between visiting the local tohunga Maori or asking the Mormon elders for

---

125. Anthropologist Ian G. Barber is cautious about accepting this perception, which was fostered by the Pakeha establishment supported by Young Maori Party leaders. Barber suggests that, for political reasons, a few cases of abuse may have been blown out of proportion, perhaps giving an unduly negative picture. Ian G. Barber, email to Marjorie Newton, dated Wellington, 14 January 1998.

126. Franklin D. Richards, Letter to Ezra F. Richards, dated 28 February 1898, copied into Ezra F. Richards, Journal, 11 April 1898.

127. New Zealand Mission, Manuscript History, 8 August 1894.

128. Bishop, Diary, 11 April, 16 May 1887, 79, 95.

129. King, *Maori*, 75.

a blessing. While the Mormon ordinance may not always have been efficacious, numerous healings credited to their administrations were recorded. At least anointing with consecrated oil and laying on hands while a blessing was pronounced could do no harm. The same could not always be said for the methods of the tohunga; fatalities resulting from their more drastic methods are well documented and prompted the New Zealand Government to pass the Tohunga Suppression Act in 1907.

The missionaries were both fascinated and repelled by the methods of the tohunga Maori. "We call to see a Saint who had become a tohunga Maori," wrote missionary Francis W. Kirkham in 1898. "She claims divine power to heal. All diseases, fever included, are treated alike. The patient must be immersed seven times in cold water. No wonder they die."[130] In the Mahia district in 1896, Elder James N. Lambert recorded that "the way of curing is very strange . . . . [T]hey cause the flesh to suffer something terrible. One way is to place them between hot rocks; another to place in boiling hot water; another to pull part of the hair out and still another to dip the person in cold water seven times." The following year, Elder Lambert found himself involved in a heated argument when he stated during a priesthood meeting that he thought it improper to use the Bible to try to heal someone. "Let me here explain that . . . they have been using the Bible ect. [sic] to cure the sick [by] . . . hitting a person, possessed by the devil, over the head with the Bible and all such stuff," he explained.[131] A Maori prophetess in the Bay of Islands in 1900 used milder methods. William B. Erekson described watching as her patients, whatever their symptoms, were bathed in the same tub of hot water. A tapu or holy stone was placed in the water to purify it, "which, no doubt, needed it badly after the first patient had been treated," wrote Elder Erekson. At the same time, the tohunga's attendants sang a chant to repel evil spirits.[132]

Mission president Ezra T. Stevenson (1898–1900) frequently preached against tohunga work and expected the Saints to forsake it. Apart from the sometimes-fatal results of the treatment meted out to patients by tohunga Maori, President Stevenson felt that Maori belief in tohunga smacked of idolatry.[133] "They seem like Israel of old," he lamented ironically to the

130. Francis W. Kirkham, Diaries, 14 March 1898, 6:47.
131. Lambert, Diaries, 18 June 1896, 3:92, and 7 August 1897, 5:123.
132. "Among the Maori—William B. Erekson to Editor, dated 5 June 1900," *Deseret Evening News*, 7 July 1900, 22.
133. Ezra T. Stevenson, Letter to President Wilford Woodruff, dated Auckland, 9 June 1898.

First Presidency, "to soon forget the blessings and mercies of the Lord, and we have deemed it wisdom to request a special fast among the Elders."[134]

The missionaries held their two-day fast at the beginning of October 1898, praying for the Lord's help. When, shortly afterwards, the New Zealand government began taking steps towards prohibiting certain practitioners and certain elements of tohunga practice, Stevenson was quietly confident that the Lord was working to overcome the problem.[135] A few years later, an Auckland paper reported that "the action of the Government in taking steps towards the suppression of the nefarious practices of the Maori tohungas has given great satisfaction to the [Mormon] elders, since they have always zealously exerted themselves in opposing those customs."[136]

With prompting from the group that became the Young Maori Party, the New Zealand government took action to improve the health and social conditions of the Maori people, in addition to trying to limit the worst excesses of the tohunga Maori. The Public Health and Maori Councils Act of 1900 divided New Zealand into nineteen Maori districts with elected councils. Native health officers were appointed with power to order the demolition of sub-standard housing and the installation of hygienic sanitary arrangements in Maori villages.[137] Charles Hardy, reporting the annual mission conference (Hui Tau) in 1902 in the *Auckland Weekly News*, stressed the complementary role of the eight mission Relief Societies, whose object was to provide for the sick and needy, and also to teach cleanliness and sanitation. "The elders realize that if they can elevate the women into a higher plane of civilized life, the children will profit in more than an equal degree, and thus the race will be advanced through that most powerful of social and religious levers, the mother," he wrote.[138]

Government laws and regulations were somewhat ineffectual; it was impossible to police every Maori village. On 12 August 1901, President Magleby noted that a leading Saint had gone to a tangi for two of his cousins who had died as a result of tohunga treatment. Though it was now a misdemeanour to prey upon the credulity of superstitious people, wrote Elder J. M. Hixson, "where there is a will there is a way, for they have succeeded quite well in evading the law by professing to have given up witch-

134. Ezra T. Stevenson, Letter to First Presidency, dated Nuhaka, 24 August 1898.

135. Ezra T. Stevenson, Letter to First Presidency (Presidents Lorenzo Snow, George Q. Cannon, and Joseph F. Smith), dated Auckland, 17 April 1899.

136. "The Mormon Mission in New Zealand," *Auckland Weekly News*, 24 April 1902.

137. Michael King, "Between Two Worlds," 287.

138. "The Mormon Mission in New Zealand."

craft entirely and resorted to mild remedies introduced by civilization. . . . But it is plain to see that . . . witchcraft is still being relied upon."[139]

When Tamaite Mate, a Latter-day Saint woman, engaged in tohunga work in the Poverty Bay District in 1902, a priesthood court was convened to decide whether to impose Church discipline on her. The court almost collapsed when her branch president, a key figure in the prosecution proceedings, confessed that he was associated with her work. It then became apparent that almost every member of both the Waiwhara and Muriwai LDS branches had been involved in one way or another. Tamaite Mate maintained that she had been instructed in healing by the spirit of a premature baby (a traditional belief). Branch members had set up a formal organisation with a committee to organise her work. Following extensive and sometimes heated discussion, the missionaries asked her to give up the supernatural elements of her work and to use only recognised herbal medicines. After much persuasion, she agreed; a new branch president was installed, and branch members begged each other's forgiveness for their involvement in the proscribed procedures.[140]

Problems with tohunga work continued to surface from time to time. Elder John W. Gardner found the people of one Maori village, "both Saints and sinners," gone "wild" over what he termed "that crazy Maori work of Satan" in 1903.[141] And in 1906, shortly before the passing of the Tohunga Suppression Act, a Maori tohunga named "Whisky Sal" recruited several leading LDS women in Te Hauke as acolytes or apprentices. The missionaries were scandalised to find the Relief Society president among them. "I gave her a month to repent and she took two," wrote Elder James King to Louis G. Hoagland, "and then came back. I asked her if she had repented and if she had done any more tohunga work during those two months. She said she would not say she had or had not . . . so we had to let it go. She is a very hard old case."[142]

The Tohunga Suppression Act (1907), introduced by Maori Members of Parliament James Carroll and Apirana Ngata "to eradicate what they saw as charlatanism in Maori folk medicine," is generally regarded as a "conspicuous failure," according to Michael King. "Few prosecutions were

139. Magleby, Journal, 12 August 1901; J. M. Hixson, "New Zealand—Superstition Still Prospers," Letter to the Editor, dated 10 March 1902, *Deseret News*, 10 April 1902 in Journal History, 10 March 1902, 5.

140. Charles B. Bartlett, Journal, 3 August–1 September 1902, 59–71, passim; New Zealand Mission, Minutes, 30–31 August 1902, 317–19.

141. Gardner and Gardner, "Day Journal of John W. Gardner," 10 October 1903, 286.

142. James King, Letter to Louis G. Hoagland, dated Te Hauke, 18 December 1906.

brought under it, victims could not or would not give evidence, [and] to-hunga practices continued in all Maori districts."[143] The act was eventually repealed in 1962. The resurgence of interest in Maori culture in the last decades of the twentieth century has been accompanied by a revival of the practice of Rongoā Māori (the traditional herbal healing methods of Maori), under the auspices of the Ministry of Health.

It is clear from Mormon records that little except the methods of some tohunga had changed by the late 1930s when Elder Robert L. Simpson (later to become the first Pacific Area president) served his first mission in New Zealand. "The Maori people felt comfortable about being Mormons while holding onto most of their Maori traditions," he commented forty years later. "The Church didn't really discourage them from carrying on in most of their traditions. The only real problem we had was a few people who believed in the Church, but when there were sick among them, they'd not only call in the Elders but think to themselves, 'Why not make sure that we've touched all the bases?' and they'd call on the old Maori tohunga to give them a blessing at the same time."[144]

Mormon Policymaking

This examination of leadership response to specific Maori cultural customs makes it clear that Church leaders in Salt Lake City were able to give New Zealand mission presidents few firm policy guidelines for accommodating Maori culture. To a very large extent, policy and praxis at any given time depended on the personality and prejudices of the in-cumbent mission president. Because these administrators changed every three years, discontinuity and inconsistency sometimes left local members confused, and institutional growth was, to some extent, hampered. Mission presidents themselves occasionally recognised this problem. Reporting an interview with a Maori priesthood leader in 1951, President Gordon C. Young wrote: "He thinks everything I have done is wrong and says the people have to change every time a new mission president comes out [from Utah]. He wonders if we are inspired when our policies differ. He may have something there."[145] It was inevitable that at times a considerable degree of misunderstanding should be manifested between Mormon missionar-ies and their Maori converts. What is remarkable is how relatively seldom such misunderstanding led to either defection by or the excommunication of Maori members, at least until the middle of the twentieth century.

---

143. King, *Maori*, 162.
144. Simpson, Oral History, 5.
145. Young, Journal, 13 February 1951.

The land rights movement of the late 1970s led to a resurgence of Maori culture and increased recognition of Maoritanga by both the New Zealand government and New Zealand society in general. This movement has coincided with the LDS Church's unprecedented international expansion. As the Church strives to socialise converts from widely differing cultures, its leaders encourage members throughout the world to prioritise those gospel principles that have universal application—faith in Christ, obedience to His teachings, and love of fellow humans—and to be willing to sacrifice some aspects of their native cultures in areas of conflict. These developments and their implications for Maori Latter-day Saints raise the question: how Maori may a Maori Mormon remain?

Chapter 5

Mormon and Maori?

Half a century ago, a scholar who examined the interaction of Mormonism with Maoritanga concluded that, in the nineteenth century, the relationship was one of acceptance and accommodation by the Mormon Church, followed by a gradual retreat until the post-World War II Church completely rejected all but the shell of Maori culture.[1] As a broad picture this is true; but a generation later, anthropologist Ian Barber more accurately suggested that Mormon Church policies towards Maori members have always oscillated between the poles of biculturalism and assimilation.[2]

While Barber's explanation of the relationship in terms of policy swings is valid, it should not be inferred from this description that the Mormon Church ever formulated explicit, official Church policies of either biculturalism or assimilation for its Maori converts. Within a very few firm guidelines from Church headquarters, individual Mormon mission presidents in New Zealand administered the mission according to their own perceptions of the compatibility of Maori culture and Mormon doctrine. As Barber has demonstrated, their decisions were not uninfluenced by socio-political trends in New Zealand.[3] But they were also swayed by their own personal preferences, perceptions, goals and biases. Instead of a gradual change from policies of biculturalism to assimilation, as Barker postulated, or even swings by decade or period, as Barber suggests, the history of the LDS Church in New Zealand shows constant fluctuations in its relationship with Maoritanga according to the outlook of the American mission presidents. Thus, while it is convenient to speak of "the Church" as either tolerating biculturalism or working

---

1. Ian R. Barker, "The Connexion: The Mormon Church and the Maori People."
2. Ian G. Barber, "Between Biculturalism and Assimilation: The Changing Place of Maori Culture in the Twentieth Century New Zealand Mormon Church," 142–69.
3. Ibid., 144.

towards assimilation, apart from the question of Maori "gathering," there *were* no Church policies—only decisions of the mission president or other priesthood leader in charge at any given time. Only to the extent that those affected by such decisions perceived them to have come from "the Church" can they be said to be Church policies.

In the 1880s, individual missionaries swung between extremes of pleased identification of some Maori customs as "Israelitish" and disapproving attribution of others to the degeneracy of these "Lamanites." But although the early missionaries consistently taught cleanliness, sobriety, and chastity as essential elements of Mormonism, the sanctions they applied to violators of Church standards were inconsistent, varying enormously from district to district and between one mission president's term and another's. Mission presidents occasionally sought First Presidency advice on problems such as Maori marriage customs (as discussed in the previous chapter), but the replies were seldom available to succeeding mission presidents and never became even unofficially "canonised" as mission policy.

For much of its history, the New Zealand LDS mission suffered from the effects of distance from Salt Lake City. General Authorities of the Church visited New Zealand only twice before World War II. Their guidance on problematical aspects of Maori culture was seldom informed by deeper research than the examples and questions supplied by the incumbent mission presidents, and their suggestions would likewise not qualify as official Church policy.

There was a clear Church policy in the nineteenth century applicable to Caucasian converts from Britain, Scandinavia, and other parts of Europe, and even Australia and New Zealand: After baptism, it was the duty of converts to gather to Zion in America as soon as possible. In practice, "by choosing to become Mormons they were also becoming Americans," literally adopting a new nationality along with a new religion as they uprooted themselves and removed to the United States.[4] As one scholar expressed it in the Church's *Ensign* magazine, gathering was "part and parcel of the conversion package."[5] The acquisition of Polynesian members, the LDS Church's first large-scale success in a non-Western society, of necessity caused some rethinking at Church headquarters of the doctrine of the gathering.

Early Polynesian Saints and the Gathering

Mormon success in the 1840s in French Polynesia began while the Church was still headquartered in Illinois and continued through the

---

4. Candadai Seshachari, "Other Voices, Other Mansions," 118.
5. Paul H. Peterson, "They Came by Handcart," 32.

Mormon exodus to the Mountainwest and the founding of Salt Lake City. Although Addison Pratt taught the principle of gathering, and many of his Polynesian converts were willing to emigrate from their island homes to the United States, the cost was prohibitive and no serious attempt was ever made. Despite the expense, Elder Pratt anticipated a future migration and wrote to Brigham Young recommending that he designate a gathering place for Pacific Islanders.[6] President Young, whose territorial claims for the potential State of Deseret stretched from Salt Lake City to the Pacific Coast, visualised a chain of Mormon settlements that would serve as way-stations for incoming immigrants and goods, as well as for missionaries departing for Asia and the Pacific. In 1853, he designated San Bernardino, California, as the gathering place for "Pacific Islanders, Asiatics and those ... accustomed to tropical climates," including American Saints from southern United States.[7]

The Mormon settlement of San Bernardino never became "Zion" for more than a handful of Polynesian Saints. Mormon missionaries were expelled from French Polynesia in 1852, when the infant settlement at San Bernardino was only months old. Six years later, in 1858, most of the Mormon settlers abandoned San Bernardino and returned to Utah to help defend it from the perceived threat of General Albert Sidney Johnston's Utah Expedition.[8]

As neither the French government nor the government of the independent kingdom of Hawaii would allow the permanent exodus of large groups of Polynesian people in any case, the LDS missionaries in Hawaii established a local gathering place on the island of Lanai. After an unsuccessful trial there,[9] Church funds were used to purchase a sugar plantation at Laie on the windward (northeastern) side of the Hawaiian island of Oahu in 1865. The plantation was intended to provide employment for gathering Polynesian Saints, and also produce cotton and sugar for the Mormon settlements in Utah.[10]

---

6. S. George Ellsworth and Kathleen C. Perrin, *Seasons of Faith and Courage: The Church of Jesus Christ of Latter-day Saints in French Polynesia: A Sesquicentennial History, 1843–1993*, 15.

7. General Epistle of the First Presidency (Brigham Young, Heber C. Kimball, and Willard Richards), 19 February 1853, cited in Edward Leo Lyman, *San Bernardino: The Rise and Fall of a California Community*, 89.

8. Lyman, *San Bernardino*, chap. 8. Lyman makes it clear that the possibility of conflict with the federal government was not the only reason the Mormons left their California outpost.

9. R. Lanier Britsch, *Moramona: The Mormons in Hawaii*, 35–49, 74.

10. Ibid., 75.

In the 1870s, Hawaiian emigration laws were relaxed. Devout Mormon converts deeply desirous of receiving their endowment and sealing ordinances began to migrate to Utah until, by the late 1880s, about seventy-five Hawaiian Saints were living in Salt Lake City. They remained unassimilated and were subjected to a degree of racial prejudice. They were economically unstable, being unqualified for anything but unskilled labouring work available only in summer, and were forced to rely on Church assistance during the winter. Returned missionaries concerned for their welfare prompted the First Presidency to purchase a ranch in Skull Valley, Tooele County, Utah, in 1889, and here the Polynesian colony of Iosepa ("Joseph," in honour of Joseph F. Smith) was founded.

The arid, isolated desert land could hardly have formed a greater contrast to the lush Hawaiian environment. Colonists had to cope with isolation, severe weather conditions, financial difficulties, and leprosy. The death rate was high.[11] Iosepa was a considerable drain on Church finances and did not become economically self-sufficient until 1907. When Church policies on gathering changed, and construction of a temple in Hawaii was announced in 1915, the First Presidency advised the Hawaiian Saints to return home and financially assisted those who wished to do so. Most returned.[12]

These experiments make it clear that no general policy of assimilation for non-Western indigenous converts was in place in the nineteenth-century LDS Church. Although the designation of Lanai, Laie, and Iosepa as Polynesian gathering places seems to indicate that the official policy was biculturalism, the location of Iosepa made a Polynesian way of life impossible; speaking Hawaiian in everyday life and in Church meetings was almost the only aspect of Hawaiian culture unchanged for the emigrants. Food, clothing, homes, education, and general lifestyle were of necessity American, yet Iosepa's isolation also made assimilation impossible. Lanai, Laie, and Iosepa were *ad hoc* responses to the problems of gathering converts from among indigenous peoples whose lifestyles were incompatible with those of the main body of the Church, rather than the result of a considered policy that promoted either assimilation, biculturalism, or any other possible outcome.

In Laie, although the Hawaiian converts remained in their home environment, the intention of the founding missionaries was never to foster Hawaiian culture, but to "elevate" the Hawaiian converts; to this extent, Laie can be regarded as an experiment in assimilation. Laie was established at a time when the Hawaiian population, like that of the Maori, was decreasing

---

11. Tracey E. Panek, "Life at Iosepa, Utah's Polynesian Colony," 65.
12. Ibid., 64–77; Britsch, *Moramona*, 122–35.

rapidly. It was a well-meant but paternalistic attempt at race regeneration, undertaken because of Mormon beliefs that the Polynesian people were lineal descendants of the house of Israel and that such regeneration and redemption were necessary to fulfil Book of Mormon prophecies.[13]

Thus, when the question of gathering Maori Saints to Utah was first referred to the First Presidency in the 1880s, the experiment at Lanai had failed and that at Iosepa had not yet begun; Laie was only partially successful in its spiritual purposes and was costing the Church considerable sums of money each year; and the Hawaiian Saints in Salt Lake City were, apparently, unsuccessful and unhappy.[14]

Maori Interest in Gathering

Within months of the first Maori baptisms in Taonoke, Elder Edward Newby reported that "the spirit of gathering is making itself manifest in H[awkes] B[ay] but as yet I do not say anything about it."[15] When Elder Henry F. McCune returned to Utah from New Zealand in January 1886, he reported that "the principle of gathering has never been preached to the Maories by the Elders but they seem to have imbibed it."[16] Two months later, Elder Ezra F. Richards told his father, Apostle Franklin D. Richards, that "the spirit of the gathering is working considerably upon some of the natives, more especially among the leading chiefs; . . . and the feeling that seems to be fast growing on them will, I think, cause a company of them to emigrate soon."[17]

The Twelve were apparently somewhat alarmed to hear this news. Apostle Richards replied by the next mail. "It is interesting to notice that the natives begin to incline to gather; but this should be conducted with great caution and prudence; for the condition of things here, during the present [anti-polygamy] crusade, are so different from their surroundings in their native lands, it would be a severe test of their faith." Instead, the apostle suggested, it might be wiser if a few "of the faithful and leading men" were to visit Utah for a few months, then return to New Zealand to testify of what they had seen and done. "[A] general gathering, in these times, would not be admissible, but might prove very disasterous [sic]," he

13. Britsch, *Moramona*, 74–75.

14. Ibid., 122–23; Panek, "Life at Iosepa," 65.

15. "More about the Maoris," *Deseret Evening News*, 13 December 1884, in Journal History, 13 December 1884, 3.

16. "A Mission to the Antipodes," *Deseret Evening News*, 10 February 1886, 14, in Utah Digital Newspapers, 10 February 1886 (accessed 27 December 2013).

17. "The New Zealand Mission," *Deseret Evening News*, 23 March 1886, in Journal History, 23 March 1886, 4.

warned.[18] At the March 1887 Hui Tau, mission president William Paxman
read to the missionaries a letter from the First Presidency in which they
counselled that the principle of tithing should be taught to the Maori, but
not the principle of gathering.[19]

The New Zealand missionaries believed that, sooner or later, the
Maori Saints would gather to Zion in America. Shortly before his release
in July 1889, President Paxman himself assured the Maori Saints of the
Hauraki District that he would "look forward with pleasure to the time
when you shall be gathered to the land of your forefathers."[20] The Saints
in Porirua, near Wellington, memorised scripture verses on several gospel topics including "the scattering and gathering of Israel," and included
these in their daily karakia (communal prayer and scripture recitations).
Many of them were "earnestly praying for the time to come when they can
gather to Zion," wrote Elder Benjamin F. Goddard in 1892.[21]

The missionaries continued to teach the doctrine of gathering, even if
they were not encouraging the Maori Saints to leave immediately. Once
the Maori translation of the Book of Mormon was published in 1889,
many of the Maori Saints came to regard the frequent prophecies contained in it that Israel would be gathered to the lands of their inheritance
from the four quarters of the earth and "the isles of the sea" as God's plan
to solve their land grievances.[22]

By 1893, the worldwide depression was hitting Utah hard. Unemploy-
ment among labourers in Salt Lake City was estimated by one source at
nearly 48 per cent[23] when Elder Goddard's mission president, William T.
Stewart, asked the First Presidency (Wilford Woodruff, George Q. Cannon, and Joseph F. Smith), for counsel on the matter of Maori gathering.
It was not a good economic climate for any new immigrants, and the First
Presidency began to encourage not only Maori Saints but converts from all

18. Franklin D. Richards to Ezra F. Richards, dated Salt Lake City, 8 April
1886, copied into Ezra F. Richards, Journal, 28 May 1886.

19. Richards, Journal, 12 March 1887.

20. Heber S. Cutler, "The Australasian Mission [report of conference at Kiri
Kiri, 6-7 July 1889]," *Deseret News Weekly*, 17 August 1889, 255.

21. Benjamin Goddard, 'Letter from New Zealand," dated Porirua, 11 July
1892, *Deseret Evening News*, 9 August 1892, 7.

22. Barber, "Between Biculturalism and Assimilation," 151. Barber lists some
two dozen explicit Book of Mormon promises that Israel would be gathered from
the isles of the sea.

23. Leonard J. Arrington, "Utah and the Depression of the 1890s," 6. Arrington
notes that the contemporary *Deseret News* doubted the accuracy of this figure but
agreed that it was "dangerously high."

countries, including those in Europe, to remain and build up the Church in their homelands. However, the Presidency wrote to Stewart, "After perusing your letter and learning therefrom their characteristics, their industry and their capability, for such work as is incidental to the opening of a new country, we have felt that a limited number of the best and most capable brethren and their families might, at the present time, be permitted to gather."[24]

The First Presidency specified that the chosen Maori Saints should travel to Utah with returning missionaries and settle in Kanab, the southern Utah hometown of William T. Stewart, whose term as mission president was drawing to a close. Before returning home, President Stewart chose a wealthy and highly respected rangatira, Hirini Whaanga, president of the Nuhaka Branch, and his third (monogamous) wife Mere. They sailed the following year and took with them Hirini's sister-in-law and two of her sons, and three other children, aged between ten and twelve, from their extended family. Described by Benjamin Goddard as "the first Maori Saints permitted to return to the ancient inheritance of their ancestors,"[25] they sailed in June 1894 and duly settled in Kanab. When Hirini Whaanga lost most of his assets as a result of bad advice from one of the ex-missionaries who took over management of his affairs, Zion's Maori Association (made up of former New Zealand missionaries) resettled them in Salt Lake City's Forest Dale Ward. Here they spent most of their time in the temple, performing temple work for their own ancestors and those of other Maori Saints in New Zealand.[26]

As a result of the struggles to establish Laie, the trials at Iosepa and the fate of the Whaanga family, the First Presidency vetoed further Maori gathering.[27] This did not stop Maori Saints from wanting to gather. "We are not preaching the gathering to the natives," Ezra F. Richards, now serv-

24. First Presidency (Wilford Woodruff, George Q. Cannon, and Joseph F. Smith), to Prest. W. T. Stewart, New Zealand, dated Salt Lake City, 14 October 1893, in William Thomas Stewart, Papers, 1878–93.

25. Phoenix [Benjamin Goddard], "Notes on the 'Hui Tau,'" *Deseret Evening News*, 19 May 1894, in Journal History, 17 April 1894, 11.

26. For a fuller account of the Whaanga family's emigration to Utah, see Marjorie Newton, *Tiki and Temple: The Mormon Mission in New Zealand, 1854*, 81–84, and Marjorie Newton, "Her Very Presence Is a Sermon: Mere Mete Whaanga."

27. New Zealand Mission, Minutes, 8 February 1897, 105. Another Maori family moved to Utah a few years after Hirini Whaanga died in 1905, but this was in the nature of a "mission call" to provide continuity in Maori temple work. General Maori immigration into Utah was still discouraged.

ing as mission president, assured the First Presidency in 1897. "In fact, 'tis with difficulty that we hold them down and keep them from emigrating."[28]

Four years later, some Maori Latter-day Saints were still speaking of gathering to Utah, and were actually beginning to organise their departure. Aware that Church leaders would not approve, John E. Magleby, now mission president, wrote to President Lorenzo Snow (who had succeeded Wilford Woodruff as Church president) proposing that a gathering place or colony should be set up in New Zealand for the Maori Saints, similar to that at Laie. He pointed out the advantages that such centralisation would bring to Church members and programs.[29] However, President Magleby was released before anything was done. His successor, Charles B. Bartlett (1902-5), agreed that the Maori Saints "should remain and sustain the hands of the Elders and assist in the redemption of their people" but did not favour the idea of a Mormon "colony" in New Zealand.[30] However, the next president, Louis G. Hoagland (1905-7), revived President Magleby's idea of establishing a Maori colony, though President Hoagland's favoured location was not New Zealand, but Mexico.[31] There was a Mormon colony at Colonia Juarez, Mexico, which provided a refuge for polygamous families from Utah.[32] President Hoagland possibly envisioned LDS Maori rangatira living there in traditional polygamous marriages, but this project was never seriously considered.

As the years passed, Maori gathering to Utah remained a constant ideal. Maori leaders Stuart Meha and Wiremu Duncan Sr. investigated social and economic conditions in Utah during their visit in 1913, and this was, in fact, one of their purposes in going. They became convinced that the First Presidency's advice was sound and that the Maori Saints should remain in their homeland. Not only would the Utah climate not suit most Maori, but there would also be no special government department in Utah regulating Maori affairs as there was in New Zealand. Meha, a well-edu-

28. Ezra F. Richards, Letter to President Wilford Woodruff, 18 January 1897, copied into Richards, Journal, 18 January 1897.

29. John E. Magleby, Letter to President Lorenzo Snow, 24 September 1901, copied into New Zealand Mission, Minutes, 204.

30. Charles B. Bartlett, Mission Journal, 14 September 1902, 93; Charles B. Bartlett, "The New Zealand Mission," *Millennial Star* 66, no. 32 (11 August 1904): 501.

31. New Zealand Mission, Manuscript History, 6 April 1906; W. Frank Atkin, 1906 notebook, in William Frank Atkin Papers, 1903-6. This notebook contains Atkins's notes of Hoagland's talks at Hui Tau, 1906.

32. B. Carmon Hardy, *Solemn Covenant: The Mormon Polygamous Passage*, 168.

cated man, realised that few of his people at that date had sufficient education to compete in the job market in Utah.[33]

A Renewed Proposal for a
Mormon "Colony" in New Zealand

The question of gathering did not die and was revived with new interest during the Great War (1914–18). By now, many of the Maori Saints wanted the Church to purchase land in New Zealand for a Maori colony, as had been done at Laie and Iosepa for Hawaiian Saints, and in American Samoa (Mapusaga, 1903) and Western Samoa (Sauniatu, 1904) for Samoan converts. However, mission president James N. Lambert and Maori leader Wiremu Duncan Sr. agreed that nothing could be done while wartime conditions pushed up the price of land. Landowners also faced financial loss as the government resumed large areas of farm acreage with the intention of subdividing it for soldier-settlement schemes after the war.[34]

With the advent of peace, the perennial question of a Maori "gathering" to Zion was again freely discussed both in Utah and New Zealand. During the November 1920 dinner at the Hotel Utah before David O. McKay and Hugh J. Cannon's departure on their world mission tour, the matter was vigorously debated by members of the New Zealand Missionary Society. "There is some beautiful country on the west coast of Mexico and central America," remarked former mission president Ezra T. Stevenson, "but it has been suggested this evening that the New Zealand Government is seriously opposed to any migration of its people, but some day, not yet...." In the meantime, Stevenson continued, the idea of a gathering place within New Zealand should be reconsidered.[35] However, the New Zealand government in the post-war years was trying to break up large estates; it already viewed the Mormon Church with suspicion and would not be likely to approve such a purchase for such a project. Even more important, Stevenson felt, was the fact that tribal rivalries were still a part of Maori life. "While the Gospel has done much to unite the hearts of the Maori yet are there old tribal competitions and jealousies . . . and while a general migration to some distant whare [home, habitation] might obliter-

33. "Impressions of Utah," *Dannevirke Evening News*, 12 November 1913, reprinted in *Te Karere* 7, no. 26 (17 December 1913): 309–11.

34. James Needham Lambert, Journal, 2 September 1916, 81.

35. New Zealand Missionary Society, "Book Prepared for David O. McKay and Hugh J. Cannon, 26 November 1920." The New Zealand Missionary Society was previously known as Zion's Maori Association.

ate all those thoughts and feelings, at least minimize them, could they be sufficiently overcome for harmony in their own land?"[36]

Stevenson's arguments prevailed. Although Elder McKay discussed the possibility of a Mormon colony in New Zealand with Dr. (later Sir) Maui Pomare, Minister for Native Affairs, during his visit to Wellington in 1921, and there was a desultory search for land after he left New Zealand,[37] no colony eventuated. A decade later, when Maori Saints raised the subject again, John E. Magleby, serving a second term as mission president, discouraged local colonisation by reminding them that New Zealand "was not their homeland and a return to America would some day be their privilege."[38]

The problematical issue of Maori gathering (or, more accurately, non-gathering) makes it clear that LDS Church leaders in Utah did not really know what to do with a large body of non-Western indigenous people who would not be likely to fit into the existing culture in Utah. The best they could do was to encourage the missionaries to socialise them until, in the words of Brigham Young to the elders in Hawaii many years earlier, they were taught "the arts of industry and those correct habits which are necessary for them to acquire to be the respected fellow-laborers of the white race in building up Zion."[39] That the same philosophy guided the New Zealand mission is clear from the approval John E. Magleby gave to early twentieth-century efforts by the New Zealand government to improve Maori living conditions and restrict the activities of tohunga Maori. The new laws and regulations would, President Magleby was sure, "have a tendency to fit [the Maori] to live the higher laws of civilization, thus rendering them more fit to migrate to the land of their nativity, where they can assist in the erecting of temples to God and build up . . . Zion on the American continent."[40]

Maori Rejection of Assimilation

Maori culture was irrevocably changed by European settlement. Not only were Maori relationships with Europeans often problematical, but the prevalent European culture inevitably also affected relationships between Maori themselves and between Maori and their traditional culture and

36. Ibid.

37. "David O. McKay, "Journal of World Mission Tour, 1921," 21 April 1921; New Zealand Mission, Manuscript History, 11 October, 1 November 1921.

38. John Ephraim Magleby, Journal, 14 February 1932, 197.

39. Brigham Young, Letter to George Nebeker, 16 July 1867, as cited in Britsch, *Moramona*, 78.

40. J[ohn] E. M[agleby] to the Elders of the Various Districts of the NZ Mission, in Magleby, Journal, 3 January 1901.

customs. Robert Joseph has summarised some of these often-overlooked consequences of the imbalance resulting from the introduction of Western culture into colonial New Zealand. "Land and natural resource loss through unjust wars, confiscations and other legal machinations wreaked havoc on the relationship between people and the natural environment. The forcible individualisation of land, property and world views in the Native Land Court disturbed the balance between members of kin groups . . . and the individualistic and economic assumptions underlying European capitalism and Western liberalism destroyed traditional tribal reciprocity economies, the equilibrium between kin, the physical and metaphysical world, the environment, and the fundamental reciprocal obligations to past, present and future generations."[41]

Most Maori, whether Latter-day Saints or not, either actively or passively rejected assimilation, which in late Victorian and Edwardian times simply reflected the prevailing philosophy of social Darwinism. Ian Barber has pointed out that the Kotahitanga (Maori parliament) was a direct evidence of resistance to assimilation, and two of its principal leaders were Mormons.[42] The Kotahitanga movement was tribally, or at least regionally, based; the Ratana movement of the 1920s was the first manifestation of a truly pan-tribal Maori movement.[43] Added to the ever-rankling consciousness of nineteenth-century land confiscation, the post-World War I generation of Maori smouldered with new grievances as Maori returned servicemen were excluded from participation in land settlement schemes. Maori also found themselves unable to collect old age pensions to which they were theoretically entitled, because civil registration of Maori births had not begun until 1913, making proof of age (and therefore eligibility) almost impossible for most of this generation.[44]

The Impact of Ratana on the LDS Church

The Christian revivalism of Maori prophet Tahupotiki Wiremu Ratana was originally intended to transcend denominational boundaries. However, he proceeded to organise a separate church in 1925 and went on to develop a dynamic political movement promising spiritual and political

41. Robert Joseph, "Intercultural Exchange, Matakite Māori and the Mormon Church," 43.

42. Barber, "Between Biculturalism and Assimilation," 145.

43. Michael King, "Between Two Worlds," 298; Pieter de Bres, *Religion in Atene: Religious Associations and the Urban Maori*, 20–21.

44. J. McLeod Henderson, *Ratana: The Man, the Church, the Political Movement*, 16. The New Zealand government accepted LDS branch records of blessings of infants as proof of age for age pensions.

redemption to Maori, based on Maori self-determination, a philosophy appealing to Maori in the grip of helpless poverty. By 1928, more than 2,000 Mormon converts had allied themselves with Ratana.[45] Barber suggests that many of these were attracted to Ratana or other Maori prophets because the Mormon missionaries had failed to fulfil their converts' expectations that the Mormons would help them "redress the grievances of God's covenant people preparatory to their final redemption."[46] Certainly the mass alignment of Maori Mormons (approximately 30 percent) with Ratana coincided with the final realisation by Maori Saints that, regardless of New Zealand government policies, Mormon Church leaders would never permit Maori Saints to gather *en masse* to Utah and that, far more relevant at the grass roots, Church leaders were not prepared to buy land and establish a Mormon Maori "colony" in New Zealand either.

Barber shows that the response of successive LDS mission presidents to the appeal of Ratana ranged from warnings about false prophets to utilising branch president Wiremu Duncan Sr. to liaise between the LDS and Ratana churches. Duncan had been ordained a high priest in 1920 by Church President Heber J. Grant during Duncan's second visit to Salt Lake City,[47] and accordingly had both Maori and Mormon mana. He was strongly attracted to the Ratana movement, and even, according to John E. Magleby, recruited Latter-day Saints for Ratana.[48] He was also offered, but declined, presidency of the Ratana Church, and assured the mission president of his loyalty to Mormonism.[49] However, when healing ordinances performed by Mormon elders failed to cure his cancer, Duncan removed to Ratana village and died there on 22 April 1928.

President Magleby's subsequent calling of faithful Maori brethren to serve as district presidents and their ordination to the office of high priest (a procedure begun on 2 September 1928, shortly after the death of Wiremu Duncan Sr.) was an attempt to counter the attraction of the Ratana church and keep his Maori flock "on-side" by giving LDS mana to more of their own leaders.[50] President Magleby, whose sympathetic understanding of Maori ways was seemingly inexhaustible, never excommunicated a

---

45. New Zealand Mission, Manuscript History, 31 December 1928.
46. Barber, "Between Biculturalism and Assimilation," 151.
47. New Zealand Mission, Manuscript History, 15 August 1920.
48. Magleby, Journal, 1928–29, 1.
49. New Zealand Mission, Manuscript History, 11 January 1927.
50. This innovation served a double purpose by freeing missionaries from these callings to concentrate on missionary work, as the Great Depression saw the number of American missionaries arriving in New Zealand fall drastically.

single Ratana defector,[51] even though joining another Church constituted evidence of apostasy and hence grounds for excommunication from the Mormon Church. Deciding that cooperation would do more good than confrontation, Magleby organised inter-faith visits to Ratana Pa and invited Ratana apostles to speak at Mormon hui. Most of the Mormon defaulters eventually returned.

Swing to Biculturalism

Nevertheless, Ratana success among Mormon congregations alerted subsequent mission presidents to the deep need of Maori to maintain their distinctive "Maoriness." Holding two 1930s Hui Tau at the model marae at Ngaruawahia, locus of the King movement, is seen by both Peter Lineham and Ian Barber as evidence of conciliation and a swing towards accommodating biculturalism in the Mormon Church in New Zealand. This is probably an accurate observation, but it was not an innovation: Hui Tau had previously been held at Ngaruawahia twice in the 1920s. On both occasions, Princess Te Puea te Hirangi and "her girls" were very involved in the program, presenting Maori culture items and speaking in conference sessions.[52]

By the time Rufus K. Hardy arrived to preside over the New Zealand Mission in 1934, none of the missionaries then serving spoke Maori. English was so widely spoken and so well understood by Maori that recent mission presidents had deemed it unnecessary for their missionaries to learn te reo. President Hardy was recalled to Utah to serve as a member of the First Council of Seventy after only fifteen months as mission president, but he returned to visit New Zealand as a General Authority of the Church when Matthew Cowley was installed as mission president in 1938. Both leaders vigorously encouraged missionaries to learn Maori and both urged Maori Saints to preserve and cherish both te reo and "the sacred ideals of their ancestors."[53]

The Role of Hui Tau

The role of the annual Hui Tau is somewhat ambiguous. Barber points out that these nationally renowned gatherings "facilitated a level of national unity and regular interaction among iwi as diverse as Ngati Koata/Ngati Kuia of the northern South Island, and Nga Puhi of the northern North Island. From such interaction, leaders among the Maori Saints encouraged

51. New Zealand Mission, Manuscript History, 31 December 1928.
52. New Zealand Mission, Manuscript History, April 1927; "Mormon Conference: Gathering at Ngaruawahia," *Auckland Star*, 9 April 1928.
53. New Zealand Mission, Manuscript History, 13 April 1938; Matthew Cowley, "The President's Page," *Te Karere* 40, no. 4 (February 1945): 33.

their people in the identification of iwi ritual and tradition with an Israel-ite legacy."[54] However, intertribal rivalries were very evident in the annual competitive Maori dance, drama, oratory, choir, and sporting events, and mission presidents sometimes recorded misgivings about this popular but divisive aspect of Hui Tau. It is interesting to observe that the two best-known and best-loved institutions of Mormonism in New Zealand in the first half of the twentieth century—the Maori Agricultural College and the annual Hui Tau—each represented an opposing philosophy: the MAC was unashamedly American, while the best-loved features of Hui Tau re-tained an almost totally Maori orientation.

Gospel Culture to Supersede National Cultures

The post-World War II efforts of Mormon mission president Gor-don C. Young and his successors to have Maori members forsake those tikanga (customs) that did not sit comfortably with American Mormon values have been outlined in Chapter 4. Once a temple was built and stakes were organised in New Zealand, beginning in 1958, it became increasingly clear that Maori Saints were expected to accept the principle that all na-tional cultures are intrinsically inferior to the gospel culture taught by the true church. In the event of conflict, Maori culture must go. "My theme to the people was always, 'Maori traditions are wonderful, and we honor the traditions of your fathers,'" said Elder Robert L. Simpson in 1978, "and it's okay to keep them alive until they conflict with the restored way of doing things. As soon as you find one of your traditions in conflict with the Res-toration, and the priesthood way of doing things, then there's only one way to go, and that's to honor your Church membership and the priesthood."[55]

Most Maori Mormons have conformed, probably with varying de-grees of complacency. Unfortunately, as has been shown, for several de-cades there was no clear definition of what Elder Simpson called "the priesthood way of doing things." There seems to have been little attempt in earlier years to distinguish between those aspects of Maoritanga that con-flicted with Mormon doctrine and those that disturbed American leaders simply because they differed from American customs that had come to be accepted as part of the practice of the institutional Church. With no clear policy of either assimilation or biculturalism to guide them, individual American leaders in New Zealand were left to do the best they could as

54. Barber, "Between Assimilation and Biculturalism," 156.
55. Robert Leatham Simpson, Oral History, 28. Elder Simpson served as New Zealand [North] Mission president (1958–61), Pacific Area Supervisor (1975–78), and Area President (1984–85).

they made crucial decisions about whether or how much to accommodate Maori culture.

Preservation of Cultural Symbols Encouraged

Although some deeply ingrained Maori funerary and marriage customs were prohibited, Maori cultural performances were not only permitted but were actively promoted. In the 1950s, an Auckland Branch (later stake) concert party performed on the wharf when every Matson liner on the trans-Pacific run was in port, and was an essential fund-raiser for the hugely expensive Auckland chapel.[56] "Each [LDS] district should have a Maori Culture Group," proclaimed a mission edict in 1957, and Maori culture classes became part of the curriculum at the new Church College of New Zealand.[57] Performances by the Maori Te Aroha Concert Party at the opening of the Church's Polynesian Cultural Centre in Hawaii, and the group's subsequent tour of western United States mainland venues, were applauded by Church leaders even though assimilationist policies were dominant at the time.

During post-World War II decades, the Maori drift from rural villages to the cities weakened tribal loyalties somewhat and fostered growth of a pan-tribal Maoritanga. Mormon Church leaders contributed to the process, coordinating meetings where pan-tribal Maori culture programs were worked out for General Authority welcomes and similar events. When the first performance of the now-annual temple pageant was planned, agreement on a script for a segment re-enacting the "Great Fleet" or canoe story was achieved only after long argument and negotiation.[58] The result was pleasing to tourists, American Church leaders, and missionaries but was less satisfactory to those Maori Saints committed to their own tribal legends. On the other hand, increasing interaction (including intermarriage) between members of different iwi (tribes) resident in New Zealand cities also helped blur tribal distinctions to some extent. According to one authority, by the 1970s a single popular version of the fleet story was becoming widely accepted in

---

56. The Matson liners *Mariposa* and *Monterey* called at Auckland during their regular Pacific crossings from San Francisco to Sydney, Australia.

57. "Maori Culture Group Potential . . . Do You Use It?" *Te Karere* 51, no. 5 (June 1957): 207; Church College of New Zealand, "Language Department Goals," in Goals and Objectives, rev. 1972.

58. Robert P. Manookin, interviewed by Marjorie Newton at Orem, Utah, 26 May 1992; notes in my possession. Traditional Maori lore tells of the first arrival of Maori in the islands of Aotearoa in a fleet of seven large waka (canoes) that landed at various points. Each major iwi (tribe) has its own "canoe story."

the larger society.[59] However, the resurgence of Maori identity in the follow-ing decades has undoubtedly affected the trend toward assimiliation in the larger society, if not within the Mormon Church.

Islander Immigration into New Zealand

Large-scale immigration of Pacific Islanders into New Zealand after World War II led to a deliberate New Zealand government policy of "in-tegration." With similar intentions, President Gordon C. Young disbanded the Auckland Rangitoto Branch, originally organised as a segregated Mao-ri branch, to which incoming Samoan, Tongan, and Cook Islands Latter-day Saints now gravitated.[60] A decade later, high councillor Kelly Harris was appointed "Chairman of Integration" in one Auckland Stake.[61] But by the 1970s, ethnic wards for Samoan- and Tongan-speaking congregations were functioning in both Auckland and Wellington, respectively New Zealand's largest city and its capital.[62] The Islander immigration to New Zealand inadvertently caused a reawakening of Maori self-identification in the LDS Church and some Maori Saints requested Maori-speaking wards. They were consistently refused, as by this date virtually all Maori Saints spoke English as their primary language.[63]

In yet another pendulum swing, and perhaps partly to defuse the de-mand for Maori wards, ethnic wards in Auckland and Wellington were disbanded in 1980–81. Their members were to be absorbed into English-speaking units. In March 1981, a rebel group organised an unauthorised Samoan ward in Westmere, part of the Auckland Harbour Stake. A simi-lar unofficial ward was organised in the Wellington suburb of Newtown. Hundreds of Samoan Latter-day Saints flocked to these alternative wards, presided over by tribal matai (family chiefs) rather than by Church-appointed bishops. Repeated counsel from stake and Pacific Area lead-ers failed to persuade these Samoan Saints to accept the Church ruling,

---

59. M. P. K. Sorrenson, *Maori Origins and Migrations: The Genesis of Some Pakeha Myths and Legends*, 85-86.

60. Gordon C. Young, Letter to First Presidency, 23 January 1951; "The Presi-dent's Page," *Te Karere* 45, no. 3 (March 1951): 76, 84.

61. "The Kauri Maori Culture Group," *The Challenger*, New Zealand Mission monthly bulletin, June 1961.

62. From the 1980s, Samoan and Tongan wards were also organised in Sydney, Melbourne, and Brisbane in Australia, as well as in California and Utah in the United States. Most Western Samoans who wished to emigrate moved to New Zealand or Australia, while American Samoans migrated to the United States.

63. Conversations with former New Zealand priesthood leaders and Maori Latter-day Saints, names withheld. Notes in my possession.

and some were excommunicated. Within a year, however, new guidelines for ethnic wards were received from Salt Lake City, and Samoan- and Tongan-language units were once again sanctioned in New Zealand.[64] To the continuing and smouldering grievance of some Maori Saints, not only were Maori-speaking wards still forbidden but even speaking Maori in any LDS Church meeting was disallowed. Barber and Gilgen highlight the irony of this situation: A Church whose proud boast had been the facility of its missionaries in te reo and its role in perpetuating Maori culture had now rejected the basis of its former success.[65]

Leadership statements and actions that wavered about the propriety of foreign-language units in English-speaking countries reinforce the present thesis that the LDS Church has never had a clear, consistent policy for non-English-speaking converts in English-speaking countries. So-called "ethnic" wards were no novelty in nineteenth- and early twentieth-century Utah, where Scandinavian, German, and Welsh congregations were permitted to conduct services in their own languages. They did not exist without controversy and were viewed with mixed feelings by many Church leaders.[66]

Ethnic units,[67] of course, represent a substitute "gathering." LDS historian Richard L. Jensen highlights the LDS Church dilemma with regard to "foreign" converts in the USA, a perfect example of the assimilation/biculturalism dichotomy. On the one hand, Jensen points out, Church leaders are confronted by a Doctrine and Covenants edict that "every man [and woman] shall hear the fulness of the gospel in his [or her] own tongue, and in his [or her] own language"; on the other, leaders ponder the Pauline exhortation that, in the kingdom of God, Church members should be "no more strangers and foreigners, but fellow citizens with the saints."[68] Nineteenth-century Mormon leaders generally regarded the former injunction as fulfilled when missionaries preached in languages spoken in their assigned mission fields. "Once transplanted or converted into American Mormondom, immigrants or converts generally have been encouraged to adapt to American Mormon

---

64. Auckland New Zealand Harbour Stake, Annual Historical Reports, 1981 and 1983; Ruby Welch, "Ethnicity amongst Auckland Mormons;" Barber and Gilgen, "Between Covenant and Treaty: The LDS Future in New Zealand," 215.

65. Ian G. Barber and David Gilgen, "Between Covenant and Treaty," 214.

66. Richard L. Jensen, "Mother Tongue: Use of Non-English Languages in the Church of Jesus Christ of Latter-day Saints in the United States, 1850-1983," 276. German-speaking units were dissolved during World War I and were not reinstituted afterward.

67. Ethnic units are now officially known in the LDS Church as "language-designated" wards or branches.

68. Doctrine and Covenants 90:11; Ephesians 2:19.

culture by learning the English language as quickly as possible," says Jensen. He points out that Apostle George A. Smith, speaking at a conference in 1867, ingenuously proposed that as God, "in His divine wisdom, revealed the gospel in the English language," it was up to non-English-speaking Latter-day Saints to take the hint and learn English.[69]

Nevertheless, it was recognised that many first-generation immigrants would never become fluent in English. It was also in the interests of Mormon missionary work in Europe to perpetuate the native languages of gathered European Saints, from whose numbers most foreign missionaries were drawn for some decades before accelerated language training classes were introduced for newly called missionaries. Thus, to some extent, foreign-language Church units in Utah were tolerated.

Echoing George A. Smith a century earlier, Church president Harold B. Lee in 1973 told European Latter-day Saints assembled in Munich for an area conference that, as the First Presidency and Quorum of the Twelve could not learn all the languages in which Mormonism was now preached, international Latter-day Saints should learn English. However, President Lee's successor, Spencer W. Kimball, took a diametrically opposed viewpoint. He believed that the Church should never force its foreign-language speaking members to learn English. "The Church is for the people and not the people for the Church," President Kimball insisted.[70]

Biculturalism—but Not for Maori

Area Presidency guidelines for ethnic wards in New Zealand in 1990 stipulated that immigrants should remain in them for limited periods, usually five years, and then transfer to an English-speaking ward.[71] These guidelines reflected the findings of non-LDS sociologist Hans Mol who examined the ethnic units of several denominations in California. Mol concluded that membership in an ethnic church congregation filled a valuable function in preventing personality disintegration and disorientation in new immigrants but that, in the long term, such ethnic churches hindered assimilation of the migrant congregation.[72] Such statements, of course, presupposed that assimilation was the desired end-purpose.

In practice, a majority of members of ethnic LDS wards in New Zealand refused to make the transition when language skills were acquired. Furthermore, many Samoan and Tongan Saints were not prepared to see

69. Jensen, "Mother Tongue," 275.

70. Ibid., 275, 288.

71. Auckland New Zealand Henderson Stake, 1990 Annual Historical Report.

72. Johannis J. [Hans] Mol, *Churches and Immigrants: A Sociological Study of the Mutual Effect of Religion and Immigrant Adjustment,* 11.

even their children and grandchildren—many, if not most, of whom had been born, raised, and educated in New Zealand and spoke English fluently—transfer to English-speaking wards or branches. Instead, according to Ruby Welch, many Islanders saw what were then known as ethnic wards as "a means of roping the [second-generation immigrants] back into the ethnic group under the control of traditional authority, i.e., the heads of families or matai. For the Samoans, therefore, the [ethnic] wards are here to stay."[73] Many leaders and members of the LDS Church in New Zealand, Australia, California, and even Utah have come to agree with Mol, who suggests that long-standing foreign-language churches tend to become patriotic societies whose main function is to perpetuate the homeland culture.[74]

Policy Set at Local Levels

Jensen sees "the ultimate goal of church leaders—total integration of minorities" receding in the late 1970s and early 1980s as the needs of ethnic congregations were considered. Highlighting the problem of discontinuity that has always existed in the Church's overseas missions, he notes that, even in America, "since most decisions concerning minorities were made at the local level, attitudes of individual bishops and stake presidents were a crucial factor."[75]

Maori, ironically, have not been a minority group in the New Zealand Mormon Church since 1884.[76] It is true, of course, that by the 1950s few Maori still spoke te reo as their primary language, but most Maori clung fiercely to its ceremonial usage. Its loss in everyday life seemed symbolic. "The Maori has finally realized that his identity as a Maori is in jeopardy," said one Maori activist in the 1970s. "His once sacred culture has been commercialized, the land of his ancestors has been taken from him and his native tongue has just about been torn out of his mouth. The Maori is quickly realising that very soon, unless severe measures are taken, his identity as a Maori will be as extinct as the Moa."[77]

---

73. Welch, "Ethnicity amongst Auckland Mormons," 5.

74. Mol, *Churches and Immigrants*, 15.

75. Jensen, "Mother Tongue," 295–96.

76. They are, however, a minority in the New Zealand population, which at the 2013 census totalled 4,242,048 of whom 14.9 percent identified themselves as Māori. Statistics New Zealand (2013), *2013 Census Quick Stats about Māori*, available from www.stats.govt.nz (accessed 3 December 2013).

77. Poata Eruera, of the Nga Tamatoa Council, quoted in Robert Macdonald, *The Fifth Wind: New Zealand and the Legacy of a Turbulent Past*, 208.

Most Maori who speak the language today do so because they have made conscious efforts to learn it, but this does not necessarily mean it has less intrinsic value for them. With government and community support, Maori language classes are offered at every educational level from preschool to university, and community adult education courses in the language and culture are widely available and well patronised. In 1987, by passing the Māori Language Act, the New Zealand Parliament enshrined Maori as an official language of New Zealand. With this legislation in place, it is difficult to see how Church leaders in New Zealand can prohibit the use of Maori in LDS meetings any more than those in Canada can prohibit French being spoken in Mormon meetings there.[78] Yet Barber and Gilgen reported Maori Saints being subjected to Church discipline for speaking Maori in a priesthood meeting in 1992.[79]

Some concessions to Maoritanga have been made by Area authorities. The Maori edition of the Book of Mormon was republished in 1989. From May 1992, the Maori language was permitted at funerals, though not, as a general rule, in other Church services except for brief mihi (greetings) or for testimony-bearing by elderly members.[80] Although regular temple sessions in Maori were scheduled when the Hamilton New Zealand Temple first opened, only from 1995 were temple sessions in Maori made available to expatriate Mormon Maori in Australia, despite the ease with which this could have been done from the opening of the Sydney Temple in 1984, and despite Samoan, Tongan, and Spanish sessions being scheduled from that date.[81] Highlighting the lack of consistent Church-wide (or even Area-wide) policies, regular temple sessions in Maori at the Hamilton New Zealand Temple were discontinued in 1997,[82] although they continue to be held in the Sydney Temple.[83]

---

78. Only the right to speak Maori in courts of law is formally legislated under the act.

79. Barber and Gilgen, "Between Covenant and Treaty," 215.

80. Office of the Pacific Area Presidency (Douglas J. Martin, Robert E. Sackley, and Rulon G. Craven), Church of Jesus Christ of Latter-day Saints, Memorandum to: Regional Representatives, Stake, Mission & District Presidents, Bishops and Branch Presidents in New Zealand, Guidelines Re: Language and Cultural Values in New Zealand, 25 May 1992, photocopy in my possession.

81. The temple ceremonies are presented by film. Tapes of the sound track in several languages are rotated according to the language scheduled for particular sessions.

82. Information supplied by an Auckland stake presidency counsellor, August 1997.

83. Temple schedule, Sydney Australia Temple, www.lds.org (accessed September 2013). As well as quarterly Maori sessions, the Sydney Temple schedules monthly sessions in Cantonese, Mandarin, and Spanish, plus four Samoan and

In 1996, Barber and Gilgen saw the language question as the aspect of Maoritanga most likely to cause conflict between Maori Saints and LDS Church leaders in the future and predicted that the LDS Church might be forced to choose the path of biculturalism in order to continue to function in an increasingly bicultural (or, as Islander immigration continues, multi-cultural) New Zealand society.[84] A large and continuing emigration of both Maori and Islander Saints to Australia has led to similar problems there.

Some Maori Saints felt that denial of optional Maori-speaking wards in both New Zealand and Australia was unjust in view of the proliferation of Samoan-speaking units in both countries. Many, if not most, first-gen-eration Western Samoan emigrants had received their elementary school-ing in both Samoan and English under the New Zealand school system that operated in Western Samoa from the 1920s; as well, many of these Sa-moan immigrants had attended one or another of the LDS schools there.[85] In addition, by the 1980s, numerous adult Samoan Latter-day Saints then attending ethnic wards in both New Zealand and Australia had actually been born in New Zealand to post-World War II Samoan immigrants; they were educated in New Zealand and spoke fluent, colloquial English with a New Zealand accent.

By the mid-1990s, it was becoming apparent to Church leaders in Utah that too few youth attending ethnic wards in America were progress-ing to missions and temple marriages (the orthodox rites of passage for Mormon youth). Consequently, in California, which had several Spanish-speaking stakes, a Tongan stake and numerous Samoan, Vietnamese, and other language-designated units, the Area Presidency in 1996 announced that 205 "ethnic" wards were to be disbanded and their members assigned to attend the English-speaking ward nearest their homes. However, after

---

three Tongan sessions each month. The current Hamilton New Zealand Temple schedule does not list any regular language sessions but notes that they may be provided as required. Temple patrons may hear any session in Maori by requesting headphones. A new temple film, designed to fit a variety of languages, has been in use in all LDS temples since mid-2013, and some members have speculated that this development presages the elimination of all language-designated sessions in all temples, as patrons may now hear the soundtrack in their preferred language during any session.

84. Barber and Gilgen, "Between Covenant and Treaty," 220.

85. By the Samoan Tripartite Convention of 1899, the Samoan islands west of longitude 171 degrees became a German protectorate, while those east of 171 degrees became an American territory. In 1920, after World War 1, the League of Nations assigned Western Samoa to New Zealand as a mandated territory, which it remained from that date until it became independent in 1962.

considerable resistance and the publication of some new research, the 1996 instruction to dissolve the ethnic wards in California was reversed late the following year. "The episode suggests a profound ambivalence at the highest levels of the church about how to handle ethnic wards," commented the *Salt Lake Tribune.* "For a church used to programmatic solutions to every problem, the issue of ethnic wards continues to be thorny."[86]

Today there *is* a Church-wide policy regarding the organisation or discontinuance of language-designated units (whether branches, wards, or stakes). But it could be seen as a policy of default: decisions on these matters are to be made by stake presidencies according to their perception of the needs of local congregations. However, all such decisions must be approved by the relevant Area Presidency before implementation.[87]

Mormon Pride in Integration

Sociologists have consistently noted the high degree of integration of Maori and Pakeha in Mormon congregations in New Zealand. "The Mormons are the most successful of all Churches in the implementation of a policy of integration," wrote Hans Mol in the 1960s. Mol warned that it should be kept in mind that, as more than two-thirds of all New Zealand Mormons were Maori, integration was perhaps more of a problem for Pakeha than for Maori members.[88] Mormon leaders tend to cite observations such as Mol's notice of Mormon integration with pride.[89] That this integration is obligatory for both Maori and Pakeha Latter-day Saints does not necessarily invalidate the observation; Church affiliation and attendance, after all, cannot be enforced. But attendance at the nearest geographical unit is expected of Mormons (except those with special permission not easily obtained) and full participation in Church life (for example, temple attendance and holding "callings") is made difficult for those perceived to be disobedient to leadership counsel.

The Great Land March of 1975 symbolised and intensified interest in and awareness of Maori culture in New Zealand society. In that year, more than 5,000 Maori marched from Te Hapua in the far north of the

86. Peggy Fletcher Stack, "In Their Own Language: Should Ethnic Mormons Have Their Own Language?" *Salt Lake Tribune,* 6 December 1997, B-1.

87. Conversation with former Area Seventy, September 2012; name withheld by request.

88. Johannis J. [Hans] Mol, "The Religious Affiliations of the New Zealand Maoris," *Oceania* 35 (December 1964): 142; Johannis J. [Hans] Mol, *Religion and Race in New Zealand,* 16, 60.

89. "Maori, Pakeha Integration Lauded in Report," *Church News,* 5 September 1964, 13 and *New Zealand Church News* 2 no. 8, October 1964, [7].

North Island to the nation's capital, Wellington, in the south. At Parliament House in Wellington, they presented a petition to the government appealing for the repeal of all statutes that could alienate Maori land and the investiture of all remaining tribal land to Maori in perpetuity. Mormon leaders, in general, disapproved of Maori activism and tried to dissuade Church members from taking part in the Land March.[90] Agitation over issues such as Maori-speaking wards and the provision of a marae at Temple View was confined to relatively few Maori Latter-day Saints, though several informal discussions indicate that a degree of resentment, or at least dissatisfaction, with Church leaders' negative decisions on some of these matters affected far more Maori Saints than the level of open disagreement would suggest.

Despite token accommodations which Barber interpreted as yet another policy swing, this time towards biculturalism, there can be no doubt that the Mormon Church ideal today is that of a homogenised, universalised "gospel culture." However, many Maori are suspicious of assimilation or integration. Recalling the story of the shark and kahawai (fish) that swam together until the shark "assimilated" the smaller kahawai,[91] these Maori want biculturalism. "We must row together, in the same direction and in unison," says Henare Te Rakihiatau, deputy administrator of the Ngai Tahu Trust Board.[92]

There can be little doubt that those Maori Mormons who are able to compartmentalise their Maori and Mormon identities are more content with Mormon Church programs than those who cling to Maoritanga and regret what they see as the assimilationist policies of Church leaders in recent decades. Church leaders, of course, see these policies as being universal rather then assimilationist, necessary to enable the Church to fill the spiritual needs of a world-wide membership.

Modern Mormonism and Maori Communalism

For a few decades after World War II, some LDS Church leaders were extremely outspoken about the evils of communism, often extending their condemnation to socialism. American mission president Gordon C. Young freely criticised New Zealand's social welfare programs and openly supported the conservative National Party. Maori sympathies, on the other hand, have traditionally turned towards the Labour Party. "Maori commu-

90. Simpson, Oral History, 8; Barber and Gilgen, "Between Treaty and Covenant," 214.

91. M. P. Shirres, "The Churches' Contribution to Race Relations in New Zealand," 67.

92. Quoted in Macdonald, *The Fifth Wind*, 304.

nalism, for want of a better word, orientates people towards socialism," said distinguished Maori soldier, diplomat, and politician Sir Charles Moihi Bennett, when questioned about the apparent paradox between his elite Oxford University education and his vice-presidency of the New Zealand Labour Party.[93]

By the 1990s, Mormon priesthood, Relief Society, and Sunday School lesson manuals seldom referred to the evils of communism or socialism, yet still occasionally ran counter to deeply ingrained Maori cultural *mores*, making yet another shift away from taha Maori necessary for dedicated Maori Latter-day Saints. Even though the perceived threat of communism had subsided, doctrinal lessons still explicitly taught (and to some extent still do) values contrary to Maori communalism. A Relief Society lesson on budgeting, as taught in a Sydney, Australia, ward one Sunday in November 1997, illustrates this point. The teacher, following the official Utah-written lesson material provided, urged the women present to set up a strict family budget and to stockpile a year's supply of food and clothing for future emergencies. The half dozen expatriate Maori women present exhibited considerable unease. Finally, one of them pointed out that traditional customs made it difficult, if not impossible, for Maori women to follow this counsel. She explained that members of her extended family in New Zealand were free to make unscheduled visits to Sydney and stay as long as they wished; furthermore, she indicated that she and her husband were expected to share all they had with any part of their extended families in times of need. "If the time comes when we need help, our [extended] families and friends will share with us," she concluded. Although she was obviously articulating a value shared by the other Maori women present, the teacher and the Australian women in the class were, in their turn, unhappy with this explanation and rejected it as a valid way of conforming to the Mormon principle of family preparedness.[94] In Western societies, prestige is frequently earned by accumulating. Even today, this concept is foreign to most Maori; mana in Maori society is achieved not by accumulating, but by sharing.

Mormon teachings such as this tend to pull Maori away from the marae, a point noted by Bennett. "I have the greatest admiration for the work the Mormons do for the Maori," he told journalist Robert Gilmore. "It shows what can be done." Nevertheless, Bennett expressed reservations

---

93. Lt. Colonel Charles Moihi Bennett, DSO, interviewed by Robert Gilmore, *Auckland Star*, 30 May 1970. Bennett, a Te Aute "old boy" who commanded the Maori Battalion from 1942 and became New Zealand's High Commissioner to Malaya, later became president of the New Zealand Labour Party.

94. Reported by class member and teacher; names withheld by request.

about statements that the Mormons respected Polynesian cultures. Apart from their disapproval of the tangi, Bennett said, "Mormons tend to discourage what I regard as a pillar of Maori culture—the marae, with the meeting house as a forum. These are vehicles for the expression of such basics of Maori culture as speech-making, genealogy, chanting and carving. The Mormons appear to respect every other aspect of Maori culture and I would like to see other churches doing likewise."[95] It seems a pity that Mormonism, which in its early years both preached and practised communalism, should today try to acculturate Maori converts to a social system that requires them to reject the communal life of the marae.

On the other hand, more and more Maori Mormons are completing tertiary education and embracing successful professional careers. Thomas Fitzgerald's research suggests that many of these Latter-day Saints have so internalised Mormon values that the marae and even rangatira descent are marginalised in their lives, replaced by their positions within the LDS Church's ward and stake leadership councils.[96] But other Maori Latter-day Saints are responding to surging Maori self-consciousness by identifying ever more strongly with Maoritanga; they see no conflict between their Mormon and Maori identities that could not be harmonised, given tolerance and sympathy from the Church hierarchy.

Cultural Conflict for Pakeha as Well as for Maori Mormons[97]

What is often overlooked is that some degree of reacculturation was also expected of New Zealand Pakeha converts to Mormonism. Americans can convert to Mormonism with minimal cultural dislocation, though some studies have suggested that Utah Mormons qualify as an ethnic group, making what Mormon historian Dean L. May terms "in-migration" difficult even for American converts.[98] But although Mormon

---

95. Bennett, *Auckland Star*, 30 May 1970.

96. Thomas K. Fitzgerald, *Education and Identity: A Study of the New Zealand Maori Graduate*, 127–29, 131–32.

97. Parts of the following discussion that apply to both Australia and New Zealand have been adapted from Marjorie Newton, "Almost Like Us: The American Socialization of Australian Converts," 12–13, 17–19.

98. Dean L. May, "A Demographic Portrait of the Mormons, 1830-1980," 40; Jan Shipps, "In the Presence of the Past: Continuity and Change in Twentieth-Century Mormonism," 20, 32 note 22; Jan Shipps, *Mormonism: The Story of a New Religious Tradition*, 187 note 23. The validity of examining Mormonism as an ethnic identity has been questioned by Armand L. Mauss, *The Angel and the Beehive: The Mormon Struggle with Assimilation*, 64–66.

Church leaders during the twentieth century ceased to expect foreign converts to remove physically to the United States and assume an American nationality, Mormon missionaries overseas continued to teach Mormon Americanism along with American Mormonism, and non-American converts must still become not just cultural Mormons but cultural American immigrants as well—or at the very least hold what might be called dual cultural citizenship in order to feel an integral part of their new church and to comprehend fully its teachings and programs. All new converts in international mission fields must decide, consciously or subconsciously, how much American culture to embrace along with the new doctrine they accept at baptism.

It was not to be expected that American Mormons could proselytise among the Maori without such cultural assumptions. James Axtell described the Christianity of Western Europe two centuries earlier as "a complicated, culture-bound product of the societies that professed it." The same description might legitimately be applied to modern Mormonism. Just as early Christian missionaries in colonial North America "always demanded of native converts more than sincere profession of a creed,"[99] so did Mormon missionaries in New Zealand. When a European converted to Christianity, says Axtell, "he remained a European in culture. But when an Indian was asked to discard his old self, he was asked to commit cultural suicide, to cease to be an Indian."[100] There is a clear parallel.

During most of the twentieth century, leadership statements reinforced the perception of a divinely ordained link between the gospel and American culture. In Hawaii in 1921, Apostle (later Church president) David O. McKay was deeply moved by the microcosmic "melting pot" he noted when he attended a flag-raising ceremony at the LDS primary school at Laie with its Hawaiian, Chinese, Japanese, Filipino, and American children. "My bosom swelled with emotion and tears came to my eyes, and I felt like bowing in prayer and thanksgiving for the glorious country which is doing so much for all these nationalities...," he wrote. "America and the Church of Christ will truly make of all nations one blood. May God hasten the day when this is accomplished."[101] These sentiments changed little over the next sixty years as the international expansion of Mormonism accelerated. "The Church by expanding worldwide in theory and practice, is

99. James Axtell, *The Invasion Within: The Contest of Cultures in Colonial North America*, 330.

100. Ibid.

101. David O. McKay, quoted in Britsch, *Moramona*, 176.

demanding extra-territorial allegiance to the United States," wrote Candadai Seshachari, a Hindu professor teaching at a Utah university, in 1980.[102]

As with Australians, few New Zealand Latter-day Saints objected to the American socialisation they experienced in the LDS Church while the gathering ethos persisted; most hoped one day to gather to Zion and become Americans themselves. When the ideal of a physical gathering was finally relinquished in the 1950s, resistance to the American cultural content of the Mormon gospel package gradually increased among some Latter-day Saints, both Maori and Pakeha.

The Mormon Church still speaks with an American accent in its foreign missions and stakes. Although it may not demand what Axtell calls "cultural suicide" from its converts,[103] the LDS Church still implicitly expects its international converts to commit what Rana Kabbani has termed "cultural treason"[104] if they wish to identify fully with Mormonism. But it is a moot point whether such full identification is possible. As Peter Lineham pointed out in 1990, "No two cultures ever do match one another exactly, and no religious message can simply be stripped of one set of cultural associations and clothed with others."[105] Nor does it seem possible for individual Maori converts to simply wash away their Maori identity in the waters of baptism.

Since February 1996, there have been more Latter-day Saints outside the United States than in it. While encouraging international members to treasure those aspects of their traditional culture that harmonise with gospel teachings,[106] Church authorities have increasingly stressed the universal nature of the Christian gospel and have attempted to remove culture-specific items from handbooks and curriculum materials. Yet despite the best efforts of the Correlation Committee, LDS Church curricula and magazine articles still portray an anaemic Americanism. It is difficult, if not impossible, for American General Authorities to preach effective sermons, or for American auxiliary board members to write effective lessons, totally divorced from their own culture, just as lay members listening cannot fully comprehend them without their own cultural referents. "Literally nothing that does not come within the range of our own cultural experience, and

---

102. Seshachari, "Other Voices, Other Mansions," 118.

103. Axtell, *The Invasion Within*, 330.

104. Rana Kabbani, *Letter to Christendom*, ix.

105. Peter J. Lineham, "The Mormon Message in the Context of Maori Culture," 92–93.

106. For example, each temple dedication is now prefaced by a program presented by the youth of each temple district and featuring local cultural traditions expressed in music and dance.

hence within [the] range of our own language, can have any meaning-ful existence for us," says historian Anthony Pagden.[107] What remains to be seen is how much the present blurring of cultural differences between modern societies will trivialise cultural tensions. If globalisation continues to see American "pop" culture, variously referred to as "Coca-colonisation" or "McDonald's culture," spread at its present pace, preservation of Maori-tanga or any other national culture may become an academic question.[108]

Thus, although Church leaders early in the twentieth century declined to establish a Mormon colony in New Zealand for Maori Saints, in a larger sense the entire Mormon mission in New Zealand has been an American cultural colony. Several generations of converts, both Maori and Pakeha, accepted dual citizenship uncomplainingly; today, some question such as-sumptions. Since World War II, all former Pacific colonies of European powers have progressively won political independence, and national self-consciousness has carried over into every aspect of life. In perpetuating and tightening central control in order to meet the challenge of unprecedented international growth, the Mormon Church is seen by some non-LDS ob-servers to be swimming against an inexorable tide of nationalism, a process that seems to them both shortsighted and counter-productive.[109]

Changing Doctrinal Emphasis in Mormon Discourse

Mormon Church leaders, however, are not likely to be influenced by such arguments, nor by their previous assignment of special status to "La-manites." While the rapid growth of the LDS Church during the last four decades[110] has meant that there may be less local autonomy than in the past, Church leaders now realise that the Church's mission has a wider perspective than in the past. "We do not emphasize racial, or cultural distinctions, in-cluding Lamanite or tribal distinctions, in the Church," said Apostle Jeffrey R. Holland, speaking at a Native American Conference on 25 July 1997 in Provo, Utah. "We are moving to that millennial day where we are all Latter-day Saints and there are no more -ites among us."[111] The necessity of ad-dressing the spiritual welfare of adherents from a wide spectrum of cultural

---

107. Anthony Pagden, *European Encounters with the New World: From Renaissance to Romanticism*, 174.

108. Wilfried Decoo, "Feeding the Fleeing Flock," 115; Marjorie Newton, "Towards 2000: Mormonism in Australia," 195.

109. Eric J. Sharpe, conversation with Marjorie Newton, May 1996; notes in my possession.

110. From 3 million in 1973 to 15 million in 2013.

111. Jeffrey R. Holland, "All Cultures Are Children of One God," *Church News*, 2 August 1997, 5.

backgrounds, together with strong scientific evidence disproving (or at least casting reasonable doubt on) long-held theories of Polynesian origins, has led to changes in many Church policies and teachings.

This development has been examined by scholars, notably by sociologist Armand Mauss and religious studies historian John-Charles Duffy.[112] Duffy demonstrates that changing world—and LDS—attitudes toward race, plus the large international growth of the Church, have, of necessity, contributed to, if not caused, Church leaders' retreat from according special status to one particular racial group of its members. As he documents, this change of direction and mission perception actually predated the "Lamanite" DNA controversy. The change in LDS attitudes about the importance of lineal descent stemmed, ironically, from President Spencer W. Kimball's momentous 1978 revelation on priesthood blessings for all worthy men, regardless of race. "The Kimball years thus witnessed both the zenith of Lamanite identification and the beginnings of its decline," writes Duffy.[113]

Duffy discusses changes in leadership rhetoric, including the lack of consensus on what different interest groups accept as official discourse. Regardless of whether one regards temple dedicatory prayers and area conference addresses by LDS General Authorities as "official" statements or not, Duffy notes that, while previous temple dedicatory prayers and area conference addresses in Central and South America and the Pacific invariably included references to Latter-day Saints in these areas as Lamanites, President Gordon B. Hinckley (1995–2008) appears to have made no reference to the Polynesian peoples as "children of Lehi" when he dedicated or re-dedicated temples in Hawaii (2000), Fiji (2000), and Samoa (2005), nor in any of the addresses he gave when he toured New Zealand in 1997 and various Pacific Islands in 2000.[114] However, President Hinckley did express his "great love for the sons and daughters of Lehi" in 1997 when he rededicated the renovated meetinghouse of the Papago Ward in Arizona, which he referred to as the "oldest, continuous Indian ward in the entire world."[115]

---

112. Armand L. Mauss, *All Abraham's Children: Changing Mormon Conceptions of Race and Lineage*; John-Charles Duffy, "The Use of 'Lamanite' in Official LDS Discourse."

113. Duffy, "The Use of 'Lamanite' in Official LDS Discourse," 122, 137.

114. Duffy, "The Use of 'Lamanite' in Official LDS Discourse," 159-60 and note 142, acknowledges that *Church News* reporters may simply have failed to include such references in their stories; but as he points out, this would have been in sharp contrast to *Church News* stories of previous General Authority visits to Central and South America and the Pacific. He also notes that President Hinckley was very aware that great numbers of Pacific Islander Latter-day Saints also have European or East Asian ancestry.

115. "Pres. Hinckley Shows 'Great Love for Sons, Daughters of Lehi,'" *Church*

As the Church has grown and spread among different races and cultures, not only have its leaders moved toward stressing universal aspects of the gospel, but they have also found it necessary to actively discourage some cultural customs that are not in harmony with the gospel the Church teaches. "Your Heavenly Father assigned you to be born into a specific lineage from which you received your inheritance of race, culture, and traditions," said Elder Richard G. Scott, a senior member the Church's Quorum of the Twelve Apostles during the Church's annual general conference in April 1998. "That lineage can provide a rich heritage and great reasons to rejoice. Yet you have the responsibility to determine if there is any part of that heritage that must be discarded because it works against the Lord's plan of happiness."[116] Another apostle, Elder Dallin H. Oaks, recently appealed to "our older members to put away traditions and cultural or tribal practices that lead them away from the path of growth and progress. We ask all to climb to the higher ground of the gospel culture, to practices and traditions that are rooted in the restored gospel of Jesus Christ."[117]

Sermons by most LDS leaders today seldom mention Lamanite descent for either American Indian or Polynesian Latter-day Saints. The very fact that the long-held belief in the Lamanite ancestry of all Native Americans and Polynesians has never been canonised by the Church[118] indicates ambivalence at the very least among its prophets. It allows the modern Church the opportunity to announce definitive changes by pointing out that these uncanonised former teachings about Native American and Polynesian origins were based on supposition or contemporary cultural beliefs rather than revelation, something that has been taught in the Church (but largely ignored) for nearly one hundred years, as Meldrum and Stephens have noted.[119]

Simon Southerton suggests that LDS Church leaders, faced with unanswerable scientific data about Native American and Polynesian origins, are trapped in a situation where they cannot make fundamental doctrinal changes without damaging the faith of millions of adherents.[120] Historically, however, Church leaders have always taught that, after numerous initial revelations to Joseph Smith, LDS prophets receive continuing, incre-

News, 20 September 1997, 6.

116. Richard G. Scott, "Removing Barriers to Happiness," *Ensign*, May 1998, www.lds.org/ensign/1998/05/removing-barriers-to-happiness?lang=eng (accessed 7 July 2013).

117. Dallin H. Oaks, "The Gospel Culture," *Ensign*, March 2012, 40-47.

118. See Chapter 1.

119. D. Jeffrey Meldrum and Trent D. Stephens, *Who Are the Children of Lehi?*, 19.

120. Simon G. Southerton, *Losing a Lost Tribe*, 206.

mental revelations as needed and requested. Some changes made over the years, such as no longer teaching that the sacrament should be taken with the right hand, have been so small as to be scarcely noticed by the general Church membership.[121] But even important early policies and practices of the Church (such as the obligation for converts to physically gather with the body of the Saints in America and the teaching and practice of plural marriage), have been reversed without negative effects on grass-roots members or on Church growth.

The LDS Church successfully weathered what was seen by critics to be a momentous about-face in June 1978, when President Spencer W. Kimball announced that henceforward "all worthy male members of the Church may be ordained to the priesthood without regard for race or color." President Kimball testified that this change of policy was in answer to earnest prayer. It was canonised by unanimous vote as Official Declaration—2 at the Church's general conference on 30 September 1978 and has been included in the Doctrine and Covenants since the 1981 edition, thus reversing a ban that had long been perceived by most Mormons as doctrine. However, the belief that black males were not eligible to hold the priesthood, like Church leaders' and members' belief that American Indians and Polynesians are Lamanites, had never been canonised. The reversal of the Church's policy on priesthood ordination attracted worldwide media attention but did not damage the faith of the great majority of Church members, who rejoiced in the change. Despite Southerton's assumption, it is not only possible but likely that a similar acceptance by the leaders of the LDS Church of modern scientific findings regarding Native American and Polynesian origins could also occur without lasting damage to the faith of members, including the faith of most Polynesian members.

What *is*—and always has been—canonised Mormon doctrine is that *all* baptised members of the Church of Jesus Christ of Latter-day Saints are descendants of Abraham and Jacob, either by direct lineage or by adoption. "As members of the Church, we are admitted into the house of Israel. We become brothers and sisters, equal heirs to the same spiritual lineage,"

---

121. "There is no rule that says with which hand we take the sacrament. We do not tell the children that they must take the sacrament with their right hand. This is frustrating and confusing to them. We stress the fact that they take the sacrament reverently." Lesson 35, "We Learn More About the Sacrament . . .," Sunday School Lesson Manual, Course 4, 1970, *We Learn about Our Heavenly Father*, 237. It was previously taught that use of the right hand to take the sacrament was based on a doctrinal principle. See "The Right Hand," in Joseph Fielding Smith, *Answers to Gospel Questions*, 1:154–58.

said Bishop Gérald Caussé during a recent general conference.[122] Formal retreat from teaching that Hagoth and his shipmates were the foreparents of the Polynesians would in no wise mean that Maori were not Israelites in the eyes of the Mormon Church. Yet for the majority of today's Maori Latter-day Saints, many of whom are third-, fourth- or fifth-generation descendants of early Maori converts who accepted the Mormon gospel because of this teaching, Lamanite descent is still a fundamental element of their self-identification. "To this day, Maori Latter-day Saints cherish the Book of Mormon as *their* story, the account of their people in distant antiquity before they sailed in their *waka* (canoes) to Aotearoa. The American missionaries may have carried it to them and the American *Pakeha* Joseph Smith may have translated it, but for well over a century it has been read as the story of *their* ancestors," writes BYU professor Grant Underwood.[123] Accepting a changed perspective on their origins may be difficult, but not devastating, for the majority of Maori Saints.

However, for a small minority, the costs of being a Maori Mormon may be too high. Apart from the question of accepting changing Mormon beliefs regarding their origins, many Maori today, including stalwart Church members, want their culture to survive and feel that it exemplifies true Christian principles—not just the outward symbols displayed for tourists, but the deepest Maori values: self-esteem nurtured by one's ascribed place in the iwi; communal responsibility exemplified by sharing and caring; connectedness demonstrated by the tangihanga; the marae as a focus and locus of Maori life; and above all, te reo.

The implied attitude of many Mormon Church leaders has been that American culture most closely approaches that of heaven; this may be so, but some non-American observers of contemporary American society, including committed Mormons, have yet to be convinced of this. While they accept in theory the ideal of a universal, "celestialised" gospel culture, it may be that in practice an ideal, universal, celestial culture is impossible to achieve in what Mormon doctrine designates a telestial world. The cumulative experience of the New Zealand Mission shows that, just as the law of tithing replaced the celestial law of consecration in the mid-nineteenth-

---

122. Gérald Caussé, First Counselor in the Presiding Bishopric, "Ye Are No More Strangers," Semi-Annual General Conference of the Church of Jesus Christ of Latter-day Saints, 6 October 2013, www.lds.org (accessed 16 October 2013). For an extended discussion of the development of and changes to LDS doctrine regarding lineage, especially as it applies to ethnic minorities, see Mauss, *All Abraham's Children*.

123. Grant Underwood, "Mormonism, the Maori and Cultural Authenticity," 140.

century Church, a cultural "law of Moses" may be needed before ordinary men and women can live a celestial cultural law.

Nevertheless, despite the problematical issues described in this book, the Mormon Church has grown steadily in New Zealand in both numbers and status until it now occupies a respectable place in New Zealand society, ranking sixth in order of size among Christian churches there. While there are many thousands of recent converts, there is also a considerable base of multi-generation Maori families strengthening the LDS Church in New Zealand. Most find spiritual satisfaction and happiness in Church attendance, participation in Church programs, and the Mormon way of life. Mormons (and many non-Mormons) believe that Mormonism contributes to the well-being of New Zealand society. Most New Zealand Mormons, both Maori and Pakeha, accept Church teachings unquestioningly and remain untroubled by deeper or more difficult issues. It remains to be seen to what extent Maori Latter-day Saints can remain both Maori and Mormon.

On the other hand, those fringe-dwelling New Zealand Latter-day Saints, Pakeha or Maori, who question what they see as Mormon cultural imperialism might well ponder the conclusions of a modern scholar speaking of another time, another place, and another people: "It is only possible . . . to travel in one direction. . . . Any possibility of return has been preempted by the journey itself."[124]

---

124. Pagden, *European Encounters with the New World*, 172.

Glossary of Maori Words

Aotearoa	Maori name for New Zealand
aroha	love, affection, regard
haakari	feast, funeral feast
haka	ceremonial posture dance
hapu	sub-tribe, kinship group, exended family
hongi	salute, greet by pressing noses
hui	ceremonial meeting or formal assembly
hui pariha	LDS district conference
hui peko	annual LDS branch conference
hui tau	annual LDS mission conference
iwi	tribe
kahawai	fish
kai	food
kainga	village
karakia	communal prayers and scripture recitation
karere	messenger
kaumatua	tribal elders, Mormon missionaries
kauwhau	sermon, speech, recitation
Kotahitanga	nineteenth-century Maori parliament
mana	authority, prestige, influence
manuhiri	visitors, guests

Maoritanga	Maori culture, way of life
marae	tribal meeting place in front of carved meeting house
mihi	greeting, welcome ceremony
mihinare	missionary
Mihinare Church	Church of England, Church Missionary Society
moko	tattoo in traditional patterns
muru	to obtain compensation, redress
noa	ordinary, the opposite of *tapu*
pa	originally a fortified village, now any village
pakeha	foreign, non-Maori
piupiu	fringed waistband
poi	small woven ball on string
puhi	virgin, betrothed
rangatira	chief, noble, gentleman
raupo	rushes
reo	language, dialect
taha Maori	Maori view of society, world
tangata	man, human being, people
tangata whenua	people of the land, original inhabitants
tangi	cry
tangihanga	funeral customs
tapu	sacred, under ceremonial religious restriction
taumau	betrothed
te	the
tikanga	customs
tiriti	treaty
tohunga	priest, expert
tumuaki	president
utu	satisfaction, payment
waiata	song, songs
waka	canoe, canoes

whakapapa	genealogy, oral recitation of ancestry
whanau	one's children, family group
whare	house
whare harehare	prison, gaol
whare karakia	prayer house
whare raupo	rush-walled house

Glossary of LDS Terminology

Terms in *italics* are defined elswhere in the glossary.

apostle   a member of the *Quorum of the Twelve* [Apostles].

bishop   presiding officer of an LDS *ward*.

branch   smallest ecclesiastical unit of an LDS mission or *stake*.

calling, called   each person holding an office ("calling") in the Church is "called" to that position by a superior *priesthood* officer.

Church   when capitalised, refers to The Church of Jesus Christ of Latter-day Saints.

conference   1. A periodic assembly of members of an LDS ecclesiastical division to vote on officers, review progress, and receive counsel. 2. An administrative area within a mission, usually comprising several congregations, changed to *District* in 1927.

counsellor   Each presiding officer has two counsellors to assist with Church work.

deacon   A male member holding the lowest office of the Aaronic or lesser priesthood.

district   A group of several *branches* in an LDS mission.

elder   1. A male member holding the first office of the Melchizedek or higher priesthood. 2. Form of address for Church authorities and male missionaries.

First Presidency	A quorum formed by the president of the LDS Church and his counsellors. The highest authority in the Church.
First Quorum of Seventy	A governing council of the Church, third in authority after the First Presidency and the *Quorum of the Twelve.*
gathering	A nineteenth-century doctrine requiring converts to join the body of the Church in North America.
General Authority	A member of the governing councils of the LDS Church.
LDS	Latter-day Saint.
priest	A male member holding the third office of the lesser or Aaronic *priesthood.*
priesthood	The lay hierarchy of the Church, divided into two orders, the lesser or Aaronic and the higher or Melchizedek priesthood.
prophet	The president of the Church is *sustained* as a "prophet, seer and revelator."
quorum	Synonym for "council" in LDS parlance.
Quorum of the Twelve [Apostles]	A governing council of the Church, part of the Melchizedek or higher *priesthood,* second only to the *First Presidency.*
release	The termination of responsibility for a Church *calling.* Like a calling, a release is given by presiding authorities.
Reorganized Church of Jesus Christ of Latter Day Saints	The smaller of the two main branches of the Mormon movement, with headquarters in Independence, Missouri. Now Community of Christ.
RLDS	Abbreviation for *Reorganized Church of Jesus Christ of Latter Day Saints.*
set apart	After being called to office in the Church, members' names are presented to the congregation for a *sustaining* vote. They are then formally set apart in that *calling* by the laying on of hands.
stake	LDS diocese, usually comprised of six to twelve *wards.*

standard works   Books canonised as scripture by the LDS Church: the Bible, the Book of Mormon, the Doctrine and Covenants and the Pearl of Great Price.

sustain   Members of a Church unit show by raised hands their willingness to accept the leadership of those *called* to preside over them.

ward   parish.

Bibliography

Shortened Citations

Journal History. Journal History of the Church of Jesus Christ of Latter-day Saints. Chronology of typed entries and newspaper clippings, 1830–present. LDS Church History Library.

LDS Church History Library. Library and Archives, History Department, Church of Jesus Christ of Latter-day Saints, Salt Lake City.

Perry Special Collections. L. Tom Perry Special Collections, Harold B. Lee Library, Brigham Young University, Provo, Utah.

Citations

Alexander, R. R. *The Story of Te Aute College*. Wellington: A. H. & A. W. Reed, 1951.

Alexander, Thomas G., and Jessie L. Embry, eds. *After 150 Years: The Latter-day Saints in Sesquicentennial Perspective*. Provo, Utah: Charles Redd Center for Western Studies, 1983.

Allen, James B., and Glen M. Leonard. *The Story of the Latter-day Saints*. Salt Lake City: Deseret Book, 1976.

"Among the Maori—William B. Erekson to Editor, dated 5 June 1900." *Deseret Evening News*, 7 July 1900, 22.

Anaru, Heteraka. Oral History Interview. Transcript. Kenneth Wayne Baldridge, Interviews, 1971–73.

Anderson, Charles. Letter to YMMIA (Young Men's Mutual Improvement Association) of Elsinore. "Correspondence: Interesting Letter from New Zealand." *Deseret Evening News*, 28 April 1885, [4].

_____. "The New Zealand Mission, 3 December 1884, Waotu." *Deseret Evening News*, 9 February 1885, [4].

Anderson, Lavina Fielding. "Prayer under a Pepper Tree: Sixteen Accounts of a Spiritual Manifestation." *BYU Studies* 33, no. 1 (1993): 55–78.

Annual Statistical Reports (Form EE) for New Zealand Mission, 1907–1921. Microfilm. LDS Church History Library.

"Appeal to Old M.A.C. Boys." *Te Karere* 43, no. 2 (February 1948): 56.

Ardern, Ian S. "A Review of the Involvement of the Church of Jesus Christ of Latter-day Saints in New Zealand Education with Specific Reference to the American Influence on the Church College of New Zealand." M.Ed. thesis, University of Waikato, 1993.

"Are the Maoris of Israelitish Origin?" *Te Karere* 8, no. 18 (9 September 1914): 212–16. This version was reprinted from *The Messenger* (renamed *Te Karere*) of 31 October 1907, copies of which have not apparently survived. It was reprinted again in 1959. (See next entry.)

"Are the Maoris of Israelitish Origin?" *Te Karere* 53, no. 6 (June 1959): 251–53, 256.

Arrington, Leonard J. "Utah and the Depression of the 1890s." *Utah Historical Quarterly* 29, no. 1 (January 1961): 3–18.

Atkin, William Frank. Papers and New Zealand Mission Journals, 1903–6 and 1916–18. 15 folders. MSS 341. Perry Special Collections.

Auckland New Zealand Harbour Stake. Annual Historical Reports, 1981, 1983. LDS Church History Library, LR 13504 Series 3.

Auckland New Zealand Henderson Stake. Annual Historical Report, 1990, LDS Church History Library, LR 515035 Series 3.

Auckland Star. Auckland, New Zealand.

Axtell, James. *The Invasion Within: The Contest of Cultures in Colonial North America*. New York: Oxford University Press, 1985.

Baldridge, Kenneth Wayne. Interviews, 1971–73. MS 4231. LDS Church History Library.

———. "The Maori Agricultural College: An Experience in Rural Education." Photocopy of typescript. Church College of New Zealand Library, Temple View, New Zealand.

Ball, D. G. Inspection Reports, Maori Agricultural College, 1929, 14 August 1930. Typescripts. National Archives of New Zealand, Wellington.

Ballif, Ariel Smith. Oral History. Interviewed by Kenneth W. Baldridge, 1972. Typescript. In Kenneth Wayne Baldridge, Interviews, 1971–73.

———. Oral History. Interviewed by R. Lanier Britsch, Provo, Utah, 1973. Typescript. MS 200 154. LDS Church History Library.

———. Oral History. Interviewed by Antony I. Bentley, Provo, Utah, 1981. Typescript. MS 2735 441. LDS Church History Library.

Barber, Ian G. "Between Biculturalism and Assimilation: The Changing Place of Maori Culture in the Twentieth Century New Zealand Mormon Church." *New Zealand Journal of History* 29, no. 2 (October 1995): 142–69.

———. Email to Marjorie Newton, dated Wellington, 14 January 1998.

———, and David Gilgen. "Between Covenant and Treaty: The LDS Future in New Zealand." *Dialogue: A Journal of Mormon Thought* 29, no. 1 (Spring 1996): 207–22.

Barker, Ian R. "The Connexion: The Mormon Church and the Maori People." M.A. thesis, Victoria University, Wellington, 1967.

Barlow, Cleve. *Tikana Whakaaro: Key Concepts in Maori Culture.* Auckland: Oxford University Press, 1991.

Barrett, Stanley M. "Matthew Cowley, President of the Pacific Mission." Harold B. Lee Library, Brigham Young University, Provo, Utah.

Barrington, John M. "Maori Attitudes to Pakeha Institutions after the Wars: A Note on the Establishment of Schools." *New Zealand Journal of Educational Studies* 6, no. 1 (May 1971): 24–28.

_____. "Maori Scholastic Achievement. A Symposium: A Historical Review of Policies and Provisions." *New Zealand Journal of Educational Studies* 1, no. 1 (May 1966): 1–14.

Bartlett, Charles Bart. Journals, 1895–97, 1902–5. MS 6846. LDS Church History Library.

_____. "The New Zealand Mission." *Millennial Star* 66, no. 32 (11 August 1904): 497–502.

Bell, A., for Director of Education. Letter to the Principal, Maori Agricultural College, Hastings, 18 October 1926. Carbon copy of typescript. Department of Education, E 3 1947/1a. National Archives of New Zealand, Wellington.

Bennett, Archibald F. "Traditions of Polynesians Give Support to Book of Mormon Story of Hagoth." *Church News*, 18 October 1947, 6–7.

Bennett, Lt. Colonel Charles Moihi. Interviewed by Robert Gilmore. *Auckland Star*, 30 May 1970.

Bennett, Jonathan Royal. New Zealand Mission Journals, 1921–23. MS 6404. LDS Church History Library.

Bennion, Lowell C. "Ben," and Lawrence A. Young. "The Uncertain Dynamics of LDS Expansion, 1950–2020." *Dialogue: A Journal of Mormon Thought* 29, no. 1 (Spring 1996): 8–32.

Bergera, Gary James, and Ronald Priddis. *Brigham Young University: A House of Faith.* Salt Lake City: Signature Books, 1985.

Berrett, William E. "Church Educational Systems [CES]." In *Encyclopedia of Mormonism: The History, Scriptures, Doctrine, and Procedure of the Church of Jesus Christ of Latter-day Saints.* Edited by Daniel H. Ludlow. 5 vols. New York: Macmillan Publishing, 1992, 1:274–76.

Biggs, Bruce. *Maori Marriage: An Essay in Reconstruction.* Wellington: Polynesian Society, 1960.

Bishop, Nelson Spicer. New Zealand Mission Diaries, 1886–89. BX 8670.1 B54. Perry Special Collections.

Bitton, Davis, and Maureen Ursenbach Beecher, eds. *New Views of Mormon History: A Collection of Essays in Honor of Leonard J. Arrington.* Salt Lake City: University of Utah Press, 1987.

"The Board of Education for the South Pacific Islands." *Te Karere* 51, no. 8 (August 1957): 262.

Book of Mormon. Salt Lake City: Church of Jesus Christ of Latter-day Saints, 1981.

Book of Mormon: Another Testament of Jesus Christ. 2d. ed. New York: Doubleday, 2006.

Book of Mormon: Another Testament of Jesus Christ. Salt Lake City: Church of Jesus Christ of Latter-day Saints, 2013.

"Book of Mormon and DNA Studies," https://www.lds.org/topics/book-of-mormon-and-dna-studies (accessed 2 February 2014).

"Boys Could Learn Lesson as Girls Grab the Grades." *Waikato Times*, 23 July 1996, 7.

Britsch, R. Lanier. "Latter-day Saint Education in the Pacific Islands." In *New Views of Mormon History: A Collection of Essays in Honor of Leonard J. Arrington*. Edited by Davis Bitton and Maureen Ursenbach Beecher. Salt Lake City: University of Utah Press, 1987, 197–211.

_____. "Maori Traditions and the Mormon Church." *New Era*, June 1981, 37–46.

_____. *Moramona: The Mormons in Hawaii*. Laie, Hawaii: Institute for Polynesian Studies, 1989.

_____. *Unto the Islands of the Sea: A History of the Latter-day Saints in the Pacific*. Salt Lake City: Deseret Book, 1986.

Brittan, S. J., G. F. Grace, C. W. Grace, and A. V. Grace, eds. *A Pioneer Missionary among the Maoris, 1850–1879: Being Letters and Journals of Thomas Samuel Grace*. Palmerston North: G. H. Bennett & Co., n.d.

Bromley, William Michael. "Introduction of the Gospel to the Maories." *Juvenile Instructor*, 22, no. 1 (1 January 1887): 6–7, 26–27, 45–46 and no. 4 (15 February 1887): 57.

Buck, Sir Peter (Te Rangi Hiroa). *The Coming of the Maori*. Wellington: Maori Purpose Fund Board and Whitcoulls, 1977.

Cannon, Hugh J. *To the Peripheries of Mormondom: The Apostolic Around-the-World Journey of David O. McKay, 1920–1921*. Edited by Reid L. Neilson. Salt Lake City: University of Utah Press, 2011.

Caussé, Gérald. "Ye Are No More Strangers." *Ensign*, November 2013, 49–51.

The Challenger. New Zealand Mission, monthly bulletin. LDS Church History Library.

"Church College of New Zealand—Ethnic Groupings." CCNZ office staff. Typescript. Courtesy CCNZ Office.

Church College of New Zealand. Goals and Objectives, rev. 1972. CR 326 7, fd. 1. LDS Church History Library.

Church of Jesus Christ of Latter-day Saints. *Proceedings of Semi-Annual General Conference, October 1923*. Salt Lake City: Church of Jesus Christ of Latter-day Saints, 1923.

Church News. Salt Lake City. Weekly supplement to *Deseret News*. Currently named *LDS Church News*.

Clark, John E. "Book of Mormon Geography." In *Encyclopedia of Mormonism: The History, Scriptures, Doctrine, and Procedure of the Church of Jesus Christ of Latter-day Saints*. Edited by Daniel H. Ludlow. 5 vols. New York: Macmillan Publishing, 1992, 1:176–79.

Clement, Russell T. "Polynesian Origins: More Word on the Mormon Perspective." *Dialogue: A Journal of Mormon Thought* 13, no. 4 (Winter 1980): 88–98.

"College Work Advancing." *Te Karere* 7, no. 12 (4 June 1913): 140–43.

"Correspondence: A Maori 'Prophet': Amasa Aldridge to Editor. Dated 29 March 1885." *Deseret Evening News*, 25 April 1885, 3.

"Correspondence: Elders Arrested by Maories [sic], Progress of the Work, Curious Customs." Edward Cliff. Letter to the Editor. Dated Hastings, Hawkes Bay, 15 July 1866. *Deseret Evening News,* 12 August 1866, [2].

"Correspondence: Interesting Letter from New Zealand. [Charles Anderson to the YMMIA (Young Men's Mutual Improvement Association) of Elsinore]." *Deseret Evening News,* 28 April 1885, [4].

Cowley, Elva Eleanor Taylor. Autobiography, n.d. In Matthew Cowley Collection, Box 2, fd. 6.

Cowley, Matthew, Collection. NZ Mission Journals, 1914–19, 1938–44, and Correspondence. MSS 1470. Perry Special Collections.

_____. Matiu Kauri [Matthew Cowley]. "He Ratapuki Ki Wairoa." *Te Karere* 9, no. 16 (4 August 1915): 185–86.

_____. Letter to Mrs. Laura Brossard [his sister], dated Salt Lake City, 30 October 1932. In Matthew Cowley Collection, Box 1, fd. 10.

_____. "Maori Chief Predicts Coming of L.D.S. Missionaries." *Improvement Era* 53, no. 9 (September 1950): 696–98, 754–56.

_____. "The President's Page: M.A.C. Old Boys' Scholarship Fund." *Te Karere* 39, no. 6 (June 1944): 138–39.

_____. "The President's Page." *Te Karere* 40, no. 4 (February 1945): 33.

Cranney, A. Garr. "Schools." In *Encyclopedia of Mormonism: The History, Scriptures, Doctrine, and Procedure of the Church of Jesus Christ of Latter-day Saints.* Edited by Daniel H. Ludlow. 5 vols. New York: Macmillan Publishing, 1992, 3:1267–69.

Crawford, Sidney. Oral History Interview. Transcript. In Kenneth Wayne Baldridge, Interviews, 1971–73.

Cummings, David W. *Mighty Missionary of the Pacific: The Building Program of the Church of Jesus Christ of Latter-day Saints—Its History, Scope and Significance.* Salt Lake City: Bookcraft, 1961.

Cusack, Carol M. "Towards a General Theory of Conversion." In *Religious Change, Conversion and Culture.* Edited by Lynette Olson. Sydney: Sydney Association for Studies in Society and Culture, 1996, 1–21.

Cutler, Heber S. "The Australasian Mission [Report of Conference at Kiri Kiri, 6–7 July 1889]." *Deseret News Weekly,* 17 August 1889, 255.

_____. Letter to his parents, dated 27 November 1889. Excerpt printed as "In Maori Land." *Deseret News Weekly,* 4 January 1890, 13–14.

Daily Universe. Student newspaper, Brigham Young University, Provo, Utah.

Dakin, J. C. *Education in New Zealand.* Newton Abbot, Devon: David & Charles, 1973.

Dansey, Harry. "A View of Death." In *Te Ao Hurihuri: Aspects of Maoritanga.* Edited by Michael King. Wellington: Hicks Smith & Sons, 1977, 173–90.

Davies, Rangi. Letter to Gordon C. Young, dated Auckland, 11 January 1953. In Gordon Claridge Young, Papers, 1948–72.

de Bres, Pieter Hendrik. *Religion in Atene: Religious Associations and the Urban Maori.* Wellington: Polynesian Society, 1971.

_____. "The Religious Affiliation and the Religious Behaviour of the New Zealand Maori—A Sociological Study of the Religious Life of the Maori in a Suburban Area." M.A. thesis, University of Auckland, n.d.

Decoo, Wilfried. "Feeding the Fleeing Flock: Reflections on the Struggle to Retain Church Members in Europe." *Dialogue: A Journal of Mormon Thought* 29, no. 1 (Spring 1996): 97–118.

Deloria, Vine, Jr. *Custer Died for Your Sins: An Indian Manifesto.* New York: Macmillan, 1969.

Deseret News. The long–lived and still–publishing *Deseret News* has changed its name periodically, and also published more than one edition (e.g., daily and weekly, morning, and evening), sometimes reverting to a formerly used name. I cite the name as it appears for the specific source I am quoting. These names include:
Deseret Evening News.
Deseret News.
Deseret News-Telegram.
Deseret Weekly News.

Douglas, Norman. "The Sons of Lehi and the Seed of Cain: Racial Myths in Mormon Scripture and Their Relevance to the Pacific Islands." *Journal of Religious History* 8, no. 1 (June 1974): 90–104.

Douglass, William, Jr. Journal Notes of William Douglas Jr., while on a Mission to New Zealand, 28 February 1891–July 1894. LDS Family History Library Film 180430. Incorrectly catalogued under William Douglas [sic] Jr.

Duffy, John-Charles. "The Use of 'Lamanite' in Official LDS Discourse." *Journal of Mormon History* 34, no 1 (Winter 2008): 118–67.

Elders' Messenger. See *Te Karere.*

Ellsworth, S. George, and Kathleen C. Perrin. *Seasons of Faith and Courage: The Church of Jesus Christ of Latter-day Saints in French Polynesia: A Sesquicentennial History, 1843–1993.* Salt Lake City: Yves R. Perrin, 1994.

Elsmore, Bronwyn. *Like Them That Dream: The Maori and the Old Testament.* Otumoetai, Tauranga, N.Z.: Tauranga Moana Press, 1985.

_____. *Mana from Heaven: A Century of Maori Prophets in New Zealand.* Otumoetai, Tauranga, N.Z.: Tauranga Moana Press, 1989.

England, Eugene. Response to Eduardo Pagan. "An Innocent Racism." *Sunstone* 15, no. 1 (April 1991), 8–9.

The Ensign of the Church of Jesus Christ of Latter-day Saints. Magazine for LDS adults, 1971–present.

Esplin, Scott C. "Closing the Church College of New Zealand: A Case Study in Church Education Policy." *Journal of Mormon History* 37, no. 1 (Winter 2011): 86–114.

The Evening and the Morning Star. Independence, Missouri. Vols. 1–2 published in Independence in 1831–32. Publication resumed in Kirtland, Ohio, and the first two volumes were reprinted with editorial changes.

Evening News. Christchurch, N.Z.

Evenson, William E. "Evolution." In *Encyclopedia of Mormonism: The History, Scriptures, Doctrine, and Procedure of the Church of Jesus Christ of Latter-day Saints.* Edited by Daniel H. Ludlow. 5 vols. New York: Macmillan Publishing, 1992, 2:478.

Farnham, Augustus. "Extracts of a Letter from Elder Augustus A. Farnham to Brigham Young, dated 14 August 1853." *Deseret News,* 8 December 1853, [96].

Fergusson, D. M., M. Lloyd, and L. J. Horwood. "Family Ethnicity, Social Background and Scholastic Achievement: An Eleven–Year Longitudinal Study." *New Zealand Journal of Educational Studies* 26, no. 1 (1991): 49–63.

Ferris, John Solomon. Journals, 1880–82. MS 1435. LDS Church History Library.

First Presidency (Wilford Woodruff, George Q. Cannon, and Joseph F. Smith). Letter to Prest. W. T. Stewart, New Zealand, dated Salt Lake City, 14 October 1893. In William Thomas Stewart, Papers, 1878–93.

Fitzgerald, Thomas K. *Education and Identity: A Study of the New Zealand Maori Graduate.* Wellington: New Zealand Council for Educational Research, 1977.

Freeman, Derek. *Margaret Mead and Samoa: The Making and Unmaking of an Anthropological Myth.* Canberra: Australian National University Press, 1983.

Gardner, Brant A. *Second Witness: Analytical and Contextual Commentary on the Book of Mormon.* 6 vols. Salt Lake City: Greg Kofford Books, 2007.

Gardner, David P. "Education." In *Encyclopedia of Mormonism: The History, Scriptures, Doctrine, and Procedure of the Church of Jesus Christ of Latter-day Saints.* Edited by Daniel H. Ludlow. 5 vols. New York: Macmillan Publishing, 1992, 2:441–46.

Gardner, Eldon J., and Alice Gardner, eds. "Day Journal of John W. Gardner in New Zealand LDS Mission, 17 July 1901 to 23 January 1904." Perry Special Collections.

Gardner, William. Diaries, 1884–1916. Microfilm. MS 2884 1–9. LDS Church History Library.

"General [Mission] Conference." *Te Karere* 1, no. 6 (15 April 1907): 56.

Godbey, Allen H. *The Lost Tribes a Myth: Suggestions Towards Rewriting Hebrew History.* New York: Ktav Publishing House, 1974.

Goddard, Benjamin. "Letter from New Zealand." Dated Porirua, 11 July 1892. *Deseret Evening News,* 9 August 1892, 7.

_____. "Mormons in Maoriland." *Deseret News,* 25 January 1894, in Journal History, 25 January 1894, 5.

_____. [pseud. "Phoenix."] "Notes on the 'Hui Tau.'" *Deseret Evening News,* 19 May 1894, in Journal History, 17 April 1894, 10.

Gordon, Sam. "General Aims and Methods Employed in the Teaching of Agriculture at the C.C.N.Z." *Te Karere* 53, no. 7 (July 1959): 300–301, 320.

"Gospel Grows in New Zealand." *Deseret Evening News,* 21 March 1908, in Journal History, 7 February 1908, 3.

Gospel Principles. Salt Lake City: Church of Jesus Christ of Latter-day Saints, 1978, rpt. 2009.

Graham, Jeanine. "Settler Society." In *The Oxford History of New Zealand,* 2d ed. Edited by Geoffrey W. Rice. Auckland: Oxford University Press, 1992, 112–40.

"The Great Native Meeting at Wairoa." *Wellington Independent,* 20 April 1867, 6.

Greenwood, Alma. "My New Zealand Mission." *Juvenile Instructor* 20, no. 13 (1 July 1885): 206–7; 20, no.14 (15 July 1885): 222–23; 20, no. 16 (15 August 1885): 251; 20, no. 17 (1 September 1885): 258; and 21, no. 1 (1 January 1886): 6–7.

———. Diary and Scrapbook, 1882–88. MSS 336. Perry Special Collections.

———. "Our New Zealand Letter." Alma Greenwood to Editor, dated 1 December 1883. *Territorial Enquirer,* 11 January 1884, in Journal History, 11 January 1884, 11.

"Growth the Growing Problem for Church." *Auckland Star,* 7 April 1982, 28.

Gudmansen, Ray [Re]. Letter to L. G. Hoagland, dated Nuhaka, 3 July1906. In Louis Gerald Hoagland, Papers, Reel 2.

"Hagoth Believed to Be Link between Polynesia and Peoples of America." *LDS Church News,* 25 July 1992, 10.

"Hagoth's Children." *Time [Magazine],* 26 May 1958, 65–67.

Halversen, A. Reed. Letter to Elder Matthew Cowley, dated 12 June 1947. In Matthew Cowley Collection, Box 1, fd. 12.

Hamon, Hixon. Oral History Interview. Transcript. Kenneth Wayne Baldridge, Interviews, 1971–73.

Hardy, B. Carmon. *Solemn Covenant: The Mormon Polygamous Passage.* Urbana: University of Illinois Press, 1992.

Hardy, Charles. Letter to unidentified correspondent. *Deseret News,* 28 July 1886, 13.

Hardy, Rufus K. Letter to David O. McKay. Dated Auckland, 3 August 1934. In David O. McKay, Scrapbooks, 1928–70, Vol. 128.

———. "With Church Leaders in New Zealand." *Deseret News,* 25 June 1938, Church Section, 7.

Harris, Kelly. Oral History Interview. Transcript. Kenneth Wayne Baldridge, Interviews, 1971–73.

Hartley, William G. "From Men to Boys: LDS Aaronic Priesthood Offices, 1829–1996." *Journal of Mormon History* 22, no. 1 (Spring 1996): 80–136.

Havard-Williams, P., ed. *Marsden and the New Zealand Mission: Sixteen Letters.* Dunedin, N.Z.: University of Otago Press, 1961.

"Headmaster of Our College Has Been Appointed." *Te Karere* 51, no. 8 (August 1957): 268.

He Poropititanga Enei: Na nga Poropiti Maori o nga wa o mua. Korongata, N.Z.: Te Karere Press, 1927. LDS Church History Library.

Henderson, G. M. Memoranda to Director of Education. Reports of Inspection of Maori Agricultural College, Hastings, 5 September 1924, 13 October 1925, 4 October 1926, 11 October 1927, 10 January 1928, 25 September 1928. Carbon copies of typescripts. National Archives of New Zealand, Wellington.

Henderson, J. McLeod. *Ratana: The Man, the Church, the Political Movement.* Wellington: A. H. & A. W. Reed, 1972.

"Here and There in the Mission: College for New Zealand." *Te Karere* 43, no. 11 (November 1948): 344.

Heyerdahl, Thor. *American Indians in the Pacific: The Theory behind the Kon-tiki Expedition.* London: George Allen & Unwin, 1952.

Highland, Genevieve A., et al., eds. *Polynesian Culture History: Essays in Honor of Kenneth P. Emory.* Honolulu: Bishop Museum Press, 1967.

Hill, Michael, and Wiebe Zwaga. "Religion." In *New Zealand Society: A Sociological Introduction.* Edited by Paul Spoonley, David Pearson, and Ian Shirley. Palmerston North, N.Z.: Dunmore Press, 1990, 278–92.

Hinckley, Gordon B. "Temple in the Pacific." *Improvement Era* 61, no.7 (July 1958): 509.

_____. "Pres. Hinckley Shows 'Great Love' for Sons, Daughters of Lehi." *Church News*, 20 September 1997, 6.

Hiroa, Te Rangi. *See* Sir Peter Buck.

Hixson, J. M. "New Zealand—Superstition Still Prospers." Letter to the Editor, dated 10 March 1902. *Deseret News*, 10 April 1902, in Journal History, 10 March 1902, 5.

Hoagland, Louis Gerald. Letter to President Hugh J. Cannon, Liberty Stake, dated Mesa, Arizona, 16 November 1920. In Hoagland Papers, 1915–41.

_____. Letter to President M. Charles Woods, dated Salt Lake City, 11 May 1937. In Hoagland Papers, 1915–41.

_____, et al. Letter to President Joseph F. Smith, dated Auckland, 24 September 1906. Copied into New Zealand Mission, Manuscript History, 31 December 1906.

_____. Notes and Report of John Welch, Principal of LDS College, to James N. Lambert, 6 May 1918. In Hoagland Papers, 1915–41.

_____. Hoagland Papers, 1905–38. Microfilm. MS 4693. LDS Church History Library.

_____. Hoagland Papers, 1915–41. Microfilm. MS 6545. LDS Church History Library.

Holden, Alan. *Family Law and You.* Dunedin, N.Z.: John McIndoe, 1987.

Holland, Jeffrey R. "All Cultures Are Children of One God." *Church News*, 2 August 1997, 5.

_____. *Christ and the New Covenant: The Messianic Message of the Book of Mormon.* Salt Lake City: Deseret Books, 1997.

_____. "True or False." *New Era*, June 1995, 64–66.

Howard, Alan. "Polynesian Origins and Migrations: A Review of Two Centuries of Speculation and Theory." In *Polynesian Culture History: Essays in Honor of Kenneth P. Emory.* Edited by Genevieve A. Highland et al. Honolulu: Bishop Museum Press, 1967, 45–101.

Howe, K[erry] R[oss]. *Where the Waves Fall: A New South Sea Islands History from First Settlement to Colonial Rule.* Sydney: George Allen & Unwin, 1984.

Hui Tau Program, 1941. Inserted in *Te Karere* 35, no. 4 (April 1941): [2].

Hunt, Brian William. *Zion in New Zealand: A History of the Church of Jesus Christ of Latter-day Saints in New Zealand, 1854–1977*. Hamilton, N.Z.: Church College of New Zealand, 1977.

"Impressions of Utah." *Dannevirke Evening News*, 12 November 1913. Rpt. in *Te Karere* 7, no. 26 (17 December 1913): 309–11.

"In Maori Land." Excerpt of a letter from Heber S. Cutler to his parents, dated 27 November 1889. *Deseret News Weekly*, 4 January 1890, 13–14.

"Interesting from New Zealand." *Deseret News*, 28 July 1886, 13.

Introduction. *Book of Mormon: Another Witness of Jesus Christ*. Salt Lake City: Church of Jesus Christ of Latter-day Saints, 1981.

Introduction. Book of Mormon: Another Witness of Jesus Christ. 2013 edition. www.lds.org/scriptures/bofm/introduction (accessed 12 April 2013).

Irwin, Geoffrey. *The Prehistoric Exploration and Colonisation of the Pacific*. Cambridge, England: Cambridge University Press, 1992.

Irwin, James. *An Introduction to Maori Religion: Its Character before European Contact and Its Survival in Contemporary Maori and New Zealand Culture*. Bedford Park, S.A.: Australian Association for the Study of Religions, 1984.

Israelson, L. Dwight. "United Orders." In *Encyclopedia of Mormonism: The History, Scriptures, Doctrine, and Procedure of the Church of Jesus Christ of Latter-day Saints*. Edited by Daniel H. Ludlow. 5 vols. New York: Macmillan Publishing, 1992, 4:1493–95.

Jensen, Elwin W. "Polynesians Descend from Lehi, According to Statements of the Prophets." 1977. Photocopy of typescript. Church College of New Zealand Library, Temple View, New Zealand.

Jensen, Richard L. "Mother Tongue: Use of Non–English Languages in the Church of Jesus Christ of Latter-day Saints in the United States, 1850–1983." In *New Views of Mormon History: A Collection of Essays in Honor of Leonard J. Arrington*. Edited by Davis Bitton and Maureen Ursenbach Beecher. Salt Lake City: University of Utah Press, 1987, 273–303.

Jenson, Andrew. "Jenson's Travels: Letter No. XXXVIII." *Deseret News Weekly*, 28 March 1896, 465.

Johnson, John. Journals, 1893–1925. Microfilm. MS 1333. LDS Church History Library.

Johnson, Lane. "Who and Where Are the Lamanites? Worldwide Distribution of Lamanites." *Ensign*, December 1975, 14–15.

Johnson, M. M. "New Zealand." *Deseret News*, 10 June 1911, in Journal History, 29 March 1911, 3.

Jones, John. "To the Aboriginals of New Zealand." *Zion's Watchman* 1, nos. 24–25 (15 December 1855): 200.

Joseph, Robert. "Intercultural Exchange, Matakite Māori and the Mormon Church." In *Mana Māori and Christianity*. Edited by Hugh Morrison, Lachy Paterson, Brett Knowles, and Murray Rae. Wellington: Huia Press, 2012, 43–72.

Journal History. *See* Shortened Citations.

Juvenile Instructor. Published monthly in Salt Lake City, originally as an independent publication, later under the title of *The Instructor* as the official magazine of the LDS Sunday School. Ceased publication when all

Church–published magazines were consolidated into three (for children, teens, and adults) in 1971. The name has since been revived as a blog, not sponsored by the LDS Church, focusing on Mormon issues.

Kabbani, Rana. *Letter to Christendom.* London: Viking Press, 1989.

"The Kauri Maori Culture Group." *The Challenger.* New Zealand Mission bulletin, June 1961.

Kawana, Eruha. Oral History Interview. Transcript. Kenneth Wayne Baldridge, Interviews, 1971–73.

Kimball, Edward L., and Andrew E. Kimball Jr. *Spencer W. Kimball: Twelfth President of the Church of Jesus Christ of Latter-day Saints.* Salt Lake City: Bookcraft, 1977.

Kimball, Spencer W. "Our Paths Have Met Again." *Ensign*, December 1975, 2–8.

King, James. Letter to Louis G. Hoagland, dated Te Hauke, 18 December 1906. In Louis Gerald Hoagland, Papers, 1905–38. Microfilm. MS 4693. LDS Church History Library, Reel 3.

King, Michael. "Between Two Worlds." In *The Oxford History of New Zealand,* 2d ed. Edited by Geoffrey W. Rice. Auckland: Oxford University Press, 1992, 285–307.

_____. *Maori: A Photographic and Social History.* Auckland: Heinemann Reed, 1984.

_____. *Moko: Maori Tattooing in the 20th Century.* Wellington: Alister Taylor, 1972.

_____, ed. *Te Ao Hurihuri: The World Moves On: Aspects of Maoritanga.* Wellington: Hicks Smith & Sons, 1977.

Kirkham, Francis Washington. Diaries, 1877–72. MSS 772. Perry Special Collections.

Knowlton, David C. "Belief, Metaphor, and Rhetoric: The Mormon Practice of Testimony Bearing." *Sunstone* 15, no. 1 (April 1991): 20–27.

Kopua, Tipi. Oral History Interview. Transcript. Kenneth Wayne Baldridge, Interviews, 1971–73.

Koopman–Boyden, Peggy G., ed. *Families in New Zealand Society.* Wellington: Methuen, 1978.

Kurian, George Thomas. *Facts on File: National Profiles: Australia and New Zealand.* New York: Facts on File, 1990.

"'Lamanite' Viewed as 'Term of Distinction.'" *Daily Universe* [student newspaper, Brigham Young University], 24 November 1986, 6.

Lambert, James Needham. Diaries, 1895–98. MS 9426. LDS Church History Library.

_____. Journals, 1916–19. MS 6457. LDS Church History Library.

_____. Letter to Matthew Cowley, dated Salt Lake City, 16 May 1924. In Matthew Cowley Collection, Box 1, fd. 8.

"Latter-day Prophets Have Indicated that Pacific Islanders Are Descendants of Lehi." *LDS Church News*, 9 July 1988, 14.

Laughton, J[ohn] G[eorge]. *From Forest Trail to City Street: The Story of the Presbyterian Church among the Maori People.* Christchurch, N.Z.: Presbyterian Bookroom for the Maori Synod of the Presbyterian Church, 1961.

LeCheminant, Dale C. "Questions and Answers: Is There Any Reference in Scripture or Other Sources of Information That Tells Where Hagoth and His Ships, Referred to in Alma 63, Went?" *New Era*, July 1979, 14–15.

Lineham, Peter J. "The Mormon Message in the Context of Maori Culture." *Journal of Mormon History* 17 (1991): 62–93.

Linford, Esther. Letters to Louis G. Hoagland, dated Whangarae, 26 February and 30 October 1906. In Louis Gerald Hoagland, Papers, 1905–38.

Loveland, Jerry K. "Hagoth and the Polynesian Tradition." *BYU Studies* 17, no. 1 (Autumn 1976): 59–73.

Ludlow, Daniel H., ed. *Encyclopedia of Mormonism: The History, Scriptures, Doctrine, and Procedure of the Church of Jesus Christ of Latter-day Saints.* 5 vols. New York: Macmillan Publishing, 1992.

Lyman, Edward Leo. *San Bernardino: The Rise and Fall of a California Community.* Salt Lake City: Signature Books, 1996.

Macdonald, Robert. *The Fifth Wind: New Zealand and the Legacy of a Turbulent Past.* London: Bloomsbury, 1989.

Maffly-Kipp, Laurie F., and Reid L. Neilson, eds. *Proclamation to the People: Nineteenth-century Mormonism and the Pacific Basin Frontier.* Salt Lake City: University of Utah Press, 2008.

Magleby, John Ephraim. "Among the Maoris, Funeral of a Chief—Queer Native Customs." Letter to the Editor. *Deseret Evening News,* 30 November 1887, [2].

———. Letters to Louis G. Hoagland, dated 8 January 1929, 25 June 1929, 30 March 1930, 19 September 1930. In Louis Gerald Hoagland, Papers, 1905–38. Microfilm. MS 4693. LDS Church History Library.

———. New Zealand Mission Journal, Papers, 1885–1937. Microfilm of holograph. MS 1557. LDS Church History Library.

Manihera, R. H. "Account of Missionary Work in New Zealand: A Copy of an Unsigned, Handwritten Manuscript Given to Louis G. Hoagland in Papawai, Wairarapa, in August 1918." In Elwin W. Jensen, Papers, n.d. MS 6429. LDS Church History Library.

Manookin, Robert P. Interviewed by Marjorie Newton at Orem, Utah, 26 May 1992. Notes in my possession.

Maori Agricultural College. *Catalogue and Announcement of the Latter-day Saints Agricultural College, 1913–1914, 1914, 1918–26, 1929–31.* Microfiche. LDS Church History Library.

"Maori Culture Group Potential . . . Do You Use It?" *Te Karere* 51, no. 5 (June 1957): 207.

"Maori, Pakeha Integration Lauded in Report." *Church News,* 5 September 1964, 13; *New Zealand Church News* 2, no. 8 (October 1964): [7].

Marsden, Samuel. Letter to Revd. J. Pratt, dated 8 Ivy Lane, 7 April 1808. In *Marsden and the New Zealand Mission: Sixteen Letters.* Edited by P. Havard-Williams. Dunedin, N.Z.: University of Otago Press, 1961, 15.

———. Letter to Revd. J. Pratt, dated Parramatta, 20 November 1811. In *Marsden and the New Zealand Mission: Sixteen Letters.* Edited by P. Havard-Williams. Dunedin, N.Z.: University of Otago Press, 1961, 36–38.

Mauss, Armand L. *All Abraham's Children: Changing Mormon Conceptions of Race and Lineage.* Urbana: University of Illinois Press, 2003.

_____. *The Angel and the Beehive: The Mormon Struggle with Assimilation.* Urbana: University of Illinois Press, 1994.

May, Dean L. "A Demographic Portrait of the Mormons, 1830–1980." In *After 150 Years: The Latter-day Saints in Sesquicentennial Perspective.* Edited by Thomas G. Alexander and Jessie L. Embry. Provo, Utah: Charles Redd Center for Western Studies, 1983, 39–69.

McLachlan, William. Letter to the Editor, dated Christchurch, 28 June 1876. *Juvenile Instructor* 11, no. 15 (1 August 1876): 172–73.

McConkie, Bruce R. *Mormon Doctrine.* Salt Lake City: Bookcraft, 1966.

McCune, H[enry] F[rederick]. Autobiography and Diaries, 1919–24. Typescript. MS 2267. LDS Church History Library.

McKay, David Lawrence. *My Father, David O. McKay.* Salt Lake City: Deseret Book, 1989.

McKay, David Oman. "Gift of Interpretation of Tongues Bestowed: Testimony of President David O. McKay, Given in an Illustrated Lecture on His World Tour of the Missions of the Church at Salt Lake City, Utah, 25 December 1934." Typescript, signed and dated 1 February 1935. MS 3645. LDS Church History Library.

_____. *Gospel Ideals: Selections from the Discourses of David O. McKay, Ninth President of the Church of Jesus Christ of Latter-day Saints.* Salt Lake City: Improvement Era, 1953.

_____. "Hui Tau." *Improvement Era* 24, no. 9 (July 1921): 770–71, 774.

_____. "Journal of World Mission Tour, 1921." Photocopy of typescript in possession of Lavina Fielding Anderson, Salt Lake City, Utah.

_____. "Ki nga Hunga Tapu o te Mihana o Niu Tirini e Noho huihui ana ki te Hui Tau ki Porirua," dated 8 November 1922. English translation attached. Carbon copy of typescript. M256.4 N563mMAO. LDS Church History Library.

_____. Letter to Professor William Lee Stokes, 15 February 1957, photocopy in my possession.

_____. Scrapbooks, 1928–70, vol. 128. LDS Church History Library.

McLachlan, William. Letter to the Editor, dated Christchurch, 28 June 1876. *Juvenile Instructor* 11, no. 15 (1 August 1876): 172–73.

Mead, Margaret. *Coming of Age in Samoa: A Study of Adolescence and Sex in Primitive Societies.* London: Penguin, 1969.

Meha, Stuart. "A Prophetic Utterance of Paora Potangaroa." *Te Karere* 43, no. 10 (October 1948): 298–99.

_____. "A Request Talk for Sunday Evening the 15th April, 1962." Photocopy of typescript. Copy in my possession, courtesy of Robert P. Manookin.

Meha, Tetuati [Stuart]. Letter to Francis W. Kirkham, dated Waiapa, 14 March 1961. MS 7956. LDS Church History Library.

Meldrum, D. Jeffrey, and Trent D. Stephens. *Who Are the Children of Lehi? DNA and the Book of Mormon.* Salt Lake City: Greg Kofford Books, 2007.

The Messenger. See *Te Karere.*

Metge, Joan. *The Maoris of New Zealand: Rautahi.* London: Routledge & Kegan Paul, 1976.

_____. "The Maori Family." In *Marriage and the Family in New Zealand.* Edited by Stewart Houston. Wellington: Sweet & Maxwell, 1970, 111–41.

Millennial Star. The Latter-day Saints Millennial Star. Published monthly by the British Mission of the Church of Jesus Christ of Latter-day Saints, 1840–1970.

"A Mission to the Antipodes." *Deseret Evening News,* 28 January 1886, in Journal History, 25 January 1886, 5.

"Missionaries and Saints of New Zealand: 'Hui Tau' at Annual Conference at Otiria." *Deseret News,* 2 June 1922, in Journal History, 17 April 1922, 4.

Mol, Johannis J. [Hans]. *Churches and Immigrants: A Sociological Study of the Mutual Effect of Religion and Immigrant Adjustment.* [The Hague: Albani], 1961.

_____. *Religion and Race in New Zealand: A Critical Review of the Policies and Practices of the Churches in New Zealand Relevant to Racial Integration.* Christchurch, N.Z.: National Council of Churches, 1966.

_____. "The Religious Affiliations of the New Zealand Maoris." *Oceania,* 35 (December 1964): 136–43.

"More about the Maoris." *Deseret Evening News,* 13 December 1884, in Journal History, 13 December 1884, 3.

Morehouse, Ric. "The Establishment of Church Education in New Zealand." Bachelor's degree, Independent Study, Brigham Young University, Provo, Utah, 1983. M260 M838e. LDS Church History Library.

"Mormon Conference: Gathering at Ngaruawahia." *Auckland Star,* 9 April 1928.

"Mormonism among the Maoris." *Deseret Evening News,* 10 February 1891, 4.

"Mormons and Maori." Letter to editor signed "Alpha." *Wairarapa Standard,* 20 August 1883.

"The Mormons and the Maori." *Evening News* (Christchurch, N.Z.), n.d. Rpt. in *Te Karere (The Messenger)* 7, no. 10 (7 May 1913): 111.

"Mormons in Maoriland." Benjamin Goddard, Letter to Mrs. Benjamin Goddard. *Deseret News,* 25 January 1894, in Journal History, 25 January 1894, 5.

"The Mormon Mission in New Zealand." *Auckland Weekly News,* 24 April 1902.

Morrell, W. P. *The Anglican Church in New Zealand: A History.* Dunedin, N.Z.: John McIndoe for Anglican Church of the Province of New Zealand, 1973.

Morton, Harry, and Carol Morton Johnston. *The Farthest Corner: New Zealand— A Twice Discovered Land.* Auckland: Century Hutchinson, 1988.

Munday, James. Oral History Interview. Transcript. Kenneth Wayne Baldridge, Interviews, 1971–73.

Murdock, John. Journal and Autobiography. MS F822. LDS Church History Library.

_____. "Extracts from a Letter from John Murdock to First Presidency." *Deseret News,* 24 July 1852, 2.

_____. Letter to Parley P. Pratt. Dated Sydney, 17 January 1852. In John Murdock, Journal and Autobiography. MS F822. LDS Church History Library.

Murphy, Thomas W. "Imagining Lamanites: Constructions of Self and Other in the Book of Mormon." Paper presented at the annual meeting of the Mormon History Association, May 1996, Snowbird, Utah. Typescript. Copy courtesy of Thomas W. Murphy.

Neilson, Reid L., ed. *To the Peripheries of Mormondom*. See Cannon, Hugh J.

Nepia, George. Oral History Interview. Transcript. Kenneth Wayne Baldridge, Interviews, 1971–73.

"News of the Church: Australia-New Zealand." *Ensign* Insert, November 1985, 115; November 1988, 81; September 1989, 83; December 1989, 82; August 1991, 84; October 1994, 82.

"News of the Church: *Encyclopedia of Mormonism* Released." *Ensign*, March 1992, 79.

Newton, Marjorie. "Almost Like Us: The American Socialization of Australian Converts." *Dialogue: A Journal of Mormon Thought* 24, no. 3 (Fall 1991): 9–20.

_____. "From Tolerance to 'House Cleaning': LDS Leadership Response to Maori Marriage Customs, 1890–1990." *Journal of Mormon History* 22 (Fall 1996): 72–91.

_____. "Her Very Presence Is a Sermon: Mere Mete Whaanga." In *Women of Faith in the Latter-days: Volume 3, 1846–1870*. Edited by Richard E. Turley and Brittany Chapman. Salt Lake City: Deseret Book, 2014.

_____. "Nineteenth-century Pakeha Mormons in New Zealand." In *Proclamation to the People: Nineteenth-century Mormonism and the Pacific Basin Frontier*. Edited by Laurie F. Maffly-Kipp and Reid L. Neilson. Salt Lake City: University of Utah Press, 2008, 228–54.

_____. *Southern Cross Saints: The Mormons in Australia*. Laie, Hawaii: Institute for Polynesian Studies, 1991.

_____. *Tiki and Temple: The Story of the New Zealand Mission of the Church of Jesus Christ of Latter-day Saints, 1854–1958*. Salt Lake City: Greg Kofford Books, 2012.

_____. "Towards 2000: Mormonism in Australia." *Dialogue: A Journal of Mormon Thought* 29, no. 1 (Spring 1996): 193–206.

"New Zealand." *Deseret News Weekly*, 8 August 1877, in Journal History, 3 August 1877, 4.

New Zealand Auckland Mission. Annual Reports for 1988 and 1989, in New Zealand Mission, Manuscript History and Historical Reports. LR 6048/3. LDS Church History Library.

New Zealand Auckland Mission. Presidents' Correspondence, 1967–1975. LR 6048 /25. LDS Church History Library.

"N[ew] Z[ealand] College Receives High Rating." *Deseret News*, 20 December 1958, in Journal History, 20 December 1958, 4.

New Zealand Education Department. Registered Private Primary Schools Statistics, Maori Agricultural College, Statistics for the Years 1924–1929. LDS Church History Library.

New Zealand Mission. Manuscript History. CR MH 6048. LDS Church History Library.

New Zealand Mission. Minutes, 1891–1915. LR 6048/11. LDS Church History Library.

"The New Zealand Mission." *Deseret Evening News*, 9 February 1885, in Journal History, 3 January 1885.

"The New Zealand Mission." *Deseret Evening News,* 23 March 1886, in Journal History, 23 March 1886, 4.

"The New Zealand Mission." *Deseret Evening News,* 20 November 1915, in Journal History, 20 November 1915, 3.

"New Zealand Missionaries Hold 'Hui Nui' in Inglewood: Elder Matthew Cowley Attends." *California Inter–Mountain News,* 10 July 1951, in Journal History, 10 July 1951, 5.

"New Zealand Missionaries—William McLachlan, Letter to George Goddard, 10 January 1876." *Deseret Evening News,* 5 March 1876, [3].

New Zealand Missionary Society. "Book Prepared for David O. McKay and Hugh J. Cannon, 26 November 1920." MS 6830. LDS Church History Library.

New Zealand South Mission. Quarterly Historical Report, 31 March 1960. New Zealand South Mission, Manuscript History. LR 5050. Church History Library.

"Nga Whakaaturanga." *Te Karere* 24, no. 3 (19 March 1930): 86.

Nibley, Hugh. *Since Cumorah.* Salt Lake City: Deseret Book, 1967.

Noble, James. Letter to Louis G. Hoagland, dated Korongata, 26 November 1905. In Louis Gerald Hoagland, Papers, 1905–38. Microfilm. MS 4693. LDS Church History Library.

Oaks, Dallin H. "The Gospel Culture." *Ensign,* March 2012, 40–47.

Office of the Pacific Area Presidency (Douglas J. Martin, Robert E. Sackley, and Rulon G. Craven), Church of Jesus Christ of Latter-day Saints. To: Regional Representatives, Stake, Mission & District Presidents, Bishops and Branch Presidents in N.Z., Memorandum: Guidelines Re: Language and Cultural Values in New Zealand, 25 May 1992, photocopy in my possession.

Olssen Erik. "Towards a New Society." In *The Oxford History of New Zealand,* 2d ed. Edited by Geoffrey W. Rice. Auckland: Oxford University Press, 1992, 254–84.

Openshaw, Roger, Greg Lee, and Howard Lee. *Challenging the Myths: Rethinking New Zealand's Educational History.* Palmerston North, N.Z.: Dunmore Press, 1993.

Orange, Claudia. "The Maori People and the British Crown (1769–1840)." In *The Oxford Illustrated History of New Zealand.* Edited by Keith Sinclair. Auckland: Oxford University Press, 1990: 21–48.

———. *The Treaty of Waitangi.* Wellington: Allen and Unwin, 1987.

Orbell, Margaret. *The Illustrated Encyclopedia of Māori Myth and Legend.* Sydney: University of New South Wales Press, 1996.

———. "The Traditional Maori Family." In *Families in New Zealand Society.* Edited by Peggy G. Koopman-Boyden. Wellington: Methuen, 1978.

Ottley, Ernest A. Diaries. Ms C2761. Perry Special Collections.

Ottley, Sidney James. Diaries. Vol. 5, 1951–52. In Sidney James Ottley Papers. Perry Special Collections.

Pagan, Eduardo. "An Innocent Racism." *Sunstone* 15, no. 1 (April 1991): 8–9.

Pagden, Anthony. *European Encounters with the New World: From Renaissance to Romanticism.* New Haven, Conn.: Yale University Press, 1993.

Panek, Tracey E. "Life at Iosepa, Utah's Polynesian Colony." *Utah Historical Quarterly* 60 (Winter 1992): 64–77.

Peck, Elbert Eugene. "Casting Out the Spell." *Sunstone* 15, no. 3 (September 1991): 12–15.

Perrott, William Rosser. Oral History. Interviewed by R. Lanier Britsch. Auckland, 1974. Typescript. MS 200 335. LDS Church History Library.

Petersen, Mark E. "Polynesians Came from America." One Hundred Thirty-second Annual General Conference of the Church of Jesus Christ of Latter-day Saints, April 6, 7, 8, 1962.

Peterson, Paul H. "They Came by Handcart." *Ensign,* August 1997, 30–37.

Peterson, Otis. "Raft Voyage 'Proves' Origin of South Sea Natives." *Church News,* 18 October 1947, 6–7.

Phelps, William Wine. "We Accidentily [sic] Came Across..." *Evening and the Morning Star* 1, no. 6 (November 1832): 44.

Phillips, Roderick. *Divorce in New Zealand: A Social History.* Auckland: Oxford University Press, 1981.

Phoenix. *See* Goddard, Benjamin.

"Photo of the Month." *Te Karere* 34, no. 10 (October 1940): 392.

Poll, Richard D. *History and Faith: Reflections of a Mormon Historian.* Salt Lake City: Signature Books, 1989.

"Porirua Native School." *Te Karere* 4, no. 26 (18 January 1911): 311.

"Porirua School Report." *Te Karere* 4, no. 6 (13 April 1910): 70–71.

Porteous, Jno., Senior Inspector of Native Schools. Letter to Director of Education, Wellington, 8 January 1929. Typescript. Maori Affairs. National Archives of New Zealand, Wellington.

"Pres. Hinckley Shows 'Great Love for Sons, Daughters of Lehi.'" *Church News,* 20 September 1997, 6.

"Reception for Visiting Maoris." *Deseret Evening News,* 4 June 1913, in Journal History, 3 June 1913, 2.

Rice, Geoffrey W., ed. *The Oxford History of New Zealand,* 2d ed. Auckland: Oxford University Press, 1992.

Richards, Ezra Foss. Journal. Ezra Foss Richards Papers, 1885–1927. Microfilm. MS 4739. LDS Church History Library.

Richards, Franklin D. Letter to Ezra F. Richards, dated Salt Lake City, 26 June 1885. Copied in Ezra Foss Richards, Journal, between 13 and 14 August 1885. Ezra Foss Richards Papers, 1885–1927. Microfilm. MS 4739. LDS Church History Library.

Roberts, William. Oral History. Interviewed by Charles Ursenbach, Harrogate, Yorkshire, 1976–77. Typescript. MS 200 286. LDS Church History Library.

Rosenvall, Erick Albert. Oral History. Interviewed by Bruce Blumell, Salt Lake City, 23 October 1973. Typescript. OH 134. LDS Church History Library.

Salt Lake Tribune. Salt Lake City.

Sanders, Sondra, Jr. Journals, 1861–1934. Microfilm. MS 807. LDS Church History Library.

Schwimmer, Erik G[abriel]. "The Cognitive Aspect of Culture Change." *Journal of Polynesian Society* 72, no. 2 (June 1965): 149–81.

———. "Mormonism in a Maori Village: A Study in Social Change." M.A. thesis, University of British Columbia, 1965.

Scott, Richard G. "Removing Barriers to Happiness." *Ensign*, May 1998. www.lds.org/ensign/1998/05/removing-barriers-to-happiness?lang=eng (accessed 7 July 2013).

Seshachari, Candadai. "Other Voices, Other Mansions." Review of *Mormonism: A Faith for All Cultures*. *Dialogue: A Journal of Mormon Thought* 13, no. 1 (Spring 1980): 117–19.

Sharpe, Eric J. Conversation with Marjorie Newton, May 1996. Notes in my possession.

———. "Manning Clark Revisited." Australian Broadcasting Commission Radio, 29 August 1993. Copy of script in my possession, courtesy of Eric J. Sharpe.

Sharpe, Kevin J., ed. *Religion & New Zealand's Future: Proceedings of the Seventh Annual Auckland Religious Studies Colloquium, May 2–3, 1981.* Palmerston North, N.Z.: Dunmore Press, 1982.

Shipps, Jan. "In the Presence of the Past: Continuity and Change in Twentieth-century Mormonism." In *After 150 Years: The Latter-day Saints in Sesquicentennial Perspective.* Edited by Thomas G. Alexander and Jessie L. Embry. Provo, Utah: Charles Redd Center for Western Studies, 1983, 3–35.

———. *Mormonism: The Story of a New Religious Tradition.* Urbana: University of Illinois Press, 1985.

Shirres, M. P. "The Churches' Contribution to Race Relations in New Zealand." In *Religion and New Zealand's Future: Proceedings of the Seventh Auckland Religious Studies Colloquium, May 2–3, 1981.* Edited by Kevin J. Sharpe. Palmerston North, N.Z.: Dunmore Press, 1982, 63–67.

Shortland, John. Oral History Interview. Transcript. Kenneth Wayne Baldridge, Interviews, 1971–73.

Shumway, Eric B. "Polynesians." In *Encyclopedia of Mormonism: The History, Scriptures, Doctrine, and Procedure of the Church of Jesus Christ of Latter-day Saints.* Edited by Daniel H. Ludlow. 5 vols. New York: Macmillan Publishing, 1992, 3:1110–12.

Simpson, Robert Leatham. Oral History. Interviewed by Gordon Irving, Salt Lake City, 1978. Typescript. MS 200 386. LDS Church History Library.

———. "The Church in New Zealand." In *Encyclopedia of Mormonism: The History, Scriptures, Doctrine, and Procedure of the Church of Jesus Christ of Latter-day Saints.* Edited by Daniel H. Ludlow. 5 vols. New York: Macmillan Publishing, 1992, 3:1014–16.

Sinclair, Keith. *A History of New Zealand.* London: Penguin Books, 1960.

———, ed. *The Oxford Illustrated History of New Zealand.* Auckland: Oxford University Press, 1990.

———. "Why Are Race Relations in New Zealand Better Than in South Africa, South Australia or South Dakota?" *New Zealand Journal of History* 5, no. 2 (1971): 121–27.

Smith, Henry A. *Matthew Cowley: Man of Faith.* Salt Lake City: Bookcraft, 1954.

Smith, Joseph Fielding. *Answers to Gospel Questions.* 5 vols. Salt Lake City: Deseret Book, 1957.

Sorenson, John L. "Digging into the Book of Mormon: Our Changing Understanding of Ancient America and Its Scripture." Part 1, *Ensign,* September 1984, 27–37; and Part 2, *Ensign,* October 1984, 12–24.

_____. *An Ancient American Setting for the Book of Mormon.* Salt Lake City: Deseret Book, 1985.

Sorrenson, M. P. K. "How to Civilize Savages: Some 'Answers' from Nineteenth-century New Zealand." *New Zealand Journal of History* 9, no. 2 (1975): 97–110.

_____. "Maori and Pakeha." In *The Oxford History of New Zealand,* 2d ed. Edited by Geoffrey W. Rice. Auckland: Oxford University Press, 1992, 141–66.

_____. *Maori Origins and Migrations: The Genesis of Some Pakeha Myths and Legends.* Auckland: Auckland University Press, 1979.

Southerton, Simon G. *Losing a Lost Tribe: Native Americans, DNA, and the Mormon Church.* Salt Lake City: Signature Books, 2004.

Southon, James. Oral History. Transcript. Kenneth Wayne Baldridge, Interviews, 1971–73.

Spoonley, Paul, David Pearson, and Ian Shirley, eds. *New Zealand Society: A Sociological Introduction.* Palmerston North, N.Z.: Dunmore Press, 1990.

Stack, Peggy Fletcher. "In Their Own Language: Should Ethnic Mormons Have Their Own Language?" *Salt Lake Tribune,* 6 December 1997, B-1.

Statistics New Zealand (2013). *2013 Census Quick Stats about Māori.* Available from www.stats.govt.nz.

Stephens, Julian Rackham. "My Life's History, or a Reasonable Facsimile of It." 1981. Microfilm. MS 9245. LDS Church History Library.

Stewart, William Thomas. Papers, 1878–93. MS 2198. LDS Church History Library.

Stevenson, Ezra T. Letter to President Wilford Woodruff, dated Auckland, 9 June 1898. New Zealand Mission, Presidents' Correspondence, 1897–1900. LDS Church History Library.

_____. Letter to First Presidency, dated Nuhaka, 24 August 1898. New Zealand Mission, Presidents' Correspondence, 1897–1900. LDS Church History Library.

_____. Letter to First Presidency (Presidents Lorenzo Snow, George Q. Cannon, and Joseph F. Smith), dated Auckland, 17 April 1899. New Zealand Mission, Presidents' Correspondence, 1897–1900. LDS Church History Library.

Stock, Eugene. *The History of the Church Missionary Society, Its Environment, Its Men and Its Work.* 4 vols. London: Church Missionary Society, 1899–1916.

Stokes, Jeremiah. *Modern Miracles: Authenticated Testimonies of Living Witnesses.* Salt Lake City: Deseret News Press, 1935.

Strong, T. B. Letter to Mr G. M. Henderson, 4 August 1928. Carbon copy of typescript. National Archives of New Zealand, Wellington.

Strother, Douglas Herbert, 1918–91. Oral History. Interviewed by R. Lanier Britsch, Auckland, 1974. Typescript. MS 200 146. LDS Church History Library.

Sunday School Lesson Manual, Course 4, 1970. *We Learn about Our Heavenly Father.* Lesson 35, "We Learn More about the Sacrament at Sunday School and Sacrament Meeting," 237–41.

Swain, Tony, and Garry Trompf. *The Religions of Oceania*. London: Routledge, 1995.

Taylor, George Shepard. Private Journal, 1920–24, Book 1. MSS 167. Perry Special Collections.

———. "Report of Sermons of David O. McKay Delivered at the Annual Conference of the New Zealand Mission of the Church of Jesus Christ of Latter-day Saints, held at Huntly, 23–25 April 1921." Typescript. MS 5919. LDS Church History Library.

Taylor, Harvey L. "The Story of LDS Church Schools." 2 vols. 1971. Photocopy of typescript. LDS Church History Library.

Te Karere/The Messenger/Elders' Messenger. Monthly newspaper of the New Zealand Mission of the Church of Jesus Christ of Latter-day Saints, 1907–60. Microfiche. LDS Church History Library.

Tonks, Warren S. Missionary Diary. In Tonks Family Biographies and Diaries, 1887–1970. MSS SC 835. Perry Special Collections.

Underwood, Grant. "Mormonism, the Maori, and Cultural Authenticity." *Journal of Pacific History* 35, no. 2 (2000): 133–46.

Wade, Alton L., and Barney Wihongi. "The Church College of New Zealand—Past, Present, Future: An Analysis." September 1974. M264.2 C561w 1974. Photocopy of typescript. LDS Church History Library.

Waikato Times. Hamilton, New Zealand.

Walker, Ranginui J. "Maori People since 1950." In *The Oxford History of New Zealand*, 2d. ed. Edited by Geoffrey W. Rice. Auckland: Oxford University Press, 1992, 498–519.

———. "Marae: A Place to Stand." In *Te Ao Hurihuri: Aspects of Maoritanga*. Edited by Michael King. Wellington: Hicks Smith & Sons, 1977, 21–34.

Walton, W. D. Letter to Louis G. Hoagland, dated Huntly, 3 September 1905. In Louis Gerald Hoagland, Papers, 1905–38. Microfilm. MS 4693. LDS Church History Library.

Ward, Alan. "Law and Law Enforcement on the New Zealand Frontier, 1840–1893." *New Zealand Journal of History* 5, no. 2 (1971): 128–49.

Watt, George D. "Discourse by Pres. Brigham Young, Tabernacle, 7 February 1858." *Deseret News*, 17 February 1858, in Journal History, 7 February 1858, 2.

Welch, John Shaw. New Zealand Missionary Journals, 1917–20. MSS A 1524. Utah State Historical Society, Salt Lake City.

Welch, Ruby. "Ethnicity amongst Auckland Mormons." M.A. thesis, University of Auckland, 1989.

Wharemahihi, Nephi. Oral History Interview. Transcript. Kenneth Wayne Baldridge, Interviews, 1971–73.

Widtsoe, John A. "Does the Kon-tiki Voyage Confirm the Book of Mormon?" *Improvement Era*, May 1951, 318–19.

Widtsoe, Osborne J[ohn] P[eter]. "The Schools of the Mormon Church." M260 W641s 1914. LDS Church History Library.

Wihongi, Rupert. Oral History Interview. Transcript. Kenneth Wayne Baldridge, Interviews, 1971–73.

Williams, H. W. *Dictionary of the Maori Language*, 7th ed. Wellington: GP Publications, 1992 printing.

Willis, Suzanne, and Jo Ann Seely. "Register of the Matthew Cowley Collection." MSS 1470. In Matthew Cowley Collection.

Wilson, William A. "The Spinners of Tales." *Sunstone* 15, no. 3 (September 1991): 50–52.

Young, Gordon Claridge. Journal. In Gordon C. Young Papers, 1948–72.

_____. Letter to Edward O. Anderson, 7 July 1951.

_____. Letter to First Presidency, dated Auckland, 23 January 1951. Carbon copy. In Gordon C. Young Papers, 1948–72, fd.5.

_____. Letter to Matthew Cowley, dated 6 February 1951. Carbon copy. In Gordon C. Young Papers, 1948–72.

_____. Letter to President David O. McKay, dated 12 May 1950. Carbon copy. In Gordon C. Young Papers, 1948–72, fd. 4.

_____. Oral History. Interview by Lauritz G. Petersen, Murray, Utah, 28 August 1972. Typescript. OH 24. LDS Church History Library.

_____. Papers, 1948–1972. Microfilm. MS 4016. LDS Church History Library.

_____. Personal Monthly Reports to First Presidency, 30 September, 30 November 1948. In New Zealand Mission, Manuscript History.

_____. "The President's Page." *Te Karere* 45, no. 3 (March 1951): 76, 84.

Zion's Watchman. Published bi-monthly by the Australasian Mission of the Church of Jesus Christ of Latter-day Saints, 1853–56.

Index

A

adultery, 114, 116–17, 119–21, 124
Aldridge, Amasa, 4
American Samoa, 157, 164 note 62, 169 note 85
Americanisation
    and gospel culture, 180
    at Church College of New Zealand, 71–72, 77
    at Maori Agricultural College, 48–50, 54–55
    in Mormonism, 173–76
Anderson, Alexander P., 132
Anderson, Charles, 10, 21, 105
Anderson, Lavina Fielding, xv
Anzac/Anzac Day, xxi, 94 and note 52, 96–97, 103, 110
Anglican Church. *See also* Te Aute College.
    missionaries, xviii–xix, 7–12, 115
    schools in New Zealand, 38–40, 43, 45
Aotearoa. *See* New Zealand.
Ardern, Ian, 76–77
Area Supervisor appointed, xxv
assimilation, 149, 152, 158–59, 162–64, 166
Auckland chapels, xxiii, xxiv, 163
Auckland Harbour Stake, 164
Auckland, Maori schools at, 45
Auckland South Stake, 64
Auckland Stake, xxiv, 63 note 103, 125 note 46
Australasian Mission, xxi, xxiii, 1, 17–18, 118 note 18
Australia, xvii, 63 note 103, 64–66
Australian Mission, xxi, xxiii
Axtel, James, 1, 174–75

B

Ballance, John, 82
Ballif, Ariel S.
    as Maori Agricultural College principal, 55, 57–58
    as mission president, 71
    attitude toward funerals, 130–31
    attitude toward Maori marriages, 124–25
    MAC alumni as local leaders, 59, 63
    on John E. Magleby, 83
    on "white and delightsome," 34, 36
Ballif, Artemisia, 51 note 58
Banks (missionary), 85 note 27
Barber, Ian G.
    on biculturalism, 161, 171
    on Kotahitanga mo Te Tiriti o Wai-tangi, 12, 159
    on policy vacillations, 149, 165, 168–69
    on tangihanga, 137
    on tohunga, 142 note 125
    scholarship of, xiv
Barker, Ian, 2, 149
Barlow, Cleve, 134, 136–37
Bartlett, Charles B., 42, 44, 120, 156
Bay of Islands, xix
Beatty, Charles, 14
Bennett, Charles Moihi, 172–73 and note 93
Bennett, Jonathan Royal, 98, 130, 138–39
Best, Elsdon, 114 note 4
Bible, xix
biculturalism, 149–50, 152, 161–62, 166, 171
Biesinger, George R., 132
Biggs, Bruce, 114

Bishop, Nelson S.
    attitude toward moko, 141
    blessing by, 142
    on funeral customs, 127–30
    on land issues, 11
    on Maori as Israelites, 19
    on Maori marriages, 116–17
black men, and priesthood ordination, 177, 179
boarding schools, 44–45, 52–53. *See also* schools.
Book of Mormon
    and changes to Introductions to 1981, 2006,
        and 2013 eds., 29–30 and note 129
    and gathering, 154
    and Maori identity, 6, 12–15, 180
    and Maori origins, 15–36
    Hawaiian translation, 22–23
    limited geography interpretation, 27–28
    Maori editions, xxiii, xxiv, xxv, 19–20, 85
        and note 27, 88–89, 117, 168
"Book of Mormon and DNA Studies," 31
    note 131
Bowles, George, 87, 121
Boyack, Clifton D., 70–71
Boyd (ship), xviii
Brigham Young University (Provo), 58
Brigham Young University-Idaho, 58
Brisbane, Australia, ethnic units in, 164 note 62
Britsch, R. Lanier, 133
Bromley, William M., 18
Brown, Hugh B., 24
Brunt, John, 54
Buck, Peter, 68

C

Cannon, George Q.
    missionary in Hawaii, 90, 92 and note 45, 98
    on gathering, 154–55
    on Hawaiians as Israelites, 16
    on Maori marriages/divorce, 118
Cannon, Hugh J.
    at Maori Agricultural College, 46–47
    with McKay at 1921 Hui Tau, 90–93,
        95, 97–98 and note 61, 103–4, 110
    world tour, 139, 157
canoe legend, 18, 163 and note 58, 180
Cantonese, temple sessions in, 168 note 83
Carroll, James, 145
Carter, Harry, 4
Catholic schools, 39
Caussé, Gérald, 180

CCNZ. *See* Church College of New Zealand.
Central America, 157
Certificate of Competency, 52
childlessness, 114, 118 note 21
Christensen, Harold T., 61
Christy, Sidney, 91, 99, 100–3, 107
Church College of New Zealand
    academic level of, 71–74 and note 137, 76–77
    Americanisation of, 64, 72, 77
    and kai house, 135
    archives of, xiv
    Church activity of alumni, 74, 77
    closing of, xxv, 37, 77
    construction of, 70
    curriculum, 73–74
    decision to build, 68–70
    enrolment statistics, 75, 76 note 157
    ethnicity of students, 73–74, 76–77
    expense of, 37, 70, 74
    faculty and staff, 64, 71–72 and note 133
    Maori culture classes, performances, 76, 163
    opening of, xxiv, 34
    problems with agricultural program, 74
        and note 148
    site of, 69–70
    sport at, 74, 76
Church Missionary Society (Anglican),
    xviii–xix, 7–12 , 38–40, 43–45
Church News, on Hagoth, 24
Church of England. *See* Anglican *and* CMS.
church schools. *See* Church College of New
    Zealand, education, Maori Agricultural
    College, *and* schools.
civil registration, of births, deaths, marriages,
    115 note 9
Clement, Russell T., 15, 26
CMS. *See* Church Missionary Society.
communal values, among Maori, 171–73, 180
communism/socialism, 171–73
conversion patterns, 3–5
Cook Islands, 73, 113 note 2, 126, 164
Cook, James, xvii, xix
Cowley, Matthew
    and Book of Mormon, 85 and note 27
    and Church College of New Zealand, 69–70
    and local LDS leaders, 61
    and Doctrine and Covenants, 79, 85–89
    and Pearl of Great Price, 85, 87, 89
    and fluency in Maori, 85, 161
    as apostle, xxiv, 85

as mission president, 61, 85
as missionary, 85–89
attitude toward Maori marriages, 123, 124
on land issues, 11
on Maori Agricultural College alumni, 67
on Maori as Israelites, 23
Craven, Rulon G., 135
Crawford, Sidney, 59, 64, 68
cultural conflict, 173–76
cultural immersion of missionaries, 7–8
"cultural suicide," 174–75
culture. *See also* Maori culture *and* gospel culture.
culture shock, 8
Cutler, Heber C., 44

D

Dannevirke Branch, 133
Dansey, Harry, 130, 131–32, 134–35, 137
Davies, Edwin L., 4
Davies, Henry, 130
Davies, Rangi, 139
de Surville, Jean Francois Marie, xviii
de Thierry, Charles Philip Hippolytus, xix
Department of Native Affairs, 38
Dickson, William H., 86
disease, xx
disfellowshipment, 126 note 49
divorce, 114–15, 118 and note 21, 123 and note 38
DNA sequencing, 27, 30–31 and note 131, 177
Doctrine and Covenants, xxiv, 86–89. *See also* Matthew Cowley.
Douglas, Norman, 15–17
Douglass, William, 141
Doxey, Graham H., 90 note 40, 91, 98, 104, 109
drunkenness, 128
du Fresne, Marion, xxvii
Duffy, John–Charles, 177
Duncan, Takare, 25
Duncan, William, Wi/Wiremu, Sr., 25, 33, 86, 88
on emigration to Utah, 156–57
ordained high priest, 160

E

earthquake, and Maori Agricultural College, 45, 51, 58, 67
education, in Mormonism, 41–44 and note 29. *See also* schools.

Education Act (1877, 1914), 39, 57
Edwards, Jonathan, 14
Elders' Messenger, xiii. See also *Te Karere*.
elders quorums, xxiv
Eliot, John, 14
Elkington, James, 68, 91
Elohim, in Mormon theology, 6, 132
Elsmore, Bronwyn, 7
Encyclopedia of Mormonism, 29, 30
endowment, and funeral customs, 132–34
England, Eugene, 34
Ensign (magazine)
on Book of Mormon setting, 27–28
on gathering, 150
Erekson, William B., 143
ethnic identity, Mormonism as, 173 and note 98. *See also* Maori.
ethnic units, policies on, 164–67, 169–70
excommunication, 116–26, 140–42, 165

F

Ferris, John S., 4, 18–19
"Fifty Reasons Why the Maoris and American Indians Are of Israelitish Origin," 22
First Presidency, 118–20, 154–55
Foster, Lawrence, xv
Freeman, Derek, 113 note 2
French Polynesia, 150–51
funerals. *See* tangihanga.

G

Gallipoli Campaign, 94 and note 52, 110
Gardner, Brant A., 35
Gardner, John W., 106, 130, 145
Gardner, William, 4, 87, 105, 121
gathering, 150–58, 175, 179
genealogy, 6
George R. Biesinger Hall, 136
German ethnic units, 165 and note 66
Gilgen, David, 137, 165, 168–69
Gilmore, Robert, 172
Goddard, Benjamin
and appointments to New Zealand Mission, 48
and Maori Agricultural College site, 46–47
and Zion's Maori Association, 25, 155
on gathering, 154–55
on land issues, 11

on Maori as Israelites, 21–22
Gorst, J. E., 54
gospel culture, 162–63, 171, 175, 178, 180
Gospel Principles, 30
Grant, Heber J., 25, 58, 122–23, 160
grave dedications, 128–29
Great Depression, 160 note 50
Great Fleet. *See* canoe legend.
Great Land March (1975), 170–71
Greenwood, Alma, 3, 10, 19–20, 128
Grey, George, 22, 38
Gudmansen, Ray, 141

H

haakari, 129
Hagoth, 13, 180
link between Native Americans and Maori, 21–22, 24–27, 29, 32, 34
haka, 95, 137–40
Halversen, A. Reed, 62, 69, 123
Hamakau, Te Hatiwira. *See* Te Hatiwira.
Hamilton New Zealand Temple. *See* New Zealand Temple.
Hamilton Stake, xxv, 63 and note 103, 139
Hamilton Teacher Training College, 76
Hamon, Hixson, 67
Hardy, Charles, 22, 36, 144
Hardy, Rufus K., 61
    and haka, 139
    and interpretation of tongues account, 99 and note 67, 100–101, 103, 106–7
    and Maori Agricultural College site, 46–47
    and Maori Doctrine and Covenants, 86
    and te reo, 161
    as mission president, 61
    attitude toward Maori marriages, 121
Harold B. Lee Library (Brigham Young University), xiv
Harris, Kelly, 59, 61, 164
Hastings Stake. *See* Hawkes Bay Stake.
Hawaii, 40, 122, 127, 151–52. *See also* Lanai *and* Laie.
Hawkes Bay/Hastings Stake, xxv, 32 and note 135, 59, 63–64 note 103, 139
healers, traditional. *See* tohunga.
healing, Mormon blessings, 142–43
Henderson, G. M., 50, 51 and note 58, 54, 57
Henderson, J. McLeod, 6
herbal healing. *See* Rongoa Maori.
Heyerdahl, Thor, 16, 26

Hinckley, Gordon B., 24–25, 177
Hinckley, Ira N., 3, 10, 128
Hixson, J. M., 144
Hoagland, Louis G., 45–47, 84, 106, 145, 156
Hobson, William, xix
Hodge, Robert P., 51
Holland, Jeffrey R., 33 and note 140, 176
hongi, 82 and note 12, 133–34
Hoperi, Paora, 128
Hui Tau, xxiii, xxiv, 90–110, 161–62
Hukarere School, 45
Huntly, New Zealand, 40, 90
Hurst, Samuel Harris, 92

I

Ihaia, Ema, 25
Ihaia, Takerei, 25
industrial training, 38
Institute for Polynesian Studies, xiii and note 5, xiv
Institute of Religion, 74
integration, 164–65, 170–71. *See* assimilation *and* ethnic units.
Io, in Maori cosmology, 6, 132
Iosepa, Utah, 152–53, 155, 157
Irwin, James, 135
Israelite, 12–36 and note 57, 153, 179–80

J

James, Rhett, 74, 75
Jensen, Richard L., xiii, 165–67
Jenson, Andrew, 10
Johnson, Elias, 80–83
Johnson, John, 106
Johnson, Lane, 35
Johnson, M. M., 23
Johnston, Albert Sidney, 151
Joseph Fielding Smith Institute for Church History, xiii, xiv
Joseph, Robert, 159
Josephites. *See* Reorganized Church of Jesus Christ of Latter Day Saints.
Jury, John A. *See* Te Whatahoro.
Juvenile Instructor, 16

K

Kahia, Hamiora Mangai, 12
Kaiapoi, xxi, xxiii, 106
Kailimai, David Keola, 92

Kanab, Utah, Maori in, 155
karakia, 129, 154
Karori Branch, xxi, xxiii
Katene, Herewini, 64
Kauleinamoku, John W., 22, 142
Kauri, Matiu. *See* Cowley, Matthew.
Kawakawa, 80–81 and note 6
Kendall, Thomas, xviii
Kimball, Spencer W.
    attitude toward haka, 139–40
    on Hagoth, 24–26
    on learning English, 166
    on Polynesians as Lehites, 25–27, 32–33
    priesthood ordination revelation, 177, 179
    visits New Zealand, xxv, 139–40
King Country, 11, 39
King, James, 145
King, Michael, 140 note 119, 141, 145
King, Philip Gidley, xvii
Kirkham, Francis W., 11, 143
Knowlton, David Clark, 111
Kofford, Greg, xiii
Kon–Tiki, 16
Korongata, 45, 47, 138
Kotahitanga mo Te Tiriti of Waitangi, 12, 159

L

labour missionaries, 64, 129–30
Labour Party, 172 and note 93
Laie, Hawaii, 56, 151–53, 157, 174
Lamanites
    Maori as, 25, 31–36, 176–78, 180
    Polynesians as, 176–79
    world membership statistics (1975), 33
Lambert, James N.
    and Book of Mormon, 85 and note 27
    and Doctrine and Covenants, 85, 86
        and note 33, 87
    and gathering place, 157
    and Maori Agricultural College site, 46, 47
    attitude toward Maori marriages, 121
    attitude toward tohunga, 143
Lanai, Hawaii, 151–53
land, 8–12, 147, 157, 159, 167
land courts, 10, 46, 120 note 29, 125
Land Wars (1860s), xx, 18, 39, 115
language–designated units. *See* ethnic units.
Laughton, John G., 11
LDS Church. *See also* schools.
    administrative office in Auckland, xxv

Board of Education, 41
History Library, xiv
membership statistics in New Zealand,
    xxi, xxiii–xxv, 12 note 28, 62, 123
Pacific Area organised, xxv
Pacific Board of Education, 70
Seminary and Institute of Religion
    programs, xxv
sixth largest in New Zealand, 181
Lectures on Faith, 89
Lee, Harold B., 166
Lineham, Peter, xv, 9–10, 12, 161, 175
Linford, Esther, 106
Lopez de Gomara, Francisco, 14
Loveland, Jerry K., 27
Loving, A. L., 91–94, 100–102. *See also*
    Reorganized Church of Jesus Christ of
    Latter Day Saints.

M

MAC. *See* Maori Agricultural College.
M.A.C. Old Boys' Association, 69
Magleby, John E.
    and local leaders, 60–62, 65, 160
    and Maori Agricultural College, 55–58
    and Ratana, 160–61
    as mission president (1900–2), 116,
        119–20, 138, 144
    as mission president (1928–32), 55–56,
        58, 60–62, 65, 84, 107, 122–23
    as persecuted missionary, 79–85
    attitude toward haka, 138
    attitude toward marriage customs,
        116–17, 119–20, 122–23, 124
    fluent Maori speaker, 85
    on conversion patterns, 4
    on English–speaking Maori, 106–7
    on funeral customs, 128–29
    on gathering place, 156, 158
    on land issues, 11
    on sealings in Hawaii Temple, 122
Mahue, Hore, 82
Mainwaring, Bernice, 51 note 58
mana, 160, 172
Mandarin, temple sessions in, 168 note 83
Manihera, 20
Maori Agricultural College, 44–68
    academically inadequate, 49, 50–52, 54–55
    agricultural emphasis of, 57
    Americanisation of, 48–50, 54

and Laie sugar plantation, 56
and U.S. academies, 56
character building, 49–50, 68
closed, xxiv, 37, 45, 58
curriculum, 57
earthquake at, 45
expense of, 37, 45, 56, 58
faculty/staff, 50–52, 57
football at, 49, 54–55
motives for founding, 42
music at, 49, 54
myths about, 58–68
opened, xxiii, 44–45
site of, 8, 45–48, 57
student numbers, 53, 67
student ages, 53–54 and note 67
student–staff ratio, 56–57 and note 76
Maori
as Israelites, 12–14, 15–36
as percentage of population, xii, 167 note 76
as soldiers, xxi
communalism, 171–73
cosmology, 6–7
English speakers, 105–7
expectation of becoming "white and
delightsome," 33–36, 41
population statistics, xx
prophets, 2–3, 159–60
proselytizing among, 17–18
Maori culture, 162–64
and identity, 167, 170–71, 180
at Hui Tau, 161–62
funeral customs, 127–37
haka, 137–40
healings by tohunga, 140–46
marriage customs, 113–27, 120 note 29
mission presidents' attitudes toward, 113–47
missionary immersion in, 7–8
performances, 76, 163, 175 note 106
seen as inferior, 31–32, 36, 41–42
Maori language (te reo)
and identity, 107, 167, 180
as official language, 168
classes, 168
discouraged at LDS meetings, 164–65, 168
missionaries learn, 7, 83
temple sessions in, 168 and note 83
written, 38
Maori Language Act (1987), xiv note 6, 168
Maori, and Mormonism

appeal of Mormonism, 1–6
as LDS leaders, 60–62
district presidents, first, xxiv, 60–62, 160
membership statistics, xii, xxi, xxiv, 120
Maori–Pakeha ratio, xi–xii
origins, 12–36; theories of, 14–15
Maori Purpose Fund, 55, 57
Maoritanga, 147, 149, 162–63, 173
marae, 135–36, 173, 180
Marama (ship), 109
Mariposa (ship), 71, 163 note 50
Marist Brothers school, at Apia, 54
marriage customs. *See* Maori culture.
Marsden, Samuel, xviii, 14, 22
Mate, Tamaite, 145
Mather, Cotton, 14
Maugham, Alvin T., 61
Maui, Hawaii, 92, 98, 108–9
May, Dean L., 173
McCune, Henry F., 19, 153
McKay, David O.
and 1921 Hui Tau miracle, 79, 89–110
and Church College of New Zealand,
70, 71
correspondence from Gordon C. Young,
123–24
dedicates New Zealand Temple, 103
on haka, poi dance, 139
on local leaders, 60, 95
on Maori Agricultural College site, 47;
on alumni, 59
on Mormon colony in New Zealand, 158
on Polynesians as Lehites, 24, 25
superiority of American culture, 174
visits New Zealand, xxiv, 59 and note
91, 70–71, 89–110
world tour of, 46, 157
McKay, Emma Ray, 98, 109
McLachlan, William, 18, 23
Mead, Margaret, 113 note 2
medical care, 142–43. *See also* tohunga.
Meha, Arapata, 142
Meha, Stuart/Tuati
and Book of Mormon revision, 85 note 27
and Doctrine and Covenants revision,
86, 88, 89
and New Zealand Temple dedication, 103
as interpreter, 91–98, 102, 104, 105
interpretation of tongues account,
99–100, 103

on emigration to Utah, 156–57
on Maori as Israelites, 13 note 57
on Maori origins, 21
visits Utah, 25
Meihana, Hohepa Otene, 3
Melbourne, Australia, 63 note 103, 164 note 62
Meldrum, D. Jeffrey, 27 note 120, 31, 178
membership. *See* Maori.
Mendenhall, Wendell B., 70
Messenger, The, 20–21. *See also* Te Karere.
Metge, Joan, 115, 125–26
Methodist missionaries, xix, 115
Mexico, 22, 156–57
Middlemiss, Clare, 99
mihi, 139
Mihinare Church. *See* Anglican Church.
millennialism, 5–6, 115
miscegenation, 117
missionaries, Mormon. *See* Mormon
missionaries.
moko, 140–41
Mol, Hans, 166, 170
Monterey (ship), 163 note 50
Mormon History Association, xii, xiv
Mormon missionaries
as branch/district leaders, 60–63
as schoolteachers, 43–44, 50–52
at land courts, 120 note 29
cultural immersion of, 7–8
evacuated in World War II, 60, 65
first in New Zealand, xxiii, 18
married men in nineteenth century, 8
and note 41
mission presidents and Maori culture,
113–47
not legal marriage celebrants, 116
Mormonism. *See* LDS Church *and* Maori.
Mount Tarawera, 84
Muriwai Branch, 145
Murphy, Thomas W., 14
myths and legends, 58–68, 79–112

N

National Party, 171
Native Land Court. *See* land courts.
Native School Code (1880), 43
Native Schools Act (1858, 1867), 38
Nephites, 25, 31–36
Nepia, Edwin, 32
Newby, Edward, 153

New South Wales, xix–xx
Newtown, Wellington, 164
New Zealand, xvii–xx, 77 note 162, 94 note
53, 164. *See also* World War I, World
War II, *and* Anzac Day.
New Zealand Government Archives, xiv
New Zealand Land Wars (1860s). *See* land wars.
New Zealand Mission, xxi, xxiii, xxiv, 62.
See also Maori *and* LDS Church.
New Zealand Missionary Society (formerly
Zion's Maori Association), 48, 157–58
and note 35
New Zealand Motor Trades and
Apprenticeship Boards, 74
New Zealand stakes, 63–64 and note 103
New Zealand Temple, xxiv
annual pageant at, 163
dedicated, 103, 124
funerals of endowed members, 132–34
language sessions in, 168 and note 83
prophesied, 95, 110
Nga Puhi, 161
Ngaruawahia, 161
Ngata, Apirana, 68, 145
Ngati Kahungunu, 3, 11
Ngati Koata/Ngati Kuia, 161
Ngati Porou, 79–84
Niagara (ship), 25
Nibley, Hugh, 35
Nopera, Eriata, 62
North Island, xviii
Nuhaka, 11, 40, 141, 155

O

Oaks, Dallin H., 178
old age pensions, 159 and note 44
Opotiki, 19
Ottley, Ernest A., 62–63, 98
Ottley, Sidney J., 139

P

Pacific Board of Education, 70
Pacific Institute, xiii note 5
Packer, Boyd K., 75
Pagden, Anthony, 176
Paige, W. E., 128
Parsons, Robert E., 24
Paxman, William, 20, 33, 116, 154
Pearl of Great Price, Maori, xxiv, 85–87, 89

Peck, Elbert Eugene, 111
Pedersen, Herschel N., 126
Peeti, Luxford, 25
Penn, William, 14
perfectibility, LDS theology of, 41
Perrott, William R., 84
Petersen, Mark E., 16–17, 24
plural marriages, among Maori, 116–18 and note 21, 125. *See also* childlessness.
poi dance, 95, 139
Poipoi, Ngawawaea, 31
policies, inconsistencies of, 146–47, 149–50, 162, 167–68
Poll, Richard, 111
polygamy/polygyny. *See* plural marriages.
Polynesian Cultural Centre (Hawaii), 163
Polynesians, 12–17. *See also* Israelites.
Pomare, Hawaii, 68, 158
Porirua, 9, 154
Porteous, John, 54
post–mortal beliefs, Maori, 132
posture dance. *See* haka.
Potangaroa, Paora. *See* Te Potangaroa.
Poverty Bay District, 145
Pratt, Addison, 15, 151
Pratt, Louisa Barnes, 15
primary schools. *See* schools *and* LDS schools.
probation, defined, 126 note 49
Proficiency Certificate examinations, 44, 52–53, 55
prophetess, Maori, 143
prophets, Maori, 2–3, 4, 115, 143, 159–60
Public Health and Maori Councils Act (1900), 144
Puketapu, 40, 90, 102
Pulehu, Maui, 92, 98

Q–R

Queen Victoria School, 45
Raiha, Sister, 91
rangatira, defined, 3 note 13; influence of, 3–5
Rangitakaiwaho, Manihera Te Whenuanui, 3
Rangitoto Branch, Auckland, 164
Ratana Church, xxiv, 2–3, 12, 60, 160
Ratana, Tahupotiki Wiremu, 159
rebaptism, 116 and note 11
Relief Society, xxiii, 144, 172
Reorganized Church of Jesus Christ of Latter Day Saints in New Zealand, 91–94, 96–98, 100–102, 110

Richards, Ezra Foss
and Book of Mormon translation, 89, 117
and marriage customs, 116, 117–19
as missionary, 31–32, 80, 83, 116
as mission president, 117–19
on gathering, 153, 155–56
on Maori schools, 43
Richards, Franklin D., 31, 117, 153
Richards, Willard, 142
Ricks College. *See* Brigham Young University-Idaho.
Ringatu, 2
Roberts, William, 125 note 46
Robertson, Dale, xiii
Roman Catholic missionaries, xix, 115
Romney, Orson D., 87, 121, 138
Rongoa Maori, 146
Rosenvall, Erick A., 64, 132
Roundy (missionary), 85 note 27
Rudd, Glen L., 135
Ruruku, Turi, 62

S

sacrament, taking with right hand, 179 and note 121
Samoa. *See also* Western Samoa *and* American Samoa.
language, 164–65, 168
LDS schools, 70
temple sessions in Samoan, 168 and note 83
Samoan Tripartite Convention (1899), 169 note 85
Samoans
English–speaking, 167
in Australia and U.S., 164 note 62
in New Zealand, 164–65, 166
San Bernardino, California, 151 and note 8
Sanders, Sondra, Jr., 89
Savage (RLDS missionary), 91–92
Scandinavian ethnic units, 165
schools, denominational, 9, 38–39, 43. *See also* Te Aute.
schools, government, 38–40, 68–69
schools, Mormon, 37, 40–44. *See also* Maori Agricultural College, Church College of New Zealand, *and* missionaries.
Schwendiman, Fred W., 91, 121
Schwimmer, Erik G., 5–6, 17, 134, 137

Scott, Patricia Lyn, xv
Scott, Richard G., 178
sealings, temple, 122. *See also* marriages.
Sells, Albert, 53
seminary program, 74, 77
Seshachari, Candadai, 175
Sharp, Leo B., 51
Sharpe, Eric J., xv, 111–12
sheep shearing, 56
Shipps, Jan, xv
Shumway, Eric, 29
Simpson, Robert L.
  and local LDS leaders, 61, 64
  on decision to build Maori Agricultural
    College, 59 and note 91
  on Maori Agricultural College alumni, 59
  on funeral customs, 129–30, 132, 133
  on Maori culture, 162
  on Polynesian origins, 28–29
  on strong LDS families, 66
  on tohunga, 146
Sinclair, Keith, 94 note 53
Skull Valley, Utah, 152. *See also* Iosepa, Utah.
Smellie, John T., 137–38
Smith, E. Wesley, 92
Smith, George A., 166
Smith, George Albert, xxiv, 25, 47, 99 note
  67, 139
Smith, Joseph
  and Book of Mormon, 28, 34
  and polygamy, 94, 96
  on education, 41
  on Lamanites, 15, 19
Smith, Joseph F.
  and Maori schools, 45
  as missionary in Hawaii, 92 and note 45
  on gathering, 154–55
  on Hagoth, 26
  on Maori marriages/divorce, 118
  on Polynesians as Lehites, 25–26
Smith, Wi, 99, 100, 103
Snow, Lorenzo, 156
social Darwinism, 159
Sorenson, John L., 27–28
Sorrenson, M.P.K., 13, 14, 115 note 7
South Island, xvii
Southerton, Simon, 27, 31, 178, 179
Southon, James, 32, 59, 64, 68
Spanish, temple sessions in, 168 and note 83
spelling conventions, xiv

Spencer, Charles, 109
sport, at Church College of New Zealand,
  37, 74, 76
St. Stephen's School, 45
Stafford administration, and schools, 38
Stephens, Julian R., 122
Stephens, Trent D., 27 note 120, 31, 178
Stevenson, Ezra T., 20, 141, 143–44, 157–58
Stewart Island, xviii
Stewart, William T., 13 note 57, 36, 82, 154–55
stick of Ephraim/ Judah, 19
Stott, F. Earl, 93, 104
Strong, Thomas, 53
Strother, Douglas H., 133
Strother, Mihi, 133
succession after Joseph Smith, 92, 104
Sunday School general board, 90, 93
Swain, Tony, 7
Sydney, Australia, 63 note 103, 134, 164
  note 62
Sydney Australia Temple, 168 and note 83

T

Takana, William/Wi/Wiremu. *See* Duncan,
  William/Wi/Wiremu, Sr.
Takoro, Karena W., 99, 101, 103
tangi/tangihanga. *See also* Maori culture,
  funeral customs.
  and Maori identity, 180
  as Maori emotional response, 108
  discussed, 127–37
  expense of, 130–31
  LDS policies regarding, 136
  missionary attitudes toward, 127–37
tapu, 127–29
Taranaki, 12, 39
Tasman, Abel, xvii
tattooing. *See* moko.
Taumata–o–Tapuhi, 40, 44, 80, 83, 84
Tawhaio (King), 3
Taylor, George Shepard, 90–91 and note
  40, 98, 104, 108–9, 121–22
Taylor, Harvey L., 70 note 128
Te Araroa, 80 note 6
Te Aroha Concert Party, 163
Te Aute College, 45, 50, 52, 67–68
Te Hatiwira/Hati, 79–84
Te Hau, Matiu, 137
Te Hirangi, Te Puea (Princess), 161

Te Karere, xxiv, 62, 86–89. *See also* The Messenger *and* Elders' Messenger.
Te Kooti, 4, 12, 14
Te Maari, Piripi, 20
Te Potangaroa, Paora 2–3
Te Rakihiatau, Henare, 171
Te Rau Aroha, 135–36
te reo. *See* Maori language.
Te Rimu, 80
Te Whatahoro (John A. Jury), 12
Te Whiti, 4, 12, 14
Teimana, Hare, 4
temple ceremonies
    attendance, of Maori in Utah, 155
    covenants, 6
    in Maori language, 168 and note 83
    sealings, 122
    garments, 133–34, 138 and note 108
Temple View Stake. *See* Auckland South Stake.
Thomas (missionary), 85 note 27
Thorowgood, Thomas, 14
Tiki and Temple: The Mormon Mission in New Zealand, 1854–1958, xii, xiii, xv, xxi, 37
Time (magazine), 34
Tingey, Clarence H., 65
tithing, 154, 180
Tofua (ship), 95, 97, 98
tohunga, 140–46 and note 125, 158
Tohunga Suppression Act (1907), 143, 145–46
Tonga, 24, 26, 50, 70, 95, 97
    Tongan language, 165, 168 and note 83, 169
Tongans, 73, 164–67, note 62
tongues, gift of interpretation of (1921), 79, 85, 96–109
Tonks, Warren S., 96–97, 103
Tory (ship), xix
tract, Maori, xxiii
Treaty of Waitangi, xix, xxi, 8, 10
tribalism, and Mormonism, 157–58, 163, 176
Trompf, Garry, 7
Tubuai, 15, 40
Turei, Mohi, 79–80, 83

U–V

Underwood, Grant, 180
Unified Church Schools System, 70 note 128
United Order, 5

United States, Samoan and Tongan units in, 164 note 62
University of Sydney, xii, xv
Utah Expedition, 151
Victoria (Queen), xix
vital statistics. *See* civil registration.

W

Waddoups, William M., 122
Wade, Alton L., 75–76
Waiapu Valley, 4, 40, 44, 79, 82, 84
Waikato district, 4, 11, 105
    and Church College of New Zealand, 69, 73, 76
    and Hui Tau (1921), 90, 102, 139
    schools, 39, 40
Waikato Hospital Nurses Training School, 76
Waikato Technical Institute, 76
Waikato University, 76
Waiomatatini, 82
Wairarapa, 2–3, 9–10, 12, 20, 106
Waiwhara Branch, 145
Waka, Tamati, 10
Wakefield, Edward Gibbon, xix
Waotu Branch, 4
Watene, George, 61
Watene, Steve, 68
Welch, Ruby, 167
Welsh ethnic units, 165
Wesleyan missionaries, 115
Western Samoa, 54, 157, 164 note 62, 169 and note 85
Westmere, Auckland, 164
Whaanga, Hirini, 91, 155 and notes 26 and 27
Whaanga, Mere, 155
whakapapa, 6, 132
"white and delightsome," 33–36, 41
"white–collar" leaders, 65
Wihongi, Barney, 71 note 133, 75, 76
Wihongi, Henere Pere, 62
Williams, Henry, xix
Wilson, William A., 111
Wiser, Wendell H., 71–72
Woodruff, Wilford, 90, 118, 154–56
Woods, M. Charles, 61
Workman, Jacob B., 23
World War I, xxi, xxiv, 94 and notes 52 and 53
World War II, xxiv
    Islander immigration into New Zealand after, 164, 169

local leaders during, 59, 60, 62, 65
urbanisation of Maori after, xx, 163

Y-Z

Young, Brigham
  and education, 41
  and State of Deseret, 151
  as Joseph Smith's successor, 92, 104
  on assimilation, 158
  on Polynesians as Israelites, 16, 24, 29
Young, Gordon C.
  and Church College of New Zealand,
    69–71, 74

and land issues, 11
and local LDS leaders, 62
at 1921 Hui Tau, 91, 95–96, 102, 103
attitude toward funerals, 130 and note 71
attitude toward haka, 139
on assimilation, 162, 164
on inconsistent policies, 146
opposes social welfare, 171
opposes traditional marriages, 123–24
on preparation for stakehood, 124–25
Young Maori Party, 142 note 125, 144
Zion's Maori Association, 25, 48, 155 *See also* New Zealand Missionary Society.

Also available from
GREG KOFFORD BOOKS

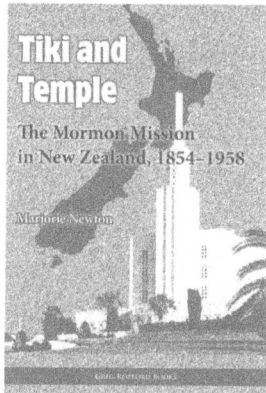

Tiki and Temple: The Mormon Mission in New Zealand, 1854–1958

Marjorie Newton

Paperback, ISBN: 978-1-58958-121-0

From the arrival of the first Mormon missionaries in New Zealand in 1854 until stakehood and the dedication of the Hamilton New Zealand Temple in 1958, Tiki and Temple tells the enthralling story of Mormonism's encounter with the genuinely different but surprisingly harmonious Maori culture.

Mormon interest in the Maori can be documented to 1832, soon after Joseph Smith organized the Church of Jesus Christ of Latter-day Saints in America. Under his successor Brigham Young, Mormon missionaries arrived in New Zealand in 1854, but another three decades passed before they began sustained proselytising among the Maori people—living in Maori pa, eating eels and potatoes with their fingers from communal dishes, learning to speak the language, and establishing schools. They grew to love—and were loved by—their Maori converts, whose numbers mushroomed until by 1898, when the Australasian Mission was divided, the New Zealand Mission was ten times larger than the parent Australian Mission.

The New Zealand Mission of the Mormon Church was virtually two missions—one to the English-speaking immigrants and their descendants, and one to the tangata whenua—"people of the land." The difficulties this dichotomy caused, as both leaders and converts struggled with cultural differences and their isolation from Church headquarters, make a fascinating story. Drawing on hitherto untapped sources, including missionary journals and letters and government documents, this absorbing book is the fullest narrative available of Mormonism's flourishing in New Zealand.

Although written primarily for a Latter-day Saint audience, this book fills a gap for anyone interested in an accurate and coherent account of the growth of Mormonism in New Zealand.

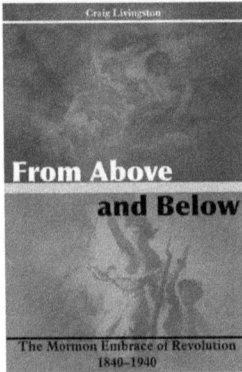

From Above and Below:
The Mormon Embrace of Revolution, 1840–1940

Craig Livingston

Paperback, ISBN: 978-1-58958-621-5

Praise for *From Above and Below*:

"In this engaging study, Craig Livingston examines Mormon responses to political revolutions across the globe from the 1840s to the 1930s. Latter-day Saints saw utopian possibilities in revolutions from the European tumults of 1848 to the Mexican Revolution. Highlighting the often radical anti-capitalist and anti-imperialist rhetoric of Mormon leaders, Livingston demonstrates how Latter-day Saints interpreted revolutions through their unique theology and millennialism."
--Matthew J. Grow, author of *Liberty to the Downtrodden: Thomas L. Kane, Romantic Reformer*

"Craig Livingston's landmark book demonstrates how 21st-century Mormonism's arch-conservatism was preceded by its pro-revolutionary worldview that was dominant from the 1830s to the 1930s. Shown by current opinion-polling to be the most politically conservative religious group in the United States, contemporary Mormons are unaware that leaders of the LDS Church once praised radical liberalism and violent revolutionaries. By this pre-1936 Mormon view, 'The people would reduce privilege and exploitation in the crucible of revolution, then reforge society in a spiritual union of peace' before the Coming of Christ and His Millennium. With profound research in Mormon sources and in academic studies about various social revolutions and political upheavals, Livingston provides a nuanced examination of this little-known dimension of LDS thought which tenuously balanced pro-revolutionary enthusiasms with anti-mob sentiments."
--D. Michael Quinn, author of *Elder Statesman: A Biography of J. Reuben Clark*

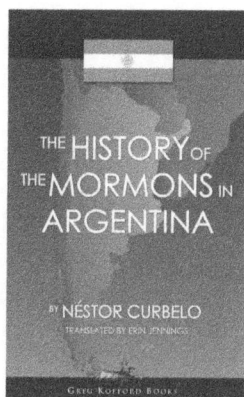

The History of Mormons in Argentina

Néstor Curbelo

English, ISBN: 978-1-58958-052-7

Originally published in Spanish, Curbelo's The History of the Mormons in Argentina is a groundbreaking book detailing the growth of the Church in this Latin American country.

Through numerous interviews and access to other primary resources, Curbelo has constructed a timeline, and then documents the story of the Church's growth. Starting with a brief discussion of Parley P. Pratt's assignment to preside over the Pacific and South American regions, continuing on with the translation of the scriptures into Spanish, the opening of the first missions in South America, and the building of temples, the book provides a survey history of the Church in Argentina. This book will be of interest not only to history buffs but also to thousands of past, present, and future missionaries.

Translated by Erin Jennings

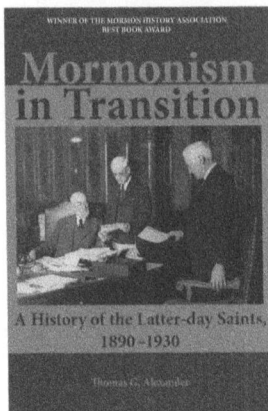

Mormonism in Transition: A History of the Latter-day Saints, 1890–1930, 3rd ed.

Thomas G. Alexander

Paperback, ISBN: 978-1-58958-188-3

More than two decades after its original publication, Thomas G. Alexander's *Mormonism in Transition* still engages audiences with its insightful study of the pivotal, early years of the Church of Jesus Christ of Latter-day Saints. Serving as a vital read for both students and scholars of American religious and social history, Alexander's book explains and charts the Church's transformation over this 40-year period of both religious and American history.

For those familiar with the LDS Church in modern times, it is impossible to study *Mormonism in Transition* without pondering the enormous amount of changes the Church has been through since 1890. For those new to the study of Mormonism, this book will give them a clear understanding the challenges the Church went through to go from a persecuted and scorned society to the rapidly growing, respected community it is today.

Praise for Mormonism in Transition:

"A must read for any serious student of this 'peculiar people' and Western history." – STANLEY B. KIMBALL, *Journal of the West*

"Will be required reading for all historians of Mormonism for some time to come." – WILLIAM D. RUSSELL, *Journal of American History*

"This is by far the most important book on this crucial period in LDS history." – JAN SHIPPS, author of *Mormonism: The Story of a New Religious Tradition*

"A work of careful and prodigious scholarship." – LEONARD J. ARRINGTON, author of *Brigham Young: American Moses*

"Clearly fills a tremendous void in the history of Mormonism." – Klaus J. Hansen, author of *Mormonism and the American Experience*

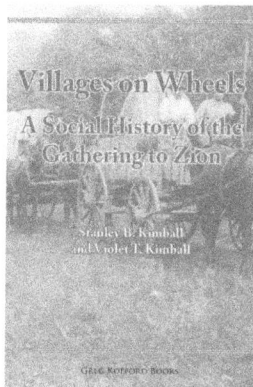

Villages on Wheels:
A Social History of the Gathering to Zion

Stanley B. Kimball and Violet T. Kimball

ISBN: 978-1-58958-119-7

The enduring saga of Mormonism is its great trek across the plains, and understanding that trek was the life work of Stanley B. Kimball, master of Mormon trails. This final work, a collaboration he began and which was completed after his death in 2003 by his photographer-writer wife, Violet, explores that movement westward as a social history, with the Mormons moving as "villages on wheels."

Set in the broader context of transcontinental migration to Oregon and California, the Mormon trek spanned twenty-two years, moved approximately 54,700 individuals, many of them in family groups, and left about 7,000 graves at the trailside.

Like a true social history, this fascinating account in fourteen chapters explores both the routines of the trail—cooking, cleaning, laundry, dealing with bodily functions—and the dramatic moments: encountering Indians and stampeding buffalo, giving birth, losing loved ones to death, dealing with rage and injustice, but also offering succor, kindliness, and faith. Religious observances were simultaneously an important part of creating and maintaining group cohesiveness, but working them into the fabric of the grueling day-to-day routine resulted in adaptation, including a "sliding Sabbath." The role played by children and teens receives careful scrutiny; not only did children grow up quickly on the trail, but the gender boundaries guarding their "separate spheres" blurred under the erosion of concentrating on tasks that had to be done regardless of the age or sex of those available to do them. Unexpected attention is given to African Americans who were part of this westering experience, and Violet also gives due credit to the "four-legged heroes" who hauled the wagons westward.

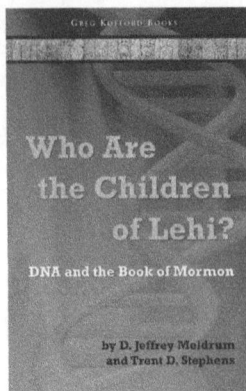

Who Are the Children of Lehi? DNA and the Book of Mormon

D. Jeffrey Meldrum and Trent D. Stephens

Hardcover, ISBN: 978-1-58958-048-0
Paperback, ISBN: 978-1-58958-129-6

How does the Book of Mormon, keystone of the LDS faith, stand up to data about DNA sequencing that puts the ancestors of modern Native Americans in northeast Asia instead of Palestine?

In *Who Are the Children of Lehi?* Meldrum and Stephens examine the merits and the fallacies of DNA-based interpretations that challenge the Book of Mormon's historicity. They provide clear guides to the science, summarize the studies, illuminate technical points with easy-to-grasp examples, and spell out the data's implications.

The results? There is no straight-line conclusion between DNA evidence and "Lamanites." The Book of Mormon's validity lies beyond the purview of scientific empiricism—as it always has. And finally, inspiringly, they affirm Lehi's kinship as one of covenant, not genes.

www.ingramcontent.com/pod-product-compliance
Lightning Source LLC
Chambersburg PA
CBHW020529270326
41927CB00006B/502